Beyond the glass ceiling

Forty women whose ideas shape the modern world

Edited by
Sian Griffiths

with an introduction by
Helena Kennedy

in association with

THE TIMES
HIGHER
EDUCATION SUPPLEMENT

Manchester University Press
Manchester and New York

distributed exclusively in the USA and Canada by St. Martin's Press

Published by Manchester University Press
Oxford Road, Manchester M13 9NR, UK
and Room 400, 175 Fifth Avenue, New York, NY 10010, USA

Distributed exclusively in the USA and Canada
by St. Martin's Press, Inc., 175 Fifth Avenue, New York, NY 10010, USA

British Library Cataloguing-in-Publication Data
A catalogue record for this book is available from the British Library

Library of Congress Cataloging-in-Publication Data applied for

ISBN 0 7190 4773 0 *hardback*
    0 7190 4954 7 *paperback*

First published 1996

00 99 98 97 96   10 9 8 7 6 5 4 3 2 1

Typeset in Great Britain
by Servis Filmsetting Ltd, Manchester

Printed in Great Britain
by Bell & Bain Ltd, Glasgow

Contents

[v]

Preface

As the first woman to edit the Times Higher Education Supplement in its 25 year history, it gives me particular pleasure to introduce this volume of profiles of women who are making an outstanding contribution to intellectual life. Most of them have featured in the columns of the paper over the past couple of years.

Women now make up around half the undergraduate population of most universities. They are out performing boys at school in some countries. But they are still only thinly represented in the upper echelons of universities. We at the THES therefore wanted, by shining a spotlight on women's achievements, to contribute to raising their profile in academic life and to encourage more women to aim higher.

After the First World War women made huge strides in professional occupations in western Europe, but those who did were often unmarried and were not therefore juggling the demands of career with those of family. Today's high fliers are more often parents with all the added pressures that brings, particularly at the crucial time in university life when academic stars break from the pack in their thirties.

It is our hope that by making more visible those who are successful, whatever their circumstances, many more women will be inspired to break through that glass ceiling which can be as much in our minds as in the minds of others.

I would like also to take this opportunity to thank the staff and contributors to the THES who have written and illustrated these profiles, and in particular, Sian Griffiths, THES features editor, herself a journalist, wife and mother.

Auriol Stevens
Editor
The Times Higher Education Supplement

Introduction

In the 1860s Sophia Jex-Blake, determined to train and practice in medicine, sought to enrol in the faculty of medicine at the University of Edinburgh in Scotland. Initially, the university accepted her enrolment, provided she received separate tuition in embarrassing subjects like anatomy. However, other students and some of the faculty took exception to Sophia Jex-Blake's presence and began a campaign of harassment and exclusion. Our heroes introduced a sheep into the lectures, which wore a placard suggesting it had greater brainpower than the woman in their midst, and certain professors of equal wit refused to teach a member of the fair sex out of respect for her delicacy and sensibilities.

Although joined in the course by a handful of other undaunted women, who provided some sustenance against the constant provocation, it became clear to Sophia that the refusal of academics to teach women would prevent any of them qualifying. There ensued a lengthy legal battle, Jex-Blake v. Senatus of the University of Edinburgh (1873) 11 McPherson 784, culminating in a ruling by their Lordships which excluded women from tertiary institutions. Passages of Lord Neave's judgment explain the rationale:

> It is a belief, widely entertained, that there is a great difference in the mental constitution of the two sexes, just as there is in their physical conformation. The power and susceptibilities of women are as noble as those of men; but they are thought to be different and, in particular, it is considered that they have not the same power of intense labour as men are endowed with. If this be so, it must form a serious objection to uniting them under the same course of academic study. I confess that, to some extent, I share this view, and should regret to see our young females subjected to the severe and incessant work which my own observation and experience have taught me to consider as indispensable to any high attainment in learning. A disregard of such an inequality would be fatal to any scheme of public instruction . . .
>
> Add to this the special acquirements and accomplishments at which women must aim, but from which men may easily remain exempt. Much

time must, or ought to be, given by women to the acquisition of a knowledge of household affairs and family duties, as well as to those ornamental
parts of education which tend so much to social refinement and domestic
happiness, and the study necessary for mastering these must always form
a serious distraction from severe pursuits, while there is little doubt that,
in public estimation, the want of these feminine arts and attractions in a
woman would be ill supplied by such branches of knowledge as a university could bestow.

Happily, there continued to be bloody-minded women who relished
'severe pursuits' and there were sustained and persistent assaults by subsequent generations of women upon the citadels of learning. Oxford
allowed women to take degrees in 1920; Cambridge witheld full
membership from them until 1948. However, a different story can be
told of the 'new' civic universities of Liverpool, Birmingham,
Manchester, Sheffield and others, which had come into being in the
latter half of the nineteenth century, making a decisive contribution to
the education of women because of their much more egalitarian ethos.
And of course, each further wave of 'new' universities, the glass and
steel campuses of the sixties and the now elevated polytechnics, has
steadily embraced women so that female students now constitute
around 50 per cent of the undergraduate population within most universities in Britain.

This canvas can be painted in comparable ways in many other countries and similar stories told of grand men expostulating on the proper
role of women. The sheer brilliance of so many female scholars can no
longer be dismissed, and the collection of stunning women included in
this book speaks to the richness and variety of their contribution to the
crucible of ideas. We could all include other favourites – Toni Morrison,
Germaine Greer, Ruth Hubbard, Lisa Jardine. The excitement is in the
impossibility of closing the list. Yet, the shameful fact remains that only
5 per cent of professorships in the United Kingdom are held by women
and 16 per cent in the United States. In the words of the historian, Janet
Sondheimer, 'professorial chairs, apparently, were designed to accom-
modate only the masculine frame'.

Why should it be that the world of academe should lag so far behind
other fields of endeavour? In her book *No Distinction of Sex? Women
in British Universities, 1870–1939*, Carol Dyhouse notes the special criticism directed at the universities, especially Oxford and Cambridge, in
the 1990 Hansard Report, 'Women at the Top'. The Commission con-

tended that it was 'wholly unacceptable that British universities should remain bastions of male power and prestige'. The report cited figures showing that most women were in low-level posts, and only a small percentage were full-time tenured members of staff.

In the intervening period some progress has taken place. We have, for example, seen the appointment of women, such as Marilyn Butler, as principals of Oxbridge colleges which were formerly all male. The new universities are employing women in slightly more generous numbers. In 1993 the Government commissioned a working party to look into the problems of UK women in science, engineering and technology, and in the following year it published a report, *The Rising Tide*, recommending ways in which hurdles can be removed. But the pace of change is testudinal.

Why are there fewer women at the top? Like many similar studies, a recent analysis showed that although youngsters enter Oxbridge universities with similar A-level results more boys than girls achieve a first-class degree (McCrum: 'The academic gender deficit at Oxford and Cambridge', *Oxford Review of Education* 1994). The author of this study suggests a number of possible explanations, including the theory that men have larger and/or better brains than women. Likewise, a recent article by Glen Wilson in the *Times Higher Education Supplement* (25 March 1994) suggests that schemes designed to help women storm male bastions will not succeed because women are innately equipped to do certain jobs and not others. 'Equal but different', he argues, suggesting that men's testosterone levels predispose them to strive for higher status within the dominance hierarchy so that they will 'sacrifice almost anything (barring sex) in order to gain power'. Hence, in this view, women find it difficult to compete with men at work. We are basically not sufficiently thrusting!

On the other hand, in a recent article in *Scientific American*, Professor M. Holloway observed that women in science commonly encounter a 'glass ceiling', and proposed that the system itself might be at fault for their failure. She suggested that women are judged in a system set up by men which reflects male standards and criteria; an argument I have myself tendered in relation to the small numbers of women appointed to the ranks of Queen's Counsel and to the Bench.

In a review of recent policy, Dr Nancy Lane of the Department of Zoology at Cambridge records that women are more likely to be interested in scientific problems if they have social relevance, and tend to work better in collaboration rather than competition. Women scientists are believed to organise their laboratories in a less hierarchical way than men, approaching problems with a different managerial style, and often having a different sociological perspective. All of these observations suggest that cultural and attitudinal differences, not innate feminine flaws, have made science a world dominated by masculine habits and behaviour. A more collaborative 'female' approach might help not just women, but also the system's overall effectiveness.

However, the undervaluing of women's skill is central to their absence from the highest echelons. The difficulty in challenging the glass ceiling which exists for women is that it is so difficult to see. The explanation is peddled that women are not present in these élite groups because of the extraordinary nature of the achievement necessary to gain a place, or a first-class degree, or a senior academic post at these centres of excellence. This fiction that the tests of excellence are neutral and that merit is an objective assessment is perpetually fostered. A *Times* editorial in 1993 explained that 'Oxford's dilemma is that equal opportunities commitments conflict with the competitive system on which the university is based'. As Professor Lisa Jardine pointed out at the time, this fails to explain why one set of competitors – highly qualified female academics – never get off the starting blocks.

Although rarely articulated, there is an unspoken residual belief that women just might not be as clever as their male colleagues. Therefore, the very few who pass muster on the male-determined academic Richter scale are wholly exceptional. It can be very tempting then for those who are given the 'exceptional' badge to believe they are truly blessed amongst women, and not to see the disadvantage faced by other female academics.

In departments with anything approaching equal numbers of women and men, the women perform exactly as well as men. And as badly – there are plenty of middlingly competent men in senior posts in our universities. (Just as I see many mediocre male judges in our courts.) But it is clear that places where women are valued are much more likely to produce their best performance.

We are inclined to believe that the academic world is one immune to prejudice – a world of genuine equal opportunity, where free expression and liberal values ensure that pure brilliance, objectively recognised, gains its reward. However, this is a myth which has to be examined.

There are no job descriptions for professorships, no personnel specifications, no stipulated criteria against which to assess the fitness of the appointee to the post. Accordingly, there are no checks against the inadvertently biased choices which regularly creep into appointment committees. Without explicit criteria, promotion panels can, with the best intentions, persist in introducing extraneous criteria which render a candidate unsuitable, when really their resistance to the candidate is because she is not what they know, what they have always had, what they can trust.

Even among the success stories told in this book, there are examples of apparent discrimination. It is to the credit of women that they rarely harp on such bad experiences, but perhaps that very *politesse* is one of our handicaps. Carole Jordan, Britain's most senior woman astronomer, has the distinction of being the first woman president of the Royal Astronomical Society. She was elected to the Royal Society, Britain's highest scientific honour, in 1990, the day after she was turned down for an Oxford readership. She is now a reader, is on the board of the UK Particle Physics and Astronomy Research Council but, at the time of writing, still had no professorship.

As deputy director of the Thomas Coram research unit at the Institute of Education, Ann Oakley saw the top job fall vacant and awarded to another candidate. She ended up heading her own research unit and gaining a personal chair.

The difficulty about using the Sex Discrimination Act, as Alison Halford, the senior policewoman, discovered to her cost, is that institutions, accused of discriminatory practice in a senior-level discretionary appointment, always insist upon the inferiority of the complainant to justify their choice. The process can be profoundly undermining to the woman and prejudicial to her opportunities elsewhere. All too often the tribunal hearing the case will share the value system of the appointing body and fail to recognise the discrimination.

One of the central components of the glass ceiling in academia is the mysterious and mystified ideal of an ungendered, disembodied academic brilliance. Germaine Greer has argued that the Oxbridge (and Ivy League) first-class degree represents a particular style of intellectual achievement to which women should not feel compelled to aspire. That is all very well, but if the world out there still rates that particular success as more valuable than any other, where does it leave women? What still has to be challenged are the very conceptions of knowledge and excellence produced and protected by a discipline or profession.

Repeatedly, within the histories recounted in this book, women find their methodology undermined or devalued.

Natalie Zemon Davis, the historian, has led the micronarrative method of constructing history through storytelling. She did this with great acclaim in *The Return of Martin Guerre*, the tale of an impostor in sixteenth-century rural France. Yet her work was subjected to an intemperate attack by the historian Robert Finlay on behalf of 'certainty', which is supposed to be achieved by the traditional historian's practice, as though that were totally neutral. In particular his offensive against Davis's historical narrative concerns itself with her methodology, which pays explicit attention to gender.

The irony of some of the attacks upon womens' work is that male scientific method is not beyond reproach. Sarah Hrdy, the anthropologist, pioneered a whole new branch of feminist primatology, showing how male-biased early animal behaviour studies have been. Carol Gilligan, the psychologist, working at Harvard under Lawrence Kohlberg, famed for his research on moral development, and Erik Erikson, an expert on self and identity, discovered that both used all-male samples for their research from which they drew universal conclusions. They were, of course, doing no more than Freud or Piaget, giving a male voice to their perspective, as lawmakers and historians and all sorts of supposedly impartial contributors to the fund of human knowledge have done before and since.

The historian, Joan Scott, argues that we have been distracted by the numbers game of trying to expand access to the universities without recognising that once 'inside' the institution, 'the subject-disciplines operate curiously consistently to remind those within that the female participant is other than the participant around whom the subject has been structured'.

Even when women seek to introduce a different perspective, the result is a frequent marginalising of their scholarship. Academics doing work specifically concerning women will be seen as narrow, their expertise as less central than those who keep closer to the orthodoxies. And so, for many women, there is early recognition that a condition of admission to these rarefied worlds is to function as honorary men. Similar choices have to be made by ambitious women in other fields. 'Hard' areas of politics like economics, foreign affairs and defence are more prestigious and the likelier roads to the top than 'soft' ministries like social services, health or education. There are the hard and soft sciences, the hard and soft areas in law, in history, in medicine. The hard areas are more highly esteemed, are heavily dominated by men, and if a woman penetrates them, and plays by the boys' rules, she will be highly regarded too.

In her paper 'The Illusion of Inclusion', Professor Lisa Jardine, Dean of English at Queen Mary and Westfield College, says 'that it is a secret fear of many women that if they choose to work on a woman author, or if they take a women's studies option or answer a feminism question in their examinations they will pay a consequence. On numerous occasions I have been tempted to dissuade a student from choosing a women's topic, because it will earn a lower grade, or will need to be "much better than normal" to gain a good one'.

These obstacles to women's recognition live within the culture of a discipline; they inhabit the interstices. Their eradication will only come about by naming the problem and exposing it wherever possible. The value of celebrating our successful women is that their stories and achievements are so diverse. Some have taken on scholarship on their own terms. Others have played by the old rules and still excelled. Their experiences are many and varied.

A number of themes do seem to emerge from their lives. As I had observed when charting the careers of senior women judges, many had unusual career patterns – only a few had travelled the main staircase route; others had gone out of the window and up the drainpipe. I suppose if you are having to avoid glass ceilings, even subconsciously, that is not so surprising. Many of the women in these pages have not followed traditional career paths: Cynthia Cockburn, for example, never went to university but her research in the 'sociology of skills' receives wide academic acclaim. She finds it 'reassuring that there are people and institutions that are open-minded and willing to judge a researcher on output rather than certification. Perhaps my career could be some encouragement to other women who find their direction late, or want to change track'. Ann Oakley and others made deliberate career choices to be with their children. None have regrets but as Uta Frith recognised: 'If I hadn't had children, I could have moved about and worked longer hours'.

Another recurring feature is the enthusiasm many women have for working collaboratively and, as Marilyn Strathern describes, blurring the boundaries between disciplines. Some of the most exciting work seems to come from eclecticism. Yet, multi-disciplinary approaches are not always lauded. Mary Douglas, for example, whose work has ranged from anthropology through sociology to religious studies, talks about the risks – including the fear of being dismissed as bizarre – of conducting research in more than one subject. Whether women are more inclined to embark on cross-disciplinary endeavours than men, I have no idea, but they seem to be less reverential about traditional demarcations.

For many of these scholars a crucial role in the launching of their careers was played by a mentor, often an enlightened man, who spurred them on, gave them a break or just treated them as another intellectual. Linda Colley refers to John Cannon, Sarah Hrdy to Prof E. O. Wilson. For others it was a parent who believed in them and their right to explore the avenues of learning. Many, while blushing at the notion of role-models, believe strongly in the importance of bringing on women in their wake. The abiding message is that we all must take responsibility for encouraging and nurturing the gifts of others, wherever we have the opportunity.

But the question remains as to whether the talents of women are different from those of men. Do women approach their research from a female perspective? Is there any difference in what men and women produce in the field of ideas? In several of these profiles the old debate between the essentialists and the relativists rises to the surface, the former arguing that there are biological causes for the different behaviour of men and women, the latter holding that masculine and feminine identities are social constructs.

The woman at the heart of this debate has been Carol Gilligan, whose book *In a Different Voice* stimulated violent debate in the women's movement when it was first published in the early eighties. It was interpreted as endorsing the idea that differences between men and women are not just the outcome of patriarchal oppression. The book concluded that women's moral perspective is different from that of men, an idea which I personally have no difficulty in accepting because it resonates so powerfully with my own perception of women's approach to law.

However, as soon as one recognises difference, there is a fear that value judgments invariably follow, in which the characteristics ascribed to women, such as care and responsibility, are low in the ranking. Unless real value is attached to the 'female' qualities, the consequence could be that women remain locked into negative identities. An intellectual, 'Brahmin' culture privileges not just abstract principles of rights and justice but also particular disciplines or modes of inquiry. Many women understandably view the 'difference' argument with alarm because it could create a cul-de-sac for women, especially when many are involved in intellectual endeavour which cannot be stereotyped in this way.

Hélène Cixous, the French intellectual, rejects the idea that recognition of difference is essentialist. She argues that the struggle for equality becomes confused with a denial of difference. Difference for her is difference 'between' not 'against' and, in celebratory style, she teaches the 'poetic of sexual difference' as a challenge to sterile conceptions of equality.

There can be no resolution of such a debate. Where there can be consensus is that women should be encouraged to be intellectually productive, in whatever ways they desire, and have their endeavours valued. I have come to the conclusion that this will only come to pass if women are included in all the 'gatekeeping' procedures and in all the processes of assessment of research and scholarship. It means that all the paraphernalia of private-sector appointing has to be introduced into the hallowed territory of academia. As Lisa Jardine says, 'It works. If you have to tick a box as to why you have discarded one candidate in favour of another you are forced to confront your own unacknowledged resistance to change'.

Out of the rich soil of these women's lives comes a wealth of ideas and evidence of intellectual rigour. For those of us who have never doubted female aptitude here is the testimony to support our faith. Women are making a difference, everywhere. We just have to make sure that even more of them do.

Helena Kennedy is a Queen's Counsel and Chancellor of Oxford Brookes University. (© Helena Kennedy)

Margaret Boden, born 1936, professor of psychology and philosophy at the University of Sussex, believes that computers can teach us a lot about human creativity.

Photograph by Neil Turner

The story of Henry Ant, composed by a computer program named Tale-Spin, is so devoid of emotion that it is ammunition for those who say computers can never be creative: 'Henry Ant was thirsty. He walked over to the river bank where his good friend Bill Bird was sitting. Henry slipped and fell in the river. He was unable to call for help. He drowned. THE END'.

The story illustrates one of the difficulties of modelling literary creativity via computer programs: writing a story depends on layers of background knowledge that we didn't even know we had. In the case of Henry Ant the programmer forgot to tell Tale-Spin that people generally notice what is happening to others near to them. Bill Bird should have noticed, and rescued, Henry Ant.

This program was written over ten years ago and more sophisticated work has been developing ever since. But much more interesting than the perpetual discussion about whether computing – from ordinary, step-by-step programming to neural networks – can ever really be creative is the question of what insight computer programs can give into human creativity: can computing science explain human originality?

One of the first people to consider this question was Margaret Boden, now professor of psychology and philosophy at the University of Sussex. Her work involved taking human concepts such as 'representation' or 'meaning' and considering whether computer programs could help in developing a scientific explanation for them. At the least, Boden managed to convince a generation of non-computer scientists that artificial intelligence was worth a glance.

[11]

Boden's living-room walls are adorned with pictures created by computers. She sits there, larger than life, amongst the pictures, a collection of antique glassware and books on myriad subjects, and describes the moment when she discovered the possibilities of artificial intelligence. It was just after she had arrived at Harvard University as a doctoral student in the early 60s.

Standing in a bookshop she read *Plans and the Structure of Behaviour* by Miller, Galanter and Pribram, which tried to apply computer programming to the whole of psychology. 'It seemed to me like a flash of lightning – a promising way of asking and perhaps answering a number of questions that I had been asking for years. It hadn't struck me that you could actually use computers to explore theories about psychology in general,' she says. 'I was an idiot.' Attempts to link the two were just beginning in the States, she says. 'The ideas were in the air but there weren't courses in it.'

She was in the right place at the right time. She was also at the right time personally: the wanderings of her background education had led her to the point at which she was ready to develop such ideas. Boden studied medical sciences and philosophy at Cambridge with the intention of becoming a psychiatrist. 'I knew nothing about universities. It wasn't till I got there that I realised you could read philosophy.' Then, just as she was going to start training at St Thomas's, she was offered a post teaching philosophy at Birmingham University. 'It was an extremely good philosophy department but I soon got bored with it. I wanted to do things that didn't really exist then, like philosophy of biology or of psychology.'

So she went to Harvard to do her doctorate in social psychology, specialising in reducing 'purposive' explanations, which explain our behaviour in terms of our intentions, to mechanistic ones, offering physical and chemical interpretations. This formed the core of her first book, *Purposive Explanation in Psychology*. 'Everything else I've written is a footnote to this,' she says. In this book Boden considered the ways in which people use the concept of purpose across a range of psychological theories. She did this by studying a psychologist who denied absolutely that there could be mechanistic explanations for people's intentions – she reinterpreted his theory using computer programs.

After this she was ready, in 1968, married with one child, to enter a centre of learning back in England which had made a commitment to the interdisciplinary approach she needed – Sussex University. 'We at

Sussex were the first in the world to offer degrees in interdisciplinary cognitive science [the branch of psychology that studies how we think and reason],' she says. She praises the university's commitment to inter-disciplinarity: 'it can only work if there is a school or a faculty which not only has a number of different subjects represented in it but also offers many courses that are interdisciplinary in that they are not just taught to people who are majors in that subject. And the staff MUST be all mixed up on the corridors.'

In the late sixties Boden wrote *Artificial Intelligence and Natural Man*, a guide for perplexed non-computer scientists to the guts and implications of AI – the attempt to build robots and computer pro-grams that can mimic human behaviour. The book tried to persuade such people that 'one could be interested in AI because of its psycholog-ical and philosophical relevance'.

In her most popular book, *The Creative Mind*, Boden strove for a sci-entific understanding of creativity. In order to avoid putting critics off at the first page she divided her investigation into four questions: could computational ideas help us understand how creativity is possible? Could computers could ever produce work that 'appears' to be creative? Could computers ever recognise that a work is creative? And could computers ever produce a work that is 'truly' creative?

To start with she avoided computer concepts completely. Instead she explored how we think in certain areas – for example, in music – in ways that may generate creative ideas. Each area is fenced in by rules and mental structures. All types of thinking – music, mathematics, litera-ture – operate within these fences, without which thought would be impossible. They keep out the unthinkable and they keep in an area in which a disciplined form of thinking can occur. Boden calls this a 'con-ceptual space'.

To explore these conceptual spaces we need mind-maps, which tell us where to go, what there is and where the limits are. We spontaneously make mind-maps of what is going on in our minds. As we get to know the subject we develop maps of our maps.

The idea of mind-maps has brought insights into the creativity of children and how it becomes more flexible as they grow up. Older chil-dren, for example, can on request draw abnormal people – perhaps with two heads or no legs. Younger children, although they can draw normal people as fluently as the older children can, just don't have the flexibil-ity to branch out into two heads or no legs. They haven't developed good internal maps of their skills, says Boden. The younger children have a skill which can be switched on but cannot be varied. The older children have explored their skill and re-described it at higher levels, breaking it down and analysing it as they go.

The conceptual space that we navigate with a mind-map is created by a 'generative system', which produces a list of cans and cannots. Crank the generator, create the space and then explore it. An example of a generative system is the one that produced Mendeleev's periodic table: exploring it led to the discovery of new chemical elements.

In order to move in a coherent way through a big conceptual space created by a generative system and described by a mind-map, we need a set of heuristics. '"Protect your queen" directs you into some chess-paths and away from others,' says Boden. New ideas can come from exploring the conceptual space. But there is a more important source of new ideas. These arise when a thinker works on his or her conceptual space and transforms it in some way. Suddenly its topography is altered or its boundaries shifted – and new ideas are possible that could not have been entertained before. It was a transformation of conceptual space, for example, that enabled Johannes Kepler, seventeenth-century astronomer, to escape from viewing planetary motion as circular and portray it as elliptical.

It may be unpleasant to think that the magical way in which a thinker has transformed a space could perhaps be written down as a set of heuristics. But Boden suggests that heuristics could do just that. The command 'consider the negative', she says, 'if applied at a relatively deep level of the generative system , can transform the space so fundamentally that very different sorts of location are created and many previous locations, indeed whole regions, simply cease to exist.'

Boden distinguishes between a novelty (for example a nonsense-sentence that has previously never been uttered) and a creative idea. 'Creative ideas are surprising, yes. They go against our expectations. But something wholly unconnected with the familiar arouses not surprise so much as bewilderment. To be sure the lack of connection with what went before may be apparent rather than real. But someone to whom the connection is not apparent will not be able to recognize the idea as *creative* (as opposed to *new*). Nor will they be able to see it as relevant to what they had regarded as the problem-domain in question: "That's not art!", "Call that poetry?"'.

Once these ideas are assimilated, Boden slips in the computer terminology. 'Fortunately,' she writes, 'a science already exists in which conceptual spaces can be precisely described: namely, artificial intelligence.'

The computer program (the person) uses a set of instructions (the heuristics) to explore a search space (conceptual space). Boden says: 'You may object: "constraints, yes. Computer programs – never!" But since creativity is a question of what thoughts can and cannot result from particular mental structures and processes, anyone seeking to understand it needs to be able to describe those structures and processes clearly, and assess their generative potential rigorously. This is why it is helpful to use AI-terms to describe the creative constraints in human minds.'

Boden's insistence that ordinary, step-by-step computer programming can give insight into creativity has been criticised, especially with the rise of parallel processing in computing – or neural networks – which are modelled far more closely on how the brain works. But Boden says: 'It is a mistake to think that sequential computer programs cannot possibly teach us anything about psychology . . . theories may identify some of the specific computational processes which, in human beings, are run in parallel. There is great excitement at present about the recent AI-work on connectionism. This is understandable, as we shall soon see. But it should not obscure the fact that step-by-step AI-models, despite their "unnatural" air, can help us investigate the contents, structures and processes of human thought.'

Boden agrees that many creative acts involve more flexible mental processes than those described in sequential programming – for example seeing an analogy where none was there before. Take the water snakes of Coleridge's 'Ancient Mariner', 'blue, glossy green, and velvet black,' which 'moved in tracks of shining white' shedding 'hoary flakes' of 'elfish light'. Luckily Coleridge's extraordinarily wide reading, which included scientific works on sea creatures, was tracked over sixty years ago by John Livingston Lowes. His conclusion was that Coleridge's genius lay in his extraordinary memory and in his inspired powers of association. To dissect this human achievement, Boden uses ideas from neural networks. These systems 'learn' as they go along rather than being programmed. Association of ideas by humans takes place via comparable processes, says Boden. Connectionist systems can recognise patterns that they have experienced before; they can recognise parts of patterns and distortions of patterns as variations on the original pattern; they can provide 'best' matches to patterns (as we would do in judging the aptness of a poetic image) and they can learn to do better. 'People who claim that computational ideas are irrelevant to creativity because *"brains are not programmed"* must face the fact that connec-

tionist computation is not the manipulation of formal symbols by programmed rules . . . we must consider the ability of neural networks to
learn to associate patterns without being explicitly programmed in
respect of *those* patterns.'

The use of the old and the new computing has produced some rivet-
ing pieces of apparent creativity – from the ludicrous Henry Ant to the
artwork on Boden's walls. Boden herself makes interesting use of analogies. Amongst the spill of them in her books are comparisons with knitting patterns and threading necklaces. One publisher asked her to
remove them on the grounds that they would not be understood. She
replied that she was fed up with analogies with radios and motor cars,
which she as a woman did not understand – men would just have to go
and find out about knitting.

Her tribulations as a woman peek out of her CV as well as her writings. Under 'posts' appears: 'Invited to Center for Advanced Study in
Behavioral Sciences, Palo Alto, in 1973, 1980 & 1990: unable to go,
because of children'. 'This is to remind people that women have it very
difficult,' she says. Her second book, *Artificial Intelligence and Natural
Man*, took five years to put together. 'I was married, I had a full-time
job, I had two babies: it took ages to write. All I could afford was help
for two days a week so I had to cram all my teaching into two days a
week and cram all my research around when the baby was asleep. But
also, I wouldn't have wanted another woman to be with my children all
that time.'

She and her husband divorced in 1981 when the children were 13 and
9. But she also says that being a woman has had advantages – her
generation was free from pressure to have a successful career and, as a
result, she followed her ideas and took risks.

She says she has encountered virtually no opposition because of her
sex. But there is opposition for other reasons. Some entirely dismiss her
area of work. Stuart Sutherland, professor emeritus at Sussex University,
where he was formerly professor of experimental psychology, reviewed
in the *Times Higher Education Supplement* in 1994 a book edited by
Boden, *Dimensions of Creativity*. He said: 'Almost all people who can
think – and many who cannot . . . believe they have something valuable
to say about creativity. Unfortunately, as *Dimensions of Creativity* . . .
amply demonstrates, most of them are wrong.'

Boden has also been criticised for writing about artificial intelligence
but not getting involved in writing computer programs. Boden says:
'There are many, many people who think that what we do is funda-

mentally incorrect. Most people who are not academics, and especially the general public, assume that it's got to be nonsense.'

Nonsense objections fall into four categories, she says: the brain-stuff argument (computers are made of non-biological material so they can't be creative); the empty program argument (computers will never grasp meaning); the consciousness argument (consciousness is essential to creativity and AI cannot be conscious) and the non-human argument (creative beings would deserve rights, computers don't have rights, therefore computers cannot be creative). She rejects the first three arguments. 'I believe that in principle computers that we have only dreamed of could produce all of the behaviour which human beings produce including what we call creative behaviour.'

Still, would such behaviour really be the result of full-blown creativity on the inside? Boden says: 'I would prefer to sit on the fence but if I was forced to come off I would say that computers can't be truly creative, for moral and political reasons. If a computer literally has creativity then it literally has desires and interests – it would be part of our ethical world. It would be a question of whether people wished to accord them this type of respect.'

Publications include:

Purposive Explanation in Psychology, 1972, Harvard University Press.
Piaget, 1979, Fontana Modern Masters Series, Collins and Harvester Press.
Minds and Mechanisms: Philosophical Psychology and Computational Models, 1981, Harvester Press/Cornell University Press.
Computer Models of Mind: Computational Approaches in Theoretical Psychology, 1988, Cambridge University Press.
(Ed.) *The Philosophy of Artificial Intelligence*, 1990, Oxford University Press.
The Creative Mind: Myths and Mechanisms, 1990, Weidenfeld and Nicolson.
(Ed.) *Dimensions of Creativity*, 1994, MIT Press.

(Aisling Irwin, © Times Higher Education Supplement)

Buried at the bottom of page one of **Jocelyn Bell Burnell**'s curriculum vitae are the words 'discovered pulsars'. That was nearly thirty years ago. Born in 1943, she is now professor of physics at the Open University.

Photograph © Jenny Matthews

It was a tiny signal that blipped out of a chattering printer, a quarter of an inch of ink among the hundreds of feet covering the daily chart. The hundreds of feet of ink represented radio signals from around the universe; the quarter of an inch was a ragged signal that was different from the rest. The woman who noticed it was Jocelyn Bell and she had just discovered pulsars, one of the major astronomical discoveries of this century. She was a mere doctoral student at the time. But that was nearly thirty years ago.

Where is she now? She is sitting in a neat suit in a tidy office at the Open University in Milton Keynes; quiet, modest and, one suspects, strict. She is on an exciting hunt for the missing supernovae in our galaxy, the stars that explode with a huge brightening radiation because their cores collapse. But her work will probably always be overshadowed by her discovery of 1967.

The pulsar is a rotating star that has reached the end of its evolutionary life and run out of nuclear fuel. It undergoes gravitational collapse into a state that is so compressed that all electrons are forced into the atomic nucleii where they combine with the protons to become neutrons. Current models of neutron stars give them a diameter of less than 10 kilometres, but they are so dense that they weigh one and a half times more than the sun. After the 1967 discovery had been told to the world, there was another pulsar discovery in the Crab nebula. This confirmed that pulsars were neutron stars that rotate and emit beamed radiation, like a lighthouse.

Discovering neutron stars supplied strong evidence that black holes existed because neutron stars represent matter on the verge of ultimate gravitational collapse to become black holes. 'I don't think anything I've done subsequently has matched that in terms of impact on the world,' says Professor Bell Burnell. 'It's extremely hard to follow. The odds are you won't do anything else comparable.'

At Cambridge University, which she joined as a PhD student to help with a new telescope for measuring electromagnetic radiation of radio frequencies that have passed through the Earth's atmosphere, she also stood out because she was a woman. To reach the stage of being a female postgraduate astronomy student had required doggedness right from the time of physics lessons at her all-female Quaker school. 'There was a very good physics teacher but very little equipment,' she says. 'We were shown a catalogue to demonstrate equipment. I decided that I wanted to do radio astronomy but the careers mistress at school hadn't even heard of it. So I wrote a letter to "Bernard Lovell, Jodrell Bank, Cheshire" and fortunately he replied.' Armed with his advice she read physics at Glasgow University. 'There were forty-nine men and me,' she says. Some of her female peers advised her to change course because of the ratio.

But she persisted and reached Cambridge where she worked under Nobel prize-winner Antony Hewish. Radio-astronomers study the radio-frequency emissions of celestial bodies. The first such emissions had been discovered about thirty-five years before. When she had finished her doctorate, 'The measurement of radio source diameters using a diffraction method', she moved to Southampton University for five years and from there to University College London's Mullard Space Science Laboratory to exploit the X-ray spectrometer, an instrument for investigating the X-ray region of the spectrum, on the Ariel V satellite.

Ariel was the first international satellite programme to develop from an offer by the National Aeronautics and Space Administration to launch foreign satellites. Number five carried experiments to study X-ray sources in space. 'It was hugely exciting,' she says. 'It set new directions in astronomy'. She and others were mapping the sky and major discoveries were tumbling down on them: transient X-ray sources and globular clusters – nearly spherical groups of tens of thousands of stars which move around the galaxies in elliptical orbits. Ariel V's main achievements were to expand knowledge about black holes and to discover a new type of star. 'It was a combination of timing and good management that did it', she says. Astronomy was the place to be and Ariel V was the satellite to be working with in 1974.

This reliance on timing has run through her life as a result of following her husband, whose job took him to different parts of the country every few years. Set up by a fine reputation early in her career, she became a part-time astrophysicist, writing letters 'on spec' to the nearest centre whenever she moved, finding a part-time job and bringing up her son the rest of the time.

This pattern took her to the Royal Observatory in Edinburgh, where she eventually became head of the James Clerk Maxwell Telescope Section in Edinburgh. The telescope, perched on a 13,800-foot mountain in Hawai, detects emissions in the part of the electromagnetic spectrum that lies between infra-red and radio waves. She then managed the Edison project, a radiatively cooled infra-red space observatory – still part-time.

In this male-dominated world she claims that she learned to be more assertive. But she was starting from a disadvantage. Back in that Quaker school it was forbidden to ask for anything at table. You could only offer it to someone else and hope that they would return the favour: 'I have had to learn to sell myself', she says.

Yet her curriculum vitae doesn't sell itself. Buried at the bottom of page one in the sixth line of explanation of her time at Cambridge are the single words: 'discovered pulsars'. This despite the significance of pulsars, which have stimulated research in many areas. Pulsars have been used as laboratories for studying matter under extreme conditions that could not be simulated on Earth. They have been used for research on the physics of the solid state and quantum liquids. They have been used to test Einstein's theory of general relativity. One exciting discovery has been a pair of neutron stars orbiting each other closely and creating ripples in space time, which spread out at the speed of light in the form of gravitational waves.

Jocelyn Bell Burnell's experience of the male physics world has had a profound effect on her. She has only written one book and it is not on astrophysics. *Broken for Life* is about the problem of suffering. It delivers the message that 'people who are hurt have quite a special service to give', she says. 'I sensed that in the circles I was moving there was a very great emphasis on being upbeat. It was getting out of balance. One could no longer acknowledge distress. I suspected that people were brushing hurt under the carpet – theirs and other people's hurt.'

She was influenced by the physics world and by the Quaker world, in which she is highly involved. She is a first assistant clerk at the annual Quaker meeting in Britain but she stresses that the Quakers avoid hierarchy and all consider themselves as servants. She was also influenced by her son's development of diabetes – his experiences surely moulded him into a person with gifts, such as empathy, to share, rather than one with a defect not to be mentioned?

'I wonder whether (brushing hurt away) is particularly true in a male dominated area,' she says. 'The element of bravado is stronger in men than in women. In physics and astronomy there's a culture that's confident and assertive. There is a distortion of the kind of values that I would like to work with.' Rather than copy her peers it seems that their influence sent the dogged part of her in pursuit of developing her own notion of values.

And now she has been using the opportunity to practise her own ideas in running a physics department. At the Open University she feels she is reaching her third great academic phase after pulsars and Ariel V. With a research student she is investigating data on a 'very curious object' in our galaxy: 'In the infra-red (region) it flares to double its flux strength in 20 seconds, stays high and then drops away. This is behaviour that is totally unknown to X-ray astronomers.' Her second project is to use radio survey data to try and find out why so few supernovae, or exploded stars, have been detected in our galaxy: 'Fifty a year are seen in other galaxies but we are not seeing them in ours'.

She finds the science exciting and she finds the students exciting. 'Teaching OU students is terrific. They're highly motivated; they're keen; they're bright. It's terrifying how many people there are out there who are capable of university education and even of PhDs.' She has also become involved in campaigns to introduce more women into science, possibly sharpened in resolve by the recent failure of her marriage. Managing the life she had created as wife and scientist was 'very difficult', she says. Nowadays there are 'fewer raised eyebrows' when young women do the same.

She finds herself increasingly put forward as a role model for young women, as the token woman on top committees and as a magnet for attracting more women into physics. She says there have been many more female applicants for jobs in her department since she joined.

On the lack of women in science in the United Kingdom and the United States she says: 'Increasingly I believe that it's something to do with the culture. In Italy the girls are not allowed to give up science. It's seen as quite normal for girls to do physics. In some countries, such as Italy, France, Mexico, Argentina the proportion of women in physics or astronomy is about 40 per cent.' She has a lot of work to do: when she was appointed to the Open University chair in 1991 she doubled the number of physics chairs held by female professors.

Publications include:

'Observation of a rapidly pulsating radio source', 1968, with A. Hewish, J. D. H. Pilkington, P. F. Scott and R. A. Collins, *Nature,* 217, pp. 709–13.

'A catalogue of X-ray spectra observed with the Ariel V proportional counter (Expt.C)', 1984, with L. Chiappetti, *Astronomy and Astrophysics Supplement,* 56, pp. 415–39.

Broken for Life, 1989, Quaker Home Service.

(Ed.) *Next Generation Infra-red Space Observatory,* 1992, with J. K. Davis and R. S. Stobie, Kluwer Academic Publishers

'Simultaneous millimetre and radio observations of Cygnus X-3 in quiescent radio state', 1995, with R. P .Fender, S. T. Garrington, R. E. Spencer and G. G. Pooley, *Monthly Notices Royal Astronomical Society,* 274, pp. 636–8.

(Aisling Irwin, © Times Higher Education Supplement)

Marilyn Butler, born 1937, erstwhile BBC producer, English professor and, since 1993, rector of Exeter College, Oxford; the first female head of a formerly male Oxbridge college.

Photograph © Ros Drinkwater

Exeter College, tucked in between the scholarly Bodleian Library and the bustling Oxford covered market, between the nerve centre of the university and the popular hub of the town. It's an appropriate place for

Marilyn Butler, a situation she obviously enjoys. For Butler, former King Edward VII professor of English in Cambridge and now rector of Exeter, has always managed to combine the scholarly and the popular in her work, spanning the outside world of journalism as well as the inner one of academe.

Her journalism training began early. Her father, Sir Trevor Evans, originally a coal miner in the Welsh valleys, rose through penny-a-line local papers to a job as industrial and labour correspondent for the *Daily Express*. His life, according to Butler, seemed 'hugely dramatic and exciting', as he led social debate in the country with his 'think-pieces' and followed every twist of the day's news as it happened. Media deadlines governed their lives. The family even chose to live in south-west London, Kingston upon Thames, because it had an all-night train service and the *Express's* last edition printed at four a.m. Six papers reached the Evans household every morning, and Butler acquired a prodigious knowledge of current affairs. She still proudly remembers beating the rest of Wimbledon High School at the age of eleven in the general knowledge quiz. It wasn't worth holding the quiz after that till she had left the school.

Her life seemed destined for the world of facts, for arguments about politics and social issues. She was planning to read history at Oxford, followed possibly by a career in journalism. But just before taking the Oxford entrance examination, she saw a production of Shakespeare's *Coriolanus*, an experience which changed her plans radically. She knew the original story of Coriolanus from Plutarch's account, but Shakespeare's version came as a revelation. 'I was completely fascinated,' she remembers, 'sitting there in the audience by the way that the play made the outcome seem inevitable, while the history made it seem accidental.' Much to the annoyance of the school, she decided suddenly to study English, 'the artistic representation of history', rather than history, which now seemed 'so straightforward by comparison, just like newspapers'.

Awarded an exhibition by St Hilda's College, she threw herself into the seriously bookish life of a typical female undergraduate in the mid fifties. But journalism and politics soon seduced her back. Philip French, now film critic for the *Observer*, commissioned her to write film reviews for the student newspaper, *Isis*. Another university paper, *Cherwell*, published her news features. The strongest pull came from Oxford's New Left, a wide grouping of students which had formed in the wake of the Suez crisis and the Soviet invasion of Hungary, and which went on to found the *New Left Review*. One of the leaders of the group was Stuart Hall, now professor of sociology at the Open University and chief creator of cultural studies as a subject. 'It was a rather heady, exciting period', he remembers, a time when students moved beyond the 'pretty backward, *belle lettriste* atmosphere' of the official Oxford literature course and met up with a wider circle of friends to discuss questions of power, culture and literature. They read Raymond Williams and F. R. Leavis, they mooted the novel argument that politics infiltrated further than the conventional political sphere, and they discussed why literature mattered to a wider society. Marilyn Butler was part of the group, 'not a student radical', Hall stresses but 'very very intelligent'.

After university, journalism briefly won the upper hand. Butler won a place on the BBC trainee scheme, and worked in the newsroom in London and later in Manchester, drawing upon her very ready sense of humour when reporting the launching of a ship which stuck halfway down the slipway. But the ephemeral nature of reporting, in which Butler felt 'after three months that I hadn't done anything', could not hold her attention. She longed for the slower thoroughness of academia, and returned to Oxford to complete a doctorate on Maria Edgeworth, the Irish contemporary of Jane Austen and Walter Scott. Over the next eight years, she wrote two books before taking up a research fellowship at St Hilda's College and subsequently a lectureship at St Hugh's.

But the leap from journalism to academia was not so wide. The years of politics and writing for a wide audience shine through Butler's work. Her style is clear, highly readable and jargon-free. Arguments are delivered as stories, literature a series of narratives. Some have seen her style as ideologically motivated. Marjorie Levinson, an American New Historicist critic, thinks it is 'subversive' of Marilyn Butler to resist the theoretical language prevalent in academic institutions. But Butler is reluctant to accept this conspiracy theory, preferring rather to see her writing as the product of 'the daughter of a man who wrote for twelve million people everyday'.

If her style is populist, her view of writers is too. Her second book, *Jane Austen and the War of Ideas*, based upon an undergraduate essay written in the inspiring days of the New Left, caused a stir when it argued that, far from apolitical studies of young women with their inner lives, Austen's novels are in fact highly political and engage in the warfare of debate of the early nineteenth century. Her fourth book, *Romantics, Rebels and Reactionaries*, maintained, among other things, that the younger Romantic poets – Byron, Shelley and Keats – were less interested in the transcendent world of the imagination than in the political effect their writing about alternative imaginary worlds would have upon their ideological opponents, other writers and their readers.

Behind these arguments is the belief that literature is not written in isolation but within the cross-currents of historical debate. Just as newspapers are influenced by their readers, a book, Butler has argued, 'is made by its public'. This notion of literature rooted in history aligns Butler closely with the New Historicism critics in America, men like Jerome McGann and Stephen Greenblatt. But she is wary of their American theorising of history. For her, literature is a place 'where there is an important debate going on', designed originally to be read by a wide cross-section of readers, and so it must be explained in a similar fashion.

This tactic of clarity and polemicism, according to Professor Janet Todd, former Cambridge colleague, places Butler 'in the forefront' of historicising criticism. But some have expressed doubts about its appropriateness for the reading of poetry. In her efforts to emphasise the social dimensions of literature rather than the imaginative, she is not so good, one Oxford colleague has suggested, 'at the delicate analysis of poetry'. But Todd agrees with Butler that English criticism had become too dominated by a certain 'patriarchal' way of looking at literature. Butler was keen to widen the number of writers studied, to resist the narrowing of literature down to those few writers whose works are 'good for a close reading technique'. 'Most writing across history has had a social meaning', she asserts. 'It has spoken to an audience that is much wider than literary practitioners and it has been accessible to a much wider audience and a less attentive audience than the modern specialist.'

This view has angered some scholars. One academic allegedly witheringly dismissed Butler's inaugural lecture as professor in Cambridge for not including a single passage of close reading. Another, the American Tom McFarland, has dramatically described Butler as 'dwelling in the foothills of Romanticism', while he prefers the peaks of the canonical poets. Butler smiles when she remembers this jibe. 'Tom obviously feels that it is very impoverishing to be stuck in the foothills but I think it is very narrowing to have this damn mountain concept.' Foothills, for Butler, offer a more socially integrated picture of cultural life: 'You get a great deal of interesting local activity around foothills, quite apart from the whole of human life actually existing at that level'.

Abandoning McFarland's traditional notion of Romanticism as a collection of canonical poets has meant that Marilyn Butler has broadened the ideas of the Romantic period. Rather than an aesthetic movement, to which only a few writers appear to conform, Romanticism, for her, implies a series of reactions from writers to the momentous events of the late eighteenth and early nineteenth centuries, and especially to the French Revolution. This different perspective allows the conservative Jane Austen and the comic Thomas Love Peacock to be considered as Romantics, as well as the traditionally Romantic poets like Wordsworth and Keats. The broadening of the term Romanticism has also resulted in the reassessment of the dates of the Romantic Age. Butler is anxious to date the Romantic period from 1760, rather than the more conventional 1789, because this allows the inclusion of various radical Enlightenment writers and gives less emphasis to the importance of Wordsworth in the 1790s.

It is probably her resistance to what Janet Todd calls the 'one-man-and-his-poem' school of criticism which has encouraged Marilyn Butler's reputation a feminist. Her first two books were about women novelists – Maria Edgeworth and Jane Austen – and she was instrumental in instituting a women's writing paper as part of the Oxford English course. At Cambridge she helped to run the women's literature graduate seminar, and she collaborated with Janet Todd in the editing of the seven-volume collection of Mary Wollstonecraft's writing, the pioneering eighteenth century feminist. This final collaboration might have caused Rachel Trickett, retired principal of St Hugh's and her DPhil supervisor, to wonder whether 'feminism went to her head' when she left for Cambridge.

But Todd thinks 'it is hard to imagine anything going to Marilyn's head', since Butler 'is such a well balanced person' who would prefer feminist issues to be incorporated into a general picture of literature. Terry Eagleton, Thomas Warton professor at Oxford, agrees that while she is a 'fellow traveller' with those who work on feminist literary theory, her own work is 'more wary of the explicitly feminist'. Feminism alone is too theoretical, too divorced from the real world, and, crucially for Butler, too narrowing.

It is partly this balanced approach which prevents Butler, surprisingly, from dwelling on her own difficulties as a woman academic. When she left the BBC for academia, she was also swayed by the fact that her new husband, David Butler, was an Oxford don and that travelling to London from Oxford for work each day would be hard. While she wrote her thesis over the next four years, she also gave birth to their three children – a 'very economical use of time'. Rachel Trickett is full of admiration, praising her 'enormous energy' and her 'tremendous ability to adapt to the situation' of combining small children and scholarly work.

But Butler offers a different perspective. She was supported by her husband for the first eight years of marriage, so that by the time she reached her first tenured position at St Hugh's College, she had completed two substantial books because time had not been distracted with teaching. Even the inevitable interruptions from small children did not spoil the reading of Jane Austen because Austen usefully did not write 'such long books' and she kept herself to 'finite chapters' which Butler could fit in between transporting children to and from school.

But whatever the degree of feminism in her work, Marilyn Butler is inevitably a role model for young women scholars. She recognises the significance of her appointment as the first female head of a former male Oxbridge college (two other women heads took up positions a couple of terms later), seeing a direct connection between her appointment and the criticism that there were not enough women professors and readers in the university. She feels the pressure to sit on numerous committees in order to be visible, to represent women. Her husband too has notoriously done his bit for the women's cause. After the all-male Oxford and Cambridge club in London refused to allow Marilyn Butler and other women to become members, David Butler dramatically ended his membership in protest, encouraging a rash of other resignations in support.

The Oxford and Cambridge has suffered a great loss, because there is no doubt that Marilyn Butler would have added to the club. She is enormously sociable, able to maintain hours on end of highly entertaining conversation and anecdote. One former Cambridge colleague recalls Butler even talking all through the night when they were flying back from America together. Students love her classes, which go on for much longer than scheduled, drawn out by Butler's stories and enthusiasm. Another former undergraduate remembers that supervisions with Marilyn Butler were always accompanied by tea or coffee, and turned into special, cosy and also inspiring events. Besides her time and her coffee, she is enormously generous with her ideas. Janet Todd confirms that 'you never spend an evening with her without going back and thinking of new things, other things you haven't thought of'. Keen to practise what she preaches, she is a regular in the polemical world of academic conferences, eager to discuss her ideas about the contemporary debates in the Romantic period, her general interest in national myths and political controversy. More specifically, her current work is on Romantic mythology and the rise of nationalism, on the collusions between writer and reader during the Romantic period, and on William Godwin.

Oxford suits her penchant for discussion. Cambridge, in contrast, while exciting was 'very demanding'. The atmosphere was 'rather rigorous', perhaps overwhelming historical debates. To her as a newcomer it seemed 'a succession of huge palaces'. Her rooms there looked over to the elegant Clare bridge across the river Cam, and were reached past the massive cathedral which is Kings College Chapel. Oxford has always appeared a 'medieval row of little houses', betraying its humble origins as simply the place where ordinary people lived who happened to be interested in ideas and learning too.

As we sit in her favourite restaurant, directly opposite the small ivy-clad quad of Exeter, discussing her life and ideas, she appears to be in her element. Owl-eyed by her big glasses and with mouth always twitching into a ready laugh or funny story, she punctures conversation occasionally to recognise friends and colleagues as they cycle past. She teases the waiters. She recalls conversations with leading figures, Nigel Lawson or Charles Taylor, founder of Canada's Socialist Party. But she remembers also to take away a big chocolate truffle for her secretary back at college. All the world's a village, it seems, a place where gossip flows and everyone's a friend. We linger to chat in the medieval narrow street as tourists and students push past to the covered market. Then she disappears through the thick wooden door to Exeter, her writing and another important meeting.

Publications include:

Jane Austen and the War of Ideas, 1975, Oxford University Press.
Peacock Displayed: A Satirist in His Context, 1979, Routledge & Kegan Paul.
Romantics, Rebels and Reactionaries, 1981, Oxford University Press.
(Ed.) *Burke, Paine, Godwin and the Revolution Controversy*, 1984, Cambridge University Press.
(Ed.) *The Works of Mary Wollstonecraft*, 1989, with Janet Todd 7 vols., 1989, W. Pickering.
(Ed.) *Maria Edgeworth's Castle Rackrent and Ennui*, 1992, Penguin.
(Ed.) *Mary Shelley, Frankenstein, The 1818 Text*, 1993, Pickering and Chatto.

(© Jennifer Wallace)

Hélène Cixous, born 1937, is professor of English Literature at the University of Paris VIII and director at the women's studies research centre. In the English-speaking world she is known primarily for her work as a feminist theorist, the creator of *écriture féminine*, but in France her work as a playwright has also brought her fame.

Photograph © Jacques Guillaume

When it comes to post-structuralist signifiers, the name of Hélène Cixous means substantially different things to different people. In the English-speaking world she is known primarily as a feminist theorist, yet many Paris theatre-goers know her above all as a playwright. In the realm of critical theory, Cixous is the creator of *écriture féminine*, whose own 'fictions' – her preferred word – have shattered the narrative form of the novel. For some of her PhD students there is the professor of English literature and James Joyce specialist, while for others she is a mentor with an original, philosophical-literary approach to women's studies.

Cixous leads a fortnightly Saturday seminar whose participants arrive from their home university by plane as well as by bus, and who have often been attending for years. She is the theorist who finds the feminist label far too limiting, the mother who mentions her children's achievements (one teaching at Cornell, the other in Paris) on the CV handed out to the visiting journalist. She is also the French intellectual whose writing is layered rather than linear, both cerebral and intensely physical, and so erudite within its radical innovations that the reader has to dismantle all those socially constructed expectations of 'the essay', 'the novel', 'the article' from the outset.

Cixous says she has 'four or five forms of written expression' and underpinning all of them is the same intensely personal involvement with language – a relationship with writing, with words and text built up from childhood, first through exposure to different languages in colonial Algeria, as the child of a German-Jewish mother and Spanish-

French-Jewish father. Then came reading. 'Ever since I knew how to read, books have been living things for me; they are events in my life alongside other major events . . . they are my parents . . . my family', she explained.

That relationship with writing continued at university with the study of English literature. At the age of twenty-two, Cixous passed the prestigious *Agrégation* 'while rocking the first baby'. Divorced when the children were still small, she says her teaching jobs, first at Bordeaux University then at the Sorbonne, helped make raising them alone while pursuing her career unproblematic. By the time the youngest child was eight, she was a professor, had published two novels and her thesis, 'The Exile of James Joyce' – 'the first', she says, 'to see that one could no longer write novels in the same way in the twentieth century'.

Cixous' love of literature did not stop her wondering 'where the women were' and the special relationship with writing had begun to take on a new dimension with the potential offered by the concept of *écriture féminine*. Feminine writing, she argues, comes from deep inside, from a place named in the Bible 'unclean' (*immonde* in French – literally out of this world) which 'precedes prohibition'. Climbing down to that place, to the 'root of writing', is difficult and exacting, taking you through the 'various doors, obstacles, walls and distances we have forged to make a life', she writes in *Three Steps on the Ladder of Writing*.

The feminine writer – usually, but not necessarily, a woman – attempts to relinquish the socially constructed self and to attain a feminine 'economy of exchange', where the 'Other' is accepted, not opposed. The concept of *écriture féminine* gives Cixous' relationship with words a militant dimension – a belief that such writing can, by overcoming 'dualistic opposition', become a form of action, initiating changes able to challenge the foundations of the state. This concern with the 'deconstruction' of the social self as a prerequisite for revolutionary action bears the mark of French feminism's 1970s '*psych et po*', psychology and politics group. Its focus on language bears the mark of Derridean thinking. Cixous has long worked closely with Jacques Derrida, of whom she has written, 'Derridean deconstruction will have been the greatest ethical critical warning gesture of our time: careful! Let us not be the dupe of logocentric authority'.

But while Derrida dissects language using what remains a classical philosophical discourse, Cixous' own language is itself innovative. Hers is an entirely personal style, at times suggestive and subjective, at times sharply analytical, entering its subject to respond from the inside, playing on the sounds and multiple meanings of words and syllables in a way which echoes psychoanalysis. Which is of course where translation of Cixous – particularly of her fictions and essays – poses enormous problems. It is hard to convey a play on words which often spurs the coining of a new or hybrid word, building up layers of meaning, different levels of 'knowledge'; it is quite impossible to convey in English the deep significance attached to the gender of nouns, which become lost in the English neuter.

More mundanely, Cixous herself has an enduring problem with the naming of the women's studies research centre at Paris VIII University she has directed since 1974. It is a problem she has still not solved. The Centre d'Etudes Féminines cannot be called women's studies, the 'most practical term' but one which has no equivalent in French. 'I could not call it feminist studies because "feminist" has an extremely precise meaning: it is a reformist demand in terms of equality and not at all in terms of difference', she stated. So she is stuck with the word 'feminine' – ridiculous too, she acknowledges, laughing – because the term she prefers, 'poetic of sexual difference', would not, she claims, be understood by the people at the ministry who accredit France's one and only women's studies doctoral course.

That concern with sexual difference has led a number of feminist theorists to label Cixous an 'essentialist' (one who believes that differences between masculine and feminine behaviour are biological, rather than socially constructed) – a charge which she refutes as being a 'stupid misrepresentation by people who haven't read me'. The novelist only became a theorist in the mid-1970s, when she saw that 'crazy comments were being made on my writing'. This decade has seen a growing polemic, in the US in particular, between essentialists and relativists (who argue that the idea of 'essential' differences between the sexes threatens to marginalise women further). For Cixous, sexual difference is first and foremost a straightforward observation of fact and an idea which 'is philosophically, simple to think'.

'There are immense areas of exchange but then there are specific areas of non-exchange and without them there would not be love . . . that point of non-comprehension is necessary.'

It is not only sexual, she argues, 'although you only have to make love to realise you cannot understand what the other is feeling', it is part of the human condition – an area where people 'move apart, look at each other without understanding each other'. This difference which is so simple to see remains a mystery and cannot be confused with the notion of essentialism, insists Cixous, who has always tried to avoid the double bind of radical feminism on the one hand and 'a system of identification in which we are all men' on the other. The deep divide that runs through US feminism is at least fertile, she points out, whereas France displays 'the most widespread aggressiveness towards the idea of sexual difference'.

'In France, the concept of equality covers everything; a universalism which represses all differences holds sway, dominates the media and travesties the idea of difference, making out that it is intolerant, that our studies are homosexual, aim to eliminate men . . . then women', she added with a smile. France may be inhospitable to women's studies in general and to the notion of sexual difference in particular, but Cixous has managed to create a haven for her research and teaching within the Centre d'Etudes Féminines and at the CIPH, the Collège Internationale de Philosophie, founded in 1984 with Derrida at the helm.

Paris VIII is the one niche in the French university system where this could have happened. Cixous' academic life has long been tied to that of the university, which she helped to set up. It was born of the May 1968 student revolt, banished from an attractive site at Vincennes near Paris, to an inaccessible and unlovely location in the northern suburb of Saint Denis, but still leaves its academics free to design their own courses.

Her university seminar is in fact held at CIPH, in the heart of the Latin Quarter, and it 'has become a ritual', she says. About a third of the participants have been attending for up to ten years and more, in some cases coming back from posts abroad – a sign that something fairly unique is to be found there. The day-long, fortnightly Saturday seminar on the poetic of sexual difference develops, through the study of great texts, a 'new form of thinking'. This Cixous describes as 'learning to read into the core of language, into signs, symptoms, traces', an approach which can serve, amongst other things, to 'read' monuments as well as writing.

She cites as an example of this transferable skill the case of a PhD student who went off for three years to Cambodian refugee camps, learned Khmer and now works in Phnom Penh on the revival of Cambodian culture while completing a thesis on sexual difference and the preservation of specific types of culture. 'This is typical of what happens in this seminar. What she is doing is intellectually daring', commented Cixous. The Cambodia project was originally triggered by a performance of one of Cixous' epic plays, *The Terrible But Unfinished Story of Norodom Sihanouk, King of Cambodia*, performed at Ariane

Mnouchkine's Théâtre du Soleil in 1985–86. While not every member of the audience was moved to get up and go to Cambodia, the theatre staff still recall that the atmosphere was so electric after the eight-hour, Shakespearean drama, that the audience could not break away and go home, sometimes for hours after the performance.

Cixous' latest dramatisation of contemporary history, *La Ville Parjure ou le Reveil des Erinyés* (The Traitor Town, or the Awakening of the Furies), explores the eternal problems of vengeance and justice as they were posed by France's contaminated blood scandal. Judicial procedures to establish responsibility for the distribution of HIV-contaminated blood products to haemophiliacs in 1985 were under way when the play was performed in 1994 and have continued since. But the play moves directly beyond such contingencies, opening with the arrival of the Furies, aroused by the cry for vengeance of a bereaved mother for the first time since Athene relegated them to their underground shrine at the end of Aeschylus' *The Eumenides*.

Drama is a unique kind of writing, she explains, because of its collaborative nature, involving not only the director and actors, but the audience. 'The writing changes totally, because you have to find words which are immediately accessible to the audience and which are as lyrical as possible, which can be shared by people living in the same epoch as you. This means the playwright has to take the present hugely into account: the political, ethical and emotional present', she commented.

It helps that the audience becomes part of the play, a fact which, she says, she only realised when she began writing for theatre. 'At *Ville Parjure*, there were spectators who cried. In a fiction, you have to write the tears.' But then, in fiction, the theme of vengeance and pardon can be developed over a hundred pages, while in a play, 'it has to be conjured up in a few words', she noted. The deconstructor of the novel accepts the conventions of the dramatic form, the characters and plot, because they are not 'weighed down by the enormous, immobile construction which surrounds them in the novel'.

Her sense of literary continuity in drama is strong – not only Aeschylus but echoes of Shakespeare ring out. Cixous refutes the charge that this makes her a learned rather than an intuitive author. Her reading is part of her make up and comes out as naturally as the rest, she maintains. 'There are a lot of Shakespeare quotes in *Ville Parjure*, but you don't have to recognise them. I enjoy it, Shakespeare enjoys it, people who recognise them enjoy it! I don't call that a display of knowledge; I call that language, which speaks with words which are very old.' So too, with her fictions.

Cixous insists on the primacy of the creative act, insists that she does not apply theories in her writing. 'I never said: "I'm going to shatter the novel". I have a great love for narrative, for the novel, where the form is a living one. But in the age of Concorde, you can no longer write as if you were in the age of the carriage. It is not a theory, the act of writing itself imposed this on me.' Cixous may not set out with a theory, but she certainly ends up with one. That interaction between theory and creativity gives tremendous drive and conviction to her theoretical work. Her explanation of her own 'non-theoretical' experience of the act of writing is followed by fervent argument: anyone writing in the traditional novel form 'still in the nineteenth century, is in something dead'.

'Ever since the word "subconscious" entered everyday vocabulary, literature changed. Some people made the most of that freedom, especially women, while others remained conservative, afraid of subconscious drives, of the liberation of writing and of language. It is almost a question of political opinion . . . but I don't want to theorise because the writer doesn't follow theories', she concluded. Echoing the idea that feminine writing 'precedes' prohibition, Cixous says that 'it is in poetry that change has always preceded itself'. Poetry has always been the form where a new freedom of expression can break through – François Villon, 'pulverising the language', John Donne 'giving primacy to the signifier' – before academic poetry puts the lid back on. Her own fiction she describes as a 'hybrid genre' of exploded narrative and poetic lyricism. But for Cixous, the prime example of *écriture féminine* is Brazilian writer Clarice Lispector. For over a decade, she has explored Lispector's texts in her seminar, analysing the features of what she calls a 'feminine economy'. This is an economy of the passions, of gifts, not of opposition, an economy of exchanges with the other, not of appropriation. Implicit in the claim that feminine writing is a form of action which could fundamentally challenge the state, is an attendant challenge to the idea that to change culture, you first have to change society. It does so by distinguishing between writing as an art form, where the form is intricately related to social context (Concorde or the carriage) and writing as exchange, independent of society and drawn from the inner depths.

The pre-eminence Cixous gives written language as a force for change draws fire from a school of Third World feminism which argues that this denies illiterate women any revolutionary role. It is also a position which appears to demand excellent writing skills of Cixous' students:

learning a 'new form of thinking' where reading becomes an infinitely demanding search for meaning is also about learning to write. 'My students are, in general, gifted at writing and able to become writers', she commented. Those students are, almost without exception, from abroad, because France has no academic teaching posts in women's studies and therefore no prospects for French postgraduates. Eric Prenowitz, a PhD student and translator of Cixous, first came across her seminar as a US physics undergraduate visiting Paris ten years ago. He admits the seminar is 'very demanding, especially as everything in the US is clear and codified'. Mara Negron did her thesis with Cixous and has now got a post in her home university teaching Puerto Rico's first course on women and literature. When she can, she will come back for the seminar. 'I go now for pleasure. Hélène awakens a passion for reading literature, she sweeps away the dust, even from the classics and always comes up with something new one hadn't seen before', she said.

Her own view of the demands made on the seminar? 'It's a question of scientific AND human rigour, of going further, making a commitment', Cixous concluded and left for a committee meeting on aid for Algerian artists and writers in exile.

Publications include:

Theory
Reading with Clarice Lispector, 1990, Minnesota University Press.
Readings, the Poetics of Blanchot, Kafka, Joyce, 1992, Minnesota University Press.
Three Steps on the Ladder of Writing, 1993, Columbia University Press.

Fiction
Jours de l'an, 1990; *L'Ange au Secret*, 1991; *Déluge*, 1992; *Beethoven à jamais*, 1993; *Photos de Racine*, 1994; *La Fiancée Juive*, 1995.

Theatre
On ne part pas, 1991 Lille.
Les Euménides, 1992–93, Théâtre du Soleil (translation).
  L'Histoire qu'on ne connaîtra jamais, 1994, Théâtre de la Ville, Paris.
  La Ville Parjure, 1994, Théâtre du Soleil.
  Black Sail, White Sail, 1995, The Sphinx Theatre, London.

(© Stella Hughes)

Sarah Coakley, born 1951, is professor of Christian theology at the Divinity School, Harvard University. Previously a theology fellow at Oxford, she is interested in exploring 'a prime problem for a Christian feminist' – the relationship between sexual desire and desire for God during contemplative prayer.

Photograph © Thomas Lingner

'My feminism, I think, was born on my knees.' Sarah Coakley, professor of Christian theology at the Divinity School, Harvard University is describing how her feminist theology has developed through the painful business of contemplative prayer.

Her thesis is paradoxical and is perceived by some feminists to have dangerous implications. Taking the 'vulnerability' and 'emptying out of self' that she sees in the Incarnate Christ, Sarah Coakley proposes the silent waiting on the Divine in prayer as a real act of empowerment for Christian feminists: 'because we can only be properly "empowered" if we cease to set the agenda, if we "make space" for God to be God'.

A woman who constantly takes cross-disciplinary risks with her theology, Sarah Coakley came relatively late to patristics, devouring the works of the early Christian Fathers in her passion to re-thread the traditions of Christian contemplation for women. She has written: 'By choosing to "make space" in this way one "practices" the "presence of God" – the subtle but enabling presence of a God who neither shouts nor forces, let alone obliterates'.

This is indeed a strange feminist language, but Sarah Coakley believes that the real long-term danger to Christian feminism is the repression of all forms of vulnerability, a failure to confront issues of fragility and suffering except through the perspective of women as victims.

Hers is a tortured yet challenging argument and it derives from her desire to work within the Christian tradition, constantly pressing for what it can be made to yield if feminist questions are put to it. Not only is she a Christian, but she is a church-goer as well and an Anglo-

Catholic one at that, a sector of the Anglican church that has produced few feminists and in places appears positively rank with misogyny. Moreover, her fieldwork into contemporary Christian practice has led her to consort with such unconventional religious groups as Charismatics and the House Church movement, an association which would give your traditionally liberal theologian heart failure.

According to Coakley, those who choose to see women who take on 'vulnerability' before God as victims, are 'failing to embrace a feminist reconceptualising of the power of the cross and resurrection'. She states: 'Only . . . by facing – and giving new expression to – the paradoxes of "losing one's life in order to save it", can feminists hope to construct a vision of the Christic "self" that transcends the gender stereotypes we are seeking to upend.'

She acknowledges that 'vulnerability' has been a taboo subject in Christian feminist writing because it can appear to condone damage to women from sexual and physical abuse, and the seeming legitimisation of this by men 'otherwise committed to disciplined religious practice and the rhetoric of cruciform redemption'.

She is exploring treacherous territory, precisely because women were perceived by the early Fathers as the ultimate temptation and barrier to effective contemplation, turning men away from their quasi-erotic journey towards God.

In addition, accounts by analytic religious philosophers of the experiences of female contemplatives like Theresa of Avila have tended to deal with the 'sudden conversion experiences', or 'they take the high points of mystical literature and work that to death without looking at all the stuff that came before'. Coakley says she is interested to see what feminist contemplation might look like philosophically worked out 'and I am certain it doesn't look like the male orgasmic version'.

The real challenge of feminist theology, she believes, is not simply to rubbish the overt misogynism of many of the Fathers, but to unpick 'albeit painfully', the connecting strands, the relationship in their writings between the sexual, the devotional, the political and the doctrinal in order to 're-thread a new tapestry, a new alignment of the sexual and the theological in which women are no longer cast as that which distracts from the divine'.

She sets this within what she regards as a contemporary feminist dilemma: a quest for individual self-determination which does not deny or undermine the significance of dependencies or relationships. However, she treads a perilous path and needless to say her critics have been vociferous. Post-Christian feminists such as theologian Daphne Hampson, at St Andrew's University, would vehemently reject the idea that 'vulnerability' can have positive value, as does a Catholic feminist like Elisabeth Schussler Fiorenza, Coakley's colleague at Harvard.

Sarah Coakley's work has been described as poetic and imaginative. Although she has only written one book, the product of a brilliant doctoral thesis on the German liberal theologian Ernst Troeltsch (1865–1923), entitled *Christ without Absolutes*, her reputation rests on published essays and lectures, two edited volumes and the books on systematic theology that are to come.

The Hulsean Lectures, entitled 'Three-Personed God' which she delivered to Cambridge in 1992 caused ripples of excitement. Those lectures are being reworked into *God, Sexuality and the Self: An Essay 'On the Trinity'* to be published by Cambridge University Press. This is to be the first of three volumes of a *théologie totale*, a cross-disciplinary approach including sociological fieldwork, the study of icons and historical and philosophical analysis. The first, on the Trinity, concentrates on what can be said positively about God; the second will deal with the unknowability of God, through the darkness and blankness experienced in contemplative prayer and the third volume will explore the use of symbolics in theology, concentrating on eucharistic ritual.

Her writing is painstaking and slow. She is a perfectionist, seeking a new and more challenging style for her *théologie totale* after the success of her first book, which she wrote while a lecturer in the religious studies department of Lancaster University. This was a lucid and concise piece of enlightening academic research which led to her being courted by the University of Chicago. Her Cambridge Hulsean lectures, delivered while she was in post as the first woman fellow at Oriel College, Oxford, displayed the same impressive scholarship, though they were more radical in style and methodology. These led to overtures from Harvard where she eventually moved to take up a tenured chair.

Coakley's theology, though scholarly, has been formed by profound personal and spiritual crises. Though she is gifted with an 'analytically obsessive mind' , a power of analysis which has earned her grudging respect from the most conservative of liberal theologians, she has constantly pushed at the boundaries of academic theological acceptability.

A bright pupil of the solid, if not stolid, Blackheath High School for Girls, from a solid middle-class church-going family, Coakley had wanted to be a theologian from an early age. At eleven her theological reading started with two books that happened to be in the house:

Honest to God by John Robinson, the then Bishop of Woolwich who sought to sweep away an oppressive, punitive vision of God, and the *Letters of Evelyn Underhill*. 'In a way,' she said, 'it was a ridiculous thing for an eleven-year-old to do.' However, the strange combination set her theological thinking on a track she pursues to this day. She stated: 'My theology in a way has been an attempt to weave together, on the one hand, profound traditions of Catholic spirituality, represented by Underhill, with a kind of creative freedom, boldness and intellectual integrity towards the tradition that Robinson represented.'

By the time she left Blackheath she was 'bursting with fury and frustration because, you know, one read the whole of *Oedipus Tyrannus* by Sophocles and I could parse every word with exactitude and never once did we stop and talk about Sophocles' tragic form or the passion and rhythm of the play.'

She compared this with the less solid but more inspired education her three brothers were receiving at Westminster. She said: 'They never learnt their regular Greek verbs like me, but I knew what I was missing.'

She proved a brilliant and assiduous student at Cambridge, emerging with a first in Part I and II of her theology degree, but again she looked on it as somewhat solid and disappointing. In a course that was biblically based she longed to grapple in more depth with the philosophy of religion and systematic theology 'which we got fairly small doses of', and to explore how historical relativism challenged the absolutist tenets of Christian doctrine.

In her last year at Cambridge she was introduced to the work of Ernst Troeltsch, which became the subject of her doctorate. Coakley stated: 'He was one of the last great German mandarins. He was not only a theologian but a philosopher, a sociologist in the very early days, living in the same house as Weber, he was interested in early psychology, he was a politician, he was a very fine historian and this inter-disciplinary texture excited me. I didn't see anyone doing this at Cambridge.'

She alighted on Troeltsch precisely because he encompassed the 'upsetting and urgent feature of the relation between faith and history'. He tackled precisely the question which was dogging her. She writes in *Christ without Absolutes*: 'The apparent choice required between these two, the Jesus of history and the Christ of faith . . . was as much a Christological bugbear in Troeltsch's generation as it is in ours.'

She worked up the material for her doctoral thesis during two years post-Cambridge as a Harkness scholar at Harvard, where she concentrated on attending philosophy lectures. This had not been possible at

Cambridge as philosophy and theology were 'strategically' placed far apart physically, though she had tried, finding herself 'always running' and 'always late' between the two departments.

She was grateful to Harvard for giving her the space to pursue her own interests, though she was shocked by the 'intellectual soupiness' of the place (it had attracted a lot of people who were 'avoiding the draft'), and although she had 'kicked over the traces of her Anglo-Catholicism', pursuing Quakerism and other avenues, she was shocked by the fact that staff and students of the Harvard Divinity School were apparently un-churched.

She eventually came under some pressure from Edward Hardy, an American friend and priest, to visit the Cowley Fathers, a stone's throw from where she lived. She said: 'The monastery was perfectly ghastly, there was a strong homo-erotic atmosphere and total fear of women. But after a while I discovered you could go to mass there at 7.30 in the morning, and you didn't have to talk to any of the monks and to my disgust something began to take root. I think it was a sort of contemplative dimension which had always been a buried strand.'

On her return to England Sarah married Dr James Farwell Coakley, an American whom she had met at Cambridge before her departure for Harvard, and the two became celebrated as the first academic couple to job share, having been offered a lectureship in religious studies at the University of Lancaster.

The move to Lancaster marked the beginning of a very painful phase for Sarah Coakley. She was attempting to finish her doctoral thesis, she was coping with early motherhood – Edith, her first child, 'rivalled the desert Fathers for feats of ascetical sleeplessness' – and she continued to move towards contemplative prayer, a great struggle which marked the 'blackest phase of my life'.

She said: 'Anyone who goes in for silent prayer of any sort is asking for a hard time. The very fact you are courting the unconscious means you are bombarded with oppressed material and you have to cope with that – so I let myself in for seven years of painful inner work and I was in a pretty bad state, but in retrospect I would say it marked a turning point in my whole intellectual development.'

'All my liberal, intellectual presumptions about Christianity began to collapse through contemplation, so that my suspicion, say, of the miraculous, as inherently incapable of chartable evidence, began to just fall away because supernatural things were happening to me. What I felt was a pressure coming to bear on me from God.'

She immersed herself in psychoanalytic literature 'to come to terms with the unconscious pressing upon me', and underwent a revolution in the God image. Her feminism, she said, was born properly here.

She came to see that the prime problem for a Christian feminist was the relationship between sexual desire and desire for God 'because no-one can spend long on their knees in silence without having to confront their own sexuality'.

What happened in contemplation was a drawing 'of one's entire life towards one source which is undeniably proto-erotic'. Mystics in the Christian tradition had unified God's love for us and our love for Him with a celibate male's version of eroticism 'firmly excluding the woman as a fatal diversion from this goal'.

'There you have the problem,' she says, 'that both made me a feminist and drives my current work. How are you going to re-thread the connections without throwing out the entire vision which I believe to be profoundly true?'

She has defended herself rigorously from feminist criticism which views this whole eroticised notion of prayer as a masculinist perversion, male sexuality writ large.

In many ways, the resolution of her personal struggles at Lancaster through a new direction in her work hardened her for the further problems she was to face at Oriel College, Oxford, an experience which turned out to be a professional nightmare. At first, the offer of a tutorial fellowship had seemed timely. Coakley had been offered a position by the University of Chicago, but the post was non-tenured and lacked the security needed before uprooting a family which now included two children (Agnes was born in 1986). In addition, 'Chip' (James Coakley) had not wished to return to the US, a society he 'has turned his back on'.

Theologically, however, the atmosphere at Oxford was extremely conservative and things did not turn out well at Oriel. Dr Rowan Williams, the Bishop of Monmouth and former Lady Margaret Professor of Divinity at Oxford, said that Oxford behaved badly and 'was hell for Sarah', though she 'had a tremendous impact on undergraduates and was extraordinarily refreshing'.

Sarah Coakley is discreet about the affair, save to say her job was made professionally impossible because she was not permitted to do the job she had been appointed to – a tutorial fellow in theology with special interests in philosophy.

She found herself caught in the 'culture wars between analytic philosophy and religion and another set of wars about relationships in the college'. After considerable unpleasantness, the college backed down from its initial position and she was finally allowed to get on with the job. By this time her students had started to do 'extraordinarily well'. She said: 'By the time I left I had been just about accepted, but I felt no temptation to stay.'

In her view 'Oxford is a very, very conservative theology faculty and I think it is committing suicide by promoting the dead hand of tradition'. She laid on the first course in feminist theology at Oxford with sensational results. Hundreds of people attended the lectures, as many men as women.

She said: 'The most surprising presence was all the conservative men, the Greek Orthodox monks who came to work with Greek Orthodox priest Kallistos Ware and conservative Catholics from St Benet's Hall, Oxford. What they couldn't understand and were absolutely fascinated by, was the fact that I was using very very traditional, serious, spiritual sources, asking questions about the relationship of sexuality and spirituality and trying to weave that into my theology. People were intrigued and would come around in droves to Oriel to talk to me further.'

It was a 'bizarre' period for Coakley, combining a huge groundswell of support with 'stolid negativity and worse' from some quarters in the college. Thankfully, Harvard intervened in all of this, offering her the Mallinckrodt Chair in Divinity. Sarah and Chip Coakley have always taken the sharing of childcare and domestic responsibilities extremely seriously, so when Harvard also offered Chip, a Syriac scholar, a tailor-made post working with Syriac manuscripts and typography and teaching Syriac in the Near-Eastern languages department, they did not hesitate to take the leap.

Coakley believes she is regarded as something of a curious oddity at Harvard, though as always she has immense pulling power with students. She said: 'It's bizarre for me to leave a place where I was regarded as so left-wing, so *outré* as to be falling off the edge, to a place where I am now regarded as so conservative and traditional as to be very suspect. Am I simply the same person who crossed the Atlantic?'

The fact that she combines the analytic philosophy of religion with theology is a little unusual. The fact that she is adding to that a profound interest in spiritual practice and feminist theory is probably unique, and the fact that this cocktail is further enriched by fieldwork, observing religious groups on the ground, such as Charismatics, is probably just plain weird. For iconoclastic feminists like Mary Daly the Coakley approach may seem so subtle and accommodating as to be downright dangerous. However, a more flexible, imaginative, less polarised feminism, based on scholarship working from within the Christian tradition, may be just the thing to move feminist theology forward in the minds of sceptics, if not antagonists. Slowly but surely Sarah Coakley is having a major theological impact.

Publications include:

Christ without Absolutes: A Study of the Christology of Ernst Troeltsch, 1988, Oxford University Press.

(Ed.) *The Making and Remaking of Christian Doctrine: Essays in Honour of Maurice Wiles*, 1993, with David A. Pailin, Oxford University Press.

'God as Trinity: an approach through prayer', in The Doctrine Commission of the Church of England, *We Believe in God*, 1987, Church House Publications, pp. 104–21.

'Mariology and "Romantic Feminism"', in Teresa Elwes (ed.), *Women's Voices*, 1992, HarperCollins, pp. 97–110

(© Elaine Williams)

Cynthia Cockburn, born 1934, a sociologist based at City University, has made the study of technology and gender within organisational contexts – trying to understand how power is deployed, often to the disadvantage of women – the theme of her research.

Photograph by Neil Turner

The life story of the microwave oven may seem an unlikely research topic for a sociologist. But then, Cynthia Cockburn has never been afraid to break new ground. A pioneer of the study of gender and technology, Cockburn's most recent research theme was an inspired choice, for the microwave neatly encapsulates the tortuous and often invisible relations between technology and gender. What happens, Cockburn wanted to know, when 'masculine engineering encounters an age-old woman's technology: cooking'?

Charting the microwave oven's trajectory from drawing-board to factory, shop and household, the research revealed how a state-of-the-art masculine 'gizmo' gets translated into a humdrum domestic appliance. Lodged squarely among the feminine 'white goods' today, it nonetheless 'retains just a whiff of aftershave' – its gender modified by all those boys and men who only reluctantly cook proper food in a conventional oven but will happily 'zap' an instant meal in a microwave.

Gender and technology are both social processes, Cockburn argues, and they help to shape each other. It's not by chance that technology becomes what it is, and not through inadequacy that women are so often excluded from the expertise called 'technological': it's the result of power-play.

Cynthia Cockburn has consistently studied technology and gender within organisational contexts, trying to understand how power is deployed – often to the disadvantage of women. 'King Kong was a rarity – and short-lived,' she writes. 'The truly powerful hold power not individually but by means of organisation and in organisations.' Not surprisingly, themes in her writing include trade unionism, work, skill and training – always seen as gendered phenomena.

Over an intellectual career spanning forty years to date, Cockburn has published eight books, contributed to thirty more and produced scores of articles, reports and pamphlets. But she has no university degree and has only briefly held a tenured academic post. I ask, incredulously, 'how did you do it?', and with a chuckle, she asks in turn, 'Where do any of us come from?'. More often than not, women do not follow traditional career paths.

Cockburn set off without any personal sense of direction when she left school at eighteen with A levels in English, French and Latin. 'My father ran a semi-family business – he was a small-scale industrialist in the thread industry in the Midlands – and my mother didn't work outside the home. They were very conservative, their perspective quite local. There weren't many books in our house. I think, looking back on it, my parents were suspicious of higher education. Neither my brother nor I were encouraged to go to university. I believe they were afraid education was something that made you a snob or turned you political. So I signed up for the local secretarial course and seemed to have acted out my mother's unfulfilled dream: to "travel the world as some important man's secretary". In short, I joined the Foreign Service typing pool.'

After seven years hammering the keyboard for diplomats at home and abroad, Cockburn left the Foreign Service and drifted into freelance journalism. In 1959 she married. Her husband was then an architectural student, and she began to study too, in her spare time, for a London University external diploma in social studies, by correspondence course. 'I'm not sure one was meant to pass on that course. The lessons were roneo-ed on green blotting paper.' But writing essays came easily, and simultaneously Cockburn's articles and photographs began to appear in newspapers and magazines. She joined the National Union of Journalists in 1961 and is still a member, thinking of herself more as a researcher/writer than as an academic.

But Cockburn quickly came to feel limitations in journalism. 'The problem is you're forced to jump from one subject to the next, drumming up opinions too quickly, and without taking responsibility for them. I began to feel uncomfortable.'

In the early 1960s, when Cockburn was writing for household and building magazines, the professor of building at University College London offered her the chance of a short-term research assistantship. That in turn led to a research post in the newly-created Centre for

Environmental Studies in 1968. 'It was a helpful period, those eight secure years in the days when researchers could get salaried jobs,' she says. 'I worked part-time, had a second baby. It was a politicising environment. We started a Marxist feminist group. And I got a good foothold in research and wrote my first research book. I learnt a lot from people there, and later, when I looked independently for research funding, I could show I'd already done something.'

That book, *The Local State* (1977), was a highly-praised study of community struggles around housing in south London and the ways in which Lambeth council tried to manage them. While Cockburn researched and wrote it she was helping to establish a local project developing print and photography for community action in the borough. This simultaneous involvement with practical skills, political action and social research – a profoundly 'connected' stance – was to become a preference in all her subsequent work.

'I try to choose research themes that have some political meaning, that provide a constituency to work for and talk to, and that also involve some hands-on manual work – typing, printing, photography', she explains.

Cynthia Cockburn's commitment to doing her own typing has not been cost-free, however. Like many writers she now has repetitive strain injury and can no longer use keyboard or pen for sustained periods. 'I'm one of the lucky ones though,' she says. 'The Department of Employment's service for the disabled has lent me a voice-activated word processor, so I can carry on. It's an immensely clever piece of technology – but not quite clever enough. Compared with typing it's so slow, so frustrating. And now I use a typist to transcribe interview tapes I feel I've lost that closeness to the material. And I worry about her hands.'

Yet the intellectual force of Cockburn's hands-on approach to sociological research is strikingly evident in her ground-breaking study of class and gender relations in the printing industry, carried out with the first of several grants from the Economic and Social Research Council. She was well prepared for it by a year as a student at the London College of Printing learning practical print production. The book that resulted was *Brothers*, published in 1983 and again in a new edition in 1991.

Her compelling account – now a classic study in the sociology of skills – charts the struggles between unions and press owners, as skilled print workers defined their occupation as a quintessentially masculine trade to prevent employers from displacing them with 'cheap' female labour. She shows how owners turned to new technology to destroy the print unions' residual control over the labour process. Technological change, in the shape of computerised origination of text and images, has now smashed the male exclusiveness of printing. Yet, as Cockburn's research shows, it does not necessarily follow that bad news for men is good news for women.

In *Machinery of Dominance* (1985), Cockburn went on to explore the impact of new technologies in warehousing, clothing manufacture and hospital X-ray departments, where she found that the old sex divisions had survived the electronic revolution. Men, even today, continue to be the technologists, and women, in the main, lower-paid operators of the new equipment. It's no wonder, she says, that while the key question in mainstream technology theory has been how to explain change, 'for feminists it's been how to explain this vexing continuity'.

For most of her research career, Cockburn has been a member of the School of Social Sciences at the City University, London, though her residence there has depended on obtaining research grants to fund her projects – from the ESRC, the Equal Opportunities Commission and the European Commission, among others. 'The advantage is that I've had no teaching or administrative responsibilities. That's been great, because dealing with a university, as far as I can see, is as time-consuming as a marriage.' Cockburn has kept a certain distance from both institutions. She and her husband have been separated 'in a friendly kind of way' since 1972. As a single parent, she worked part-time for fifteen years to look after their two daughters. 'But I couldn't have done it without childcare from some pretty special women.'

Probably Cockburn's most widely used work today is her in-depth study of men's responses to positive action for sex equality in four organisations, published in 1991 as *In the Way of Women*. Documenting the dispiriting set-backs of 'equal opportunities' policies, Cockburn argues that they can be little more than cosmetic so long as the organisational relations of technology and work remain unreformedly masculine. The book shows 'women struggling and some men blocking', Cockburn says. Yet she draws out the positive potential for alliances between women and other disadvantaged groups, who do after all continue to challenge organisations. 'If I produce knowledge it is only by making connections between things other people tell me. Almost everything I've learnt I've learnt from women at the coalface – at work, in unions.' She hopes her work helps to 'clarify problems and formulate solutions, revealing connections that make sense to people and showing the imaginative ways forward women are inventing'.

Feminist analysis does not always have the influence it should among the predominantly male academics pursuing social studies of technology, work and organisations. 'An honourable few are beginning to be "gender sensitive" and to realise these are gendered phenomena,' says Cockburn, 'but by and large you can still guess the sex of an author from the works cited in the bibliography. Men tend to cite other men; women read both mainstream and feminist theory.' Yet she refuses to be downcast by this. 'I want my work to be sound, but I've never cared two pins for being part of the mainstream. I think you have to choose at present. I'm writing for women and for feminists.' And with a lack of individualism unusual in academia, she adds: 'It's really of no significance whether I'm personally cited or acknowledged. I think it's got to be the movement as a whole, eventually reshaping general thinking, not any one of us making it into the canon'.

Cockburn turns to metaphor to help me to understand how she thinks about her academic work. 'It's like threads in some kind of tapestry. The story of *Brothers*, for instance, was a strand I stitched into it. What you hope is that others will find it trustworthy, pick up the theme, entwine it with their own. If not, it'll be discarded. If you're lucky you get a chance to rework the motif and develop it. Feminist analysis and story-telling has been weaving an impressive fabric. But all too often, men seem to prefer to work a separate cloth.'

For the past ten years, Cynthia Cockburn has been actively concerned with building links between women in Europe. During the Cold War years she was involved in a women's group taking non-violent direct action against missiles and militarism. She helped to organise the European Forum of Socialist Feminists when it began in 1985 and was quick to make working contacts with women in Eastern and Central Europe when this became possible.

Cockburn's latest book, *Bringing Technology Home* (1994), edited jointly with Ruza Furst-Dilic, was her first opportunity to do cross-national research. The result of a five-year collaboration between women scholars from Russia, Yugoslavia and six other countries across the breadth of Europe, it creatively brings together studies of 'domestic' technologies as diverse as food robots, video-phones and the electronic house. The microwave oven study – which was carried out with Susan Ormrod at City University, London – was the British contribution, and the full account of that project was published as *Gender and Technology in the Making* (1993).

'It was a really good opportunity for intensive cooperative working across cultural boundaries,' Cockburn says. 'We didn't know each other before the project began, and we each influenced the others politically and intellectually, during the process of the work. There was stress and strain but also a lot of affection in the group.' Cockburn's introduction to the book is a fascinating account of 'our debate about our differences'.

Currently, Cockburn is continuing to work with a team of five women from European Union member states on the problem of getting better representation of women in the newly emerging European trade-union structures. 'Brussels is terribly alienating for women. We are hoping to run innovative workshops at shop steward level to try to help women working in different industries such as air transport or industrial cleaning, to share experience across national boundaries. For me, it is a sort of "action research" – being involved in change but analysing the process rigorously as it goes along.'

What next? 'I've just turned 60, and it is difficult to know how to react to that. Perhaps it's time to start taking more risks.' 'A novel', I wondered? 'No, I'm too prosaic', she replied quickly, but photography could be an option. Her photographs are an engaging addition to *Gender and Technology in the Making*. 'You know, if I could choose my own skills, I'd like to be able to write like John Berger and take photographs like Jean Mohr and create wonderful books like their *The Seventh Man*. I'll never have their voice and eye. But I do want to do more documentary work – writing plus photography.' 'What on?' 'In the first instance, on the peace movement, working cross-culturally to investigate the kinds of conciliation processes that are happening as people try to rebuild communities in place like Bosnia or Northern Ireland', she says.

Despite all her achievements, Cynthia Cockburn remains the most open and unpretentious of scholars. 'Not having a degree I always felt hesitant about being a researcher, and put in that extra bit of effort,' she says. 'I greatly respect people who've achieved a formal education and in many ways I regret I haven't. But it's reassuring to find there are people and institutions that are open-minded and willing to judge a researcher on output rather than certification. Perhaps my career could be some encouragement to other women who find their direction late, or want to change track.'

Publications include:

The Local State: Management of Cities and People, 1977, Pluto Press
Brothers: Male Dominance and Technical Change, 1983 and 1991, Pluto Press.
Machinery of Dominance: Women, Men and Technical Know-how, 1985, Pluto Press and North Eastern University Press.
In the Way of Women: Men's Resistance to Sex Equality in Organisations, 1991, Macmillan and ILR Press.
Gender and Technology in the Making, 1993, with Susan Ormrod, Sage Publications.
(Ed.) *Bringing Technology Home: Gender and Technology in a Changing Europe*, 1994, with Ruza Furst-Dilic, Open University Press.

(© Gail Vines)

Photograph by Neil Turner

Linda Colley, born 1949, is Richard M. Colgate professor of history and director of the Lewis Walpole Library, Yale University. Among the most gifted of the historians attracted from Britain to the US in the last twenty years, Linda Colley is nevertheless a historian of her native country, a significant and original contributor to the never-ending debate on national identity.

'The happiest women, like the happiest nations, are those that have no history.' Too bad that George Eliot is no longer around to defend that line from *The Mill on the Floss*. The debate between her and Linda Colley, Richard M Colgate professor of history at Yale University, would be worth travelling a long way to attend.

History, and its role in the identity of nations, has been not only a means to happiness but the weapon with which Colley has smashed a succession of glass ceilings on either side of the Atlantic. Before joining the transatlantic brain drain in 1982 she was the first woman fellow in history at Christ's College, Cambridge. This was where she met her husband, David Cannadine, then also a Cambridge history fellow.

Colley's promotion to the Yale chair came in 1990 and she can point to a formidable list of prestigious public lectures set to continue into the foreseeable future – she is already booked to deliver the 1997 Trevelyan lectures in Cambridge and Wiles lectures in Belfast, the first woman asked to give either series.

She and her husband, both best-selling writers of social history, married in 1982. David Cannadine also holds an American chair and the couple make the familiar crossing from Gatwick (they have a home in a small Norfolk village where they retreat each summer to write) to New York regularly. Yale has granted Colley semesters on sabbatical to carry out engagements in Britain, breaks which she has also used to work on her books.

Her next is provisionally titled *Another Face of Power: The British Female Elite before the Vote* and it represents a new departure for her in two senses. While she is careful to point out that this will not be 'a piece of women's history primarily', it will be her first book in which female experience forms the centrepiece, rather than merely a significant element. And, covering the years between 1700 and 1918, it will take her for the first time beyond the period on which she has built her career and reputation – eighteenth-century and pre-Victorian Britain.

A friend once noted a talent for 'finding topics in need of resuscitation'. Like many talents it was one displayed early, in Colley's choice of eighteenth-century British history as a speciality: 'I have never been able to share the view of it as a dullish valley between the excitements of the seventeenth and nineteenth centuries', she says.

Enthusiasm and ability – also displayed early, as she recorded the highest finals grades ever awarded by Bristol University's department of history – still need careful nurturing. At Bristol she found a mentor in John Cannon, subsequently professor at Newcastle. Cannon had been a pupil of Lewis Namier, making it easy to constuct a dynastic line, reinforced by her subsequent graduate work with John Plumb at Cambridge, back to the mid-century godfather of eighteenth-century British studies.

The influence is undoubtedly there – and acknowledged fully in her biographical study of Namier, published in 1989 – but she also regards his microsurgical, high-political focus as an important factor in the unfashionability of his period: 'I think Namier convinced a lot of people that it was a horribly difficult and complex period, and rather scared them off'.

No such difficulties with Cannon, whom she remembers happily as an inspiring teacher of broad intellectual interests: 'He was concerned not just with the politics of the period, but the broader culture, arts and other aspects of life. And an important part of my interest in the eighteenth century was that I was drawn to the aesthetics, to the art and architecture of the time'.

The influence of that enthusiasm is to be seen most sharply in her most recent book, *Britons: Forging the Nation, 1707–1837* (1992), in which the art and artefacts are not used merely as attractive illustrations but as an integral element, underpinning the text's analysis of mores and power relations: 'Art and artefacts are as valid as historical evidence as printed or manuscript text', she argues.

Even so her doctoral work was, in its subject-matter at least, on a subject that Namier would have recognised and approved – the Tory Party, during the reign of George II (1727–60). But here again that gift for resuscitation was at work. History, as we are often reminded, tends to be written by the winners. And while the Tories were never absolute losers – she points out that they retained a number of local and regional strongholds and maintained the allegiance of numerous substantial landowners – they were excluded from national power throughout this period.

She denies that personal political allegiance has anything to do it: 'I am not a Tory. But I did see real historical purpose in examining the landscape of eighteenth-century politics through the eyes and voices of the Tories, rather than the Whigs whose viewpoint had previously dominated the historical record'.

If the subject-matter is Namierite, the reference to 'voices' points to another historical tradition – that of the radical practitioners of history from below, the likes of E. P. Thompson, Eric Hobsbawm and Christopher Hill, who rescued from obscurity the marginalised rebels and radicals of British history. No modern British historian is immune from their influence and certainly nobody like Colley, in her mid-forties, who started work as a historian in the 1960s and 1970s, will have been unaffected by the excitement that their pioneering work generated.

But to be influenced is not the same as accepting an orthodoxy. She notes: 'History and historians are changing and developing all the time, and every generation likes to rebel against previous orthodoxies –

Namier for instance was an Aunt Sally figure for a lot of young historians in the sixties and seventies. This can be a fairly circular process, but
it is also one of intellectual progress.'

The less gifted may accept an orthodoxy, sometimes to the exaspera-
tion of those whose ideas they are accepting – New Zealand historian
James Belich, whose reworking of the nineteenth-century Maori Wars
demolished traditional interpretations, has been heard to complain that
'I intended to stimulate debate, but I seem to have replaced one orthodoxy with another'. The more talented will be found among the rebels,
rejecting old orthodoxies, or the revisionists, synthesising the old along
with their own insights and intellectual style. And this is where Linda
Colley is to be found – eschewing membership of any particular
'school' and developing an individual approach that nevertheless carries
traces both of Namierite precision and the sympathetic imagination of
Thompson and Hobsbawm.

That style is to be seen in her choice of 'voices'. The historians of the
60s and 70s rescued the working-class radicals of the eighteenth and
nineteenth century from ill-merited obscurity. And that approach
generates its own revision – just as historians of the modern British
working class like John Benson argue that too much attention has been
devoted to the political and union activist, so she argues that greater
attention is needed to the majority who accepted the orthodoxies of the
day, including the commercial classes: 'The tendency has been to concentrate on the disadvantaged and the discontented and the evidence of
dissent – crime, riots and radicalism. And that was quite right. But we
also need to remember the broader picture, and the majority who were
not radicals or dissident'.

Like journalists, historians are naturally drawn to the discontinuous,
the dramatic and the exceptional. But there are dangers in this, illustrated among other things by issues of national identity. Most nations
have their own notion of 'exceptionalism' – Paul Kennedy, professor of
history at Yale, pointed out that one argument regularly used by critics
of his belief that the United States was no more immune than any other
great power to the ills of overstretch and relative decline was 'But
America is different'. *Britons*, focusing on the creation of a British
national identity in the eighteenth century, has the myth of British
'exceptionalism' – Britons' sense of themselves as singular and superior
– as an important theme.

While published in 1992, *Britons'* gestation period began in the
1980s, a time when personal experience lent itself to a questioning of

national identity: 'I think being in America has helped more than it has hindered. There is no problem with sources – the Yale library is brilliant and we also have the Yale Centre for British Art, based on the Paul Mellon collection. It gets me away from the day to day detail of life among British historians, with endless detailed debates about who is saying or writing what – and I feel able to be more daring. But being away from that world also means that I don't get people saying to me "Did you see that article in the Transactions of the Shropshire Antiquarian Society?" – keeping right up to date in that way is a little more difficult.'

Once the project was conceived British politics contrived to give ever-greater relevance to her project. At one level this was a piece of good fortune, meaning that the eventual issue of the book received even wider notice than would otherwise have been the case, but catching the *Zeitgeist* has often been a skill of the best historians. As golfer Gary Player, congratulated on his good fortune, said, 'Yes, and the more I practice, the luckier I get'.

She emphasises that *Britons* was in no way intended as a tract for modern Britain, but it emphasised for her the extent to which misunder-standing of history and national identity still permeates our politics: 'The right for instance consistently talks of Britain when it means England – Great Britain did not exist before 1707 and is an archipelago rather than an island, but we get references to Britain as a 1000-year-old monarchy'.

On the left she notices discomfort with the concept of patriotism and the assumption that it is a peculiarly right-wing characteristic: 'This ignores the fact that for much of the eighteenth and nineteenth centuries there was a radical view of patriotism, seeing it as support for the inter-ests of the whole nation as against the narrow interests of the landed and privileged.'

And the right in particular, she notes, has been prone to assumptions about British exceptionalism – one example being Michael Portillo's outburst about corruption in other European countries. Colley argues that just as continuity demands as much attention as change, so should parallels be treated as seriously as divergences: 'An extremely important element in the British self-image of the eighteenth century was that of a Protestant state ranged against Catholic France. But it was not pecu-liarly British – the Dutch and the Swedes saw themselves in similar terms'.

Part of defining an identity is finding something to define yourself against, and here she restates the importance of France – large, powerful, Catholic, authoritarian and much too close for comfort – in the formation of British national identity. And she notes the continuing relevance of such feelings: 'A poll in 1992 found that while the French distrust the British more than any other people in Europe, the British distrust the French more than any other nation in the world. There may have been two World Wars against Germany this century, but rivalry with and fear of France goes back for centuries and left a far deeper impression on us than on the French because for most of the time they were more powerful and more threat to us than we were to them. In eighteenth-century Britain Francophobia was very largely the product of feelings of vulnerability. It is possible to overstate divergences, but it strikes me as no fluke, and very typical of the relationship, that when Paris is the world centre for women's fashions London should be the same for men.'

More surprising to the modern reader is the vital role played by Protestantism: 'Britain has ceased to be self-consciously a Protestant country since 1945. People see Ulster as a freak, but Ulster attitudes are merely those that were prevalent across Britain for most of the last few hundred years. The fact that John Major can even contemplate negotiating over its future rather shows the extent to which we have ceased to be a Protestant nation.'

Next on the list of those to be rescued come those pre-enfranchisement women, members of the political élite in all but voting rights. Here again the aesthetic element will play its role: 'Issues like styles of display – both in jewellery and dress – and the development of conceptions of etiquette, will play an important part. One of the important questions is to examine how power was understood and perceived.'

And she points out that women often wielded power in more readily understood ways. 'Many women controlled substantial landholdings, and it has been estimated that around a fifth of the appointments to Church of England livings in the nineteenth century were made by women.'

Another question of possible personal interest is how far those women were conscious and resentful of their exclusion. Her own career, though highly successful in a largely male-dominated world, has not been driven by any such feelings. Though she is well aware of the way in which other female academics have been restricted and also of the limitations facing all women: 'For instance a young woman academic who is intellectually aggressive is likely to be regarded as strident where a similar attitude will be accepted in a man', she has rarely felt disadvantaged, though she was, coming as she did from a lower-middle-class Northern background, the first of her family to go to university.

She says: 'It was possibly a matter of luck. I had a sister rather than a brother, went to an all-girls school and then into a history department that had a tradition of extremely bright female students. So it was not until I went to Cambridge that I even ran across the thought that men might be brighter than women. And by then I was confident and mature enough, with my ideas formed, to be able to cope with those attitudes where they occurred.'

Should she ever start to wonder whether male historians get a better deal she can always ask her husband. (In 1988 David Cannadine was appointed to a chair at Columbia University in New York, and followed his wife out to the States after six weary years of shuttling backwards and forwards.) But it seems unlikely that such an inquiry will be necessary. Several generations rather than one may have passed since *Mill on the Floss*, but it seems clear that George Eliot is as badly in need of revision as any historian.

Publications include:

In Defiance of Oligarchy: The Tory Party 1714–60, 1982, Cambridge University Press.
Namier, 1989, Weidenfeld and Nicholson.
Britons: Forging the Nation 1707–1837, 1992, Yale University Press.

(Huw Richards, © Times Higher Education Supplement)

Photograph © Gail Bryan

Mary Daly, born 1929, is associate professor in the Department of Theology at Boston College, where she teaches feminist ethics.

Mary Daly scores high in American academe's wacky stakes. Her books are full of capital letters and made-up words. In fact she has produced her own dictionary, which she calls *Websters' First New Intergalactic Wickedary of the English Language*, containing her favourite words 'crone' (great hag of history, survivor of the perpetual witch craze of patriarchy), 'blob' (windowless, airless, lifeless) and 'blobular' (having the characteristics of a blob, example, Blob Hope).

It is amazing to discover that this lesbian feminist philosopher, who is no longer a Catholic, no longer even a Christian, is an associate professor of theology at Jesuit-run Boston College. She will never achieve full professorship, she says, even though she is in her late sixties, has seven degrees, three of them doctorates, enthusiastic student support and has written five major books. The official reason? She is not considered scholarly enough.

Daly's reputation has, however, spread far and wide as a radical feminist thinker. She may be *persona non grata* in the Catholic Church but she is a heroine to feminists, a self-confessed 'revolting hag', a 'Spinster' who 'weaves cosmic tapestries in her own time/space'.

To the Catholic theologians in Boston, however, she is a thorn in the flesh. 'They don't want a woman like me', she says simply. Boston College tried to get rid of her in 1968, the year in which her first book, *The Church and the Second Sex,* came out. The treatise was pretty tame by the standards of her later work, but it laid into the Catholic Church, and that was inflammatory stuff for the period. 'Christianity, and the Catholic Church in particular, has not yet faced its responsibility to exorcise the devil of sexual prejudice,' she wrote. 'In fact, it has lagged behind the rest of the world on this issue.' The theologians decided against renewing Daly's contract, but they reckoned without the students. There were months of demonstrations, and Boston College had to back down.

Mary Daly has been a fixture – albeit unwelcome – on Boston's academic scene ever since. She seems to enjoy her abrasive relationship with 'academentia', as she rudely describes her fellow academics. She has certainly gone out of her way to make no compromises. But, then, she delights in being outrageous. In the early 1970s, for example, as she was becoming more and more of a radical feminist, she decided to teach the men separately from the women. 'Now that I could really do my own work and teach radical feminism, I saw that the boys were an obstruction in the class because young women were influenced by their presence,' she explains. 'They (the women) would hold things back or they would ask different questions.'

Daly has kept the sexes apart ever since. In 1971 she began to teach her first feminist classes called 'The Women's Revolution and Theological Development' and 'Women's Liberation and the Church'. She describes 1971 as 'a Sparkling year, a Stunning year'. It was during 1971 that she staged what she calls 'the Harvard Memorial Exodus'. She had been invited to give a sermon at Harvard University's church, the first woman to have received such an invitation in the church's 336-year history. 'To simply accept would be to agree to being used as a token,' she writes in her autobiography, *Outercourse*. 'To refuse would seem like forfeiting an opportunity. I tried to think of a creative solution.'

Her answer was to accept, but to engineer a dramatic walk-out from patriarchal religion. From the pulpit she invited the congregation to walk out. As she describes it, hundreds of men and women stampeded out of the church.

The following year she broke another taboo when she came out as a lesbian. At that time she also began work on her second book, *Beyond God the Father*, which carries the subtitle *Toward a Philosophy of Women's Liberation*. In it she asserts that the women's revolution is a spiritual revolution. It is the search for ultimate meaning, she says, which some would call God. In that book she also makes clear her fascination with language and lays the ground for the creation of new words: 'women have had the power of naming stolen from us', she says. 'We have not been free to use our own power to name ourselves, the world, or God . . . Women are now realizing that the universal imposing of names by men has been false because partial . . . The liberation of language is rooted in the liberation of ourselves.' By the autumn of 1974, this book was being used as a required text in universities and seminaries across America.

Daly's work is taught in women's studies and also in theology – though not in the élite Roman Catholic institutions.

When she wasn't writing Mary Daly was chatting and politicking with friends, people she calls 'Cronies' or 'Tigers'. They provided her with support, laughter, suggestions. 'I wrote and wrote my heart out,' she explains. 'I wrote like a house afire. I knew that I was on the right Spiral.'

All this New Age stuff is a bit bewildering to the uninitiated, but Mary Daly is serious about it. She divides her life into four spiral galaxies. The first she calls 'Be-speaking, that is foretelling, speaking of what will be', which includes the writing of her first book and goes from birth to 1971. Be-speaking brings about psychic and/or material change by means of words, she says. The second galaxy, 'Be-falling', involves 'breakthrough' and 're-calling', i.e. giving words new names. That represents the period when she began to see through the 'foreground past', as she explains it, to the 'background past'. She adds: 'I found that Breaking through to knowledge of a Prepatriarchal Pagan Past opened the possibility for Radical Naming'. She puts the Harvard Memorial Church Exodus into the second galaxy as well as her writing of *Beyond God the Father*. Around 1975 she says she was hurled in the direction of the third spiral galaxy, which she calls 'Be-witching: Moments of Spinning'.

In that period she became much more active in her creative intellectual work, she says. She moved beyond reacting to 'patriarchally defined methods of thinking' to creating her own ideas in the book for which she is best known: *Gyn/Ecology: The Metaethics of Radical Feminism*. In that book Mary Daly describes radical feminism as the journey of women becoming. It is very much what she calls an 'Otherworld Journey' because it is a discovery and a creation of a world other than patriarchy. To get to the Otherworld, you have to go through three passages – discovery, exorcism and ecstasy. The 'First Passage' tells of the exuberance of discovery as the voyager breaks through the barriers of obsolete myths and confronts Daly's nightmares, male mystification and deception, what she calls 'patriarchal myths'. In the 'Second Passage', which is the darkest part of the journey, the voyager is introduced to the global dimensions of Goddess-murder, in Daly's words, 'the killing of the divine spark of female be-ing'. Daly looks at the rituals of Indian suttee or widow-burning, Chinese footbinding, African genital mutilation, the massacre of witches in Renaissance Europe and modern American gynaecology and psychotherapy. The happy process of women's own unfolding forms the 'Third Passage' as the Voyager moves into the Otherworld.

In conversation Mary Daly laughs and jokes, and enjoys being silly. While she was writing *Gyn/Ecology* she was rolling on the floor, doubled over with mirth. As she explains in her autobiography: 'When we were discussing a passing reference in the manuscript to "pope paul the sixth," we concluded that he should be referred to as "sixth (sic, sick)". This "title" evoked ludicrous associations. At times, of course, there was a temptation to write "sic" or "sick" after almost every word'.

After the book appeared, however, Daly found she was being monitored in the classroom at Boston College. Three 'visitors', one of them a Catholic priest, sat in on her feminist ethics class. Daly and her students asked them to leave. They did so, and filed complaints saying they had been verbally assaulted and threatened with physical assault. The dean of the graduate school formally reprimanded Daly and ordered her to send letters of apology. There were more visits from some of the original visitors, as well as the chairman of the theology department. And more complaints. Monitors began to appear in all of her classes.

Daly retaliated by instructing her students to sit in a circle. This meant that the monitor of that class, who turned out to be Father Robert Daly, the theology department chairman, found himself sandwiched between two large feminists. Meanwhile Mary Daly lectured the group on the witchhunts in Western Europe during the Renaissance, alluding to the role of Jesuits in such atrocities and reading from letters written by the aforementioned Father Daly and his colleagues as examples of a continuing witchcraft. The wretched Father Daly was then asked to respond. He could not comment on 'substantive matters,' he said, and was only doing his duty, having been sent as a monitor by the university administration. All of which was faithfully recorded by two student newspaper reporters present.

The upshot was that the monitoring stopped and Mary Daly was left alone – at least for the time being – to teach her band of supporters. Why not move to a place which appreciated her more? 'No,' she says. 'One of the things you come to realize as you become more and more of a radical feminist is that very, very few women have the courage, the guts and the integrity to pursue that direction, and they're constantly willing to be tokenised. I was very lucky, I had the opportunity to see through it all when I was fired (when the college put her on a terminal contract) and I am just kind of gutsy. I will not kneel for them. But there are very few colleagues who really can do that.'

The end of the 1970s, the period after *Gyn/Ecology* came out, was electrifying, says Daly. The women's movement was at its peak and Daly travelled the country talking about her book. She drove and flew north, east, south, west, descending on colleges and universities, women's bookstores, restaurants and coffee houses, she says in her auto-biography. 'I was beyond jet lag. I was flying in Spirals.' By contrast, the 1980s were deeply depressing to her, a time of backlash against women and a time when Republican presidents Reagan and Bush were in the White House.

That was when she wrote *Pure Lust*. She describes it as 'elemental' feminist philosophy and in it she examines phallic lust as opposed to 'pure' lust. The latter, she says, is a life-affirming force that enables women to connect with nature and themselves. In *Pure Lust* she has a go at what she calls 'ascetic' heroes, people like T.E. Lawrence, Dag Hammarskjöld and Mahatma Gandhi, who took a vow of celibacy and tested it by sleeping with young girls. And she ends up by urging women to transform themselves, to break away from the 'cockocratic' codes and find their own way, free of patriarchal control. Daly acknowledges that *Pure Lust* is a dense book, much more difficult to read than her earlier works, but she is proud of it, she says, because of its richness and because it goes further than anything she has written before.

Today she is hard at work on *Quintessence*, her latest book project. And she is living in the fourth spiral galaxy, which she describes as 'the age of cronehood in feminism'. The fourth galaxy began as she was writing her autobiography, *Outercourse*, which is a lively romp through Mary Daly's life and thoughts, with much reference to time/space travel. It is dedicated to her mother, Anna, 'who launched my Craft and refuels it constantly in the Expanding Now, and to Other Foresisters and Cronies across Time who have stayed on Course in their own unique ways and who know who they Are'.

Daly's mother was very important to her. 'She wanted me to have everything that she had not had', says Daly, who came from a poor Irish-American background, growing up in Schenectady, in upper New York state. (The Irish link is cherished and Daly loves to visit the country of her ancestors.) Her father was a travelling salesman who sold ice-cream freezers and who published a book, *What Every Ice-Cream Dealer Should Know*, which Daly says is beautifully written. Both parents had to leave school at a young age to find work.

Daly's mother never promoted the idea of marriage and children, says her daughter. She always said she had desired only one child, and that one a daughter. Daly grew up therefore on a rock-solid and confident foundation, which was to stand her in good stead in all those tussles with the Catholic theologians. Her mother also actively discouraged her from helping with any of the housework. Whenever young Mary made a half-hearted attempt to help with the washing-up, her mother told her to 'go and do your own work dear'. Daly writes: 'What that meant to me when I was eight, nine and fifteen was, essentially, that I had to find out what my work was, and go do it'.

Mary did well in school, though she was a trouble-maker, and managed to survive the rigours of American teen culture. She describes the junior and senior proms (the school dances) as 'grim', but she attended them, asking a bashful boy to take her. 'The whole prom phenomenon was an inescapable mind-fuck, masked as pure delight', she comments. All the while she was desperate to acquire a decent education, and began saving money at the age of 12, working at supermarket check-outs and stashing her hard-earned income away. Her first degree was in English at The College of St Rose, a single-sex, Catholic, liberal arts establishment. There followed an MA in English at Catholic University in Washington DC on a full-tuition scholarship, and a PhD in theology at St Mary's College, Notre Dame, Indiana. During this time her greatest dream had been to study philosophy, and she found she was able to do this at St Mary's because she was introduced to Thomas Aquinas. 'I badly wanted to go on in philosophy,' she explains. 'That was still haunting me, so I tried to get in to the PhD programme at the University of Notre Dame in philosophy, but the priests wouldn't let me in because I was a woman.'

In desperation Daly moved east to a job teaching theology and philosophy at a small Catholic college in Massachusetts. But this was not what she wanted to be doing. She wanted to be teaching interesting courses to the brightest students. In a burst of ambition, she applied to the school of sacred theology at Catholic University so that she might acquire the highest of higher degrees. 'They wouldn't even answer my letters,' she says. 'They bounced my letters back and forth . . . and finally they said they couldn't admit me because I was a woman.'

So she went to one of only two countries in Europe in which Catholic women were allowed to study theology with Catholic men – Switzerland – and enrolled at the University of Fribourg. Everything was taught in Latin by Dominican priests from all over the world, so they all spoke this dead language with differing accents. Daly understood nothing at first, but gradually the fog lifted. She kept herself alive by teaching philosophy to young men in the junior year-abroad programme of Georgetown University and in two other American programmes. And she had a great time, doing very well in her exams and riding a motorbike around town. She was fascinated by Europe, by its 'aura', its smells and its ancient roots. 'From the minute I landed there, I never wanted to go', she says.

Altogether Daly spent seven years in Fribourg. Halfway through her mother joined her, and there began a happy period living and travelling together. She got her doctorate in theology and decided to accumulate a third PhD, in philosophy. 'So I was launched on what might have seemed to be my career as the world's oldest child prodigy', she says. She was now in her late thirties. It was while she was writing her dissertation in philosophy that she got a letter from a British publisher inviting her to write a book on women and the church. In 1965 the contract for *The Church and the Second Sex* was signed, and she began work. Eventually she was kicked out of Switzerland for having the wrong visa (she was no longer a student, yet was on a student visa), which was how she came to be at Boston College. Daly hated leaving Europe and returned to America with what she calls 'distaste and dismay'. She chose Boston because it was as close as she could get to Europe.

The struggles she has encountered appear to have inspired her creative work. Certainly, her applications for full professorships in 1975 and 1989, and the subsequent rejections, seem to have spurred her on to greater acts of rebellion. She resents deeply being kept in poverty on her associate professorship (salary: less than $40,000 a year) but she says she no longer covets the status. Mary Daly has moved on.

Today she is almost a grand old dame of feminist philosophy, taught on women's studies and theology courses. As virtually the first leading figure in feminist theology in the 1970s she blazed the trail against patriarchy in religion, educating people in the theology of protest and analysing religious symbols and traditions from a radical woman's perspective. Professor Sheila Daveney, who teaches religion at the University of Denver, teaches Daly as 'one of the historical figures'. Daly is still a prominent figure on the American lecture circuit, drawing big crowds to hear her speak. But as she has become more interested in language and spiral galaxies, she has rather left mainstream America behind.

Publications include:

The Church and the Second Sex, 1968 1985, Beacon Press.

Beyond God the Father: Toward a Philosophy of Women's Liberation, 1973, 1985, Beacon Press.

Gyn/Ecology: The Metaethics of Radical Feminism, 1978, 1990, Beacon Press.

Pure Lust: Elemental Feminist Philosophy, 1984, 1992, HarperSanFrancisco.

Websters' First New Intergalactic Wickedary of the English Language, Conjured in Cahoots with Jane Caputi, 1987, Beacon Press.

Outercourse: The Be-Dazzling Voyage: Containing Recollections from My Logbook of a Radical Feminist Philosopher (Be-ing an Account of My Time/Space Travels and Ideas – Then, Again, Now, and How), 1992, HarperSanFrancisco.

(© Lucy Hodges)

Photograph © Rob Judges

Kay Davies, born 1951, is professor of molecular genetics, Oxford University. She played a key role in tracking down the gene linked to the progressive wasting disease, muscular dystrophy.

Sometimes, a scientist's career lifts like a surfer catching a wave. A combination of ripe problems and apt techniques appears at just the right time, and someone who was drifting is off, riding the crest of discovery.

Kay Davies had that experience in the late 1970s, and she is still going. It was then that she discovered genes. The talk was of genetic diagnosis, of gene mapping, perhaps even of gene therapy. And for a frankly uninspired protein chemist, the world changed: 'I realised that there was something exciting to do in science'.

It is hard to credit that this businesslike woman, with her 26-page CV listing nearly 200 papers, her recent chair in genetics at Oxford, her role in understanding the causes of the muscle-wasting disease muscular dystrophy, secure in her accomplishments but still only in mid-career, ever had doubts about science. But that is how she tells the story.

She read chemistry as an Oxford undergraduate, won prizes, and was prevailed upon to stay on for a doctorate. She did it, as much as anything, in order to avoid regretting not doing it. 'I can't have been completely bored or else I wouldn't have done it, but I was not a fired-up PhD student.' And she enjoyed the fact that it was tough going, moving toward biochemistry, setting up techniques, making them work. 'I worked quite hard at it – if you're going to do it, you might as well do it well.'

She did it well enough to earn a Royal Society post-doctoral fellowship, which took her to a lab on the outskirts of Paris, 'to learn something about proteins'. But having proved herself, the motivation began to flag. 'I spent more time skiing and playing tennis, I have to say.' Fortunately for her career, she also took the opportunity to look beyond the bench to the rest of science. 'That was the great advantage of those days,' she says, as if 1979 were an age ago, 'you could actually try different things. You never felt there was any urgency to get a tenured position. You could actually explore bits of science and see what really interested you.'

Her chemical education had not brought any contact with genetics. Now, with the 'new genetics' just taking shape, that was what caught her interest. Genes were being manipulated in new ways, cut up with enzymes, patched together, and grown in bacteria. At the same time, the principles of the new mapping techniques which would ultimately lead to the human genome programme (the goal of which is to identify all the genes in humankind) were emerging. There was the promise of the discovery of many genes involved in human disease.

The young Davies learnt the techniques of 'cloning', or making copies of pieces of DNA – the genetic material – of interest, at the Pasteur Institute, then quickly moved back to London to join the group led by Professor Bob Williamson at St Mary's Hospital. It was

1980 and, as she recalls, 'not only did my interest explode; the whole field exploded'.

A decade and a half on, and she has a central role in the British contribution to applying the new genetics. An explosion in knowledge, unlike the physical kind, makes new connections. It needs strategists and entrepreneurs, and people who try and channel the flow. Inevitably, they get drawn into the politics of science, as Davies has in writing reports for the Academia Europea and the Office of Science and Technology. The trick is to balance this with the research, and she recently took a crucial decision to stick with the science, after a plum Medical Research Council job threatened to become more politics than research.

The job was to direct the council's new Clinical Sciences Centre at the Royal Postgraduate Medical School in Hammersmith, a flagship for the council's efforts to marry basic science with clinical research. Davies, who is interested above all in genetic disease, was invited to lead this effort, and build the new institute around the new genetics. But the new venture fell foul of government restructuring of London's health service. She spent many hours in meetings thrashing out the implications: 'I was having to spend an enormous amount of time, turning up at meetings trying to persuade people that, you know, the muscle clinic needed to stay at the Hammersmith because the muscle research depended on it, and the department of haematology needed to be protected'.

This wasn't what she was there for: 'I felt that as leader of that institution I needed to be leading from the front with the science, not the politics'. So she quit and went back to Oxford. 'If the best way of protecting the science base is for me to go back and do pure basic research, then I'll go back and do pure basic research for five years. What I won't do is stay in London and try and do that when I know I can't if I have all those other responsibilities.'

The extra responsibilities she is keen on are ones which make the research more effective, like editing the new journal *Human Molecular Genetics*. She admits ruefully that this 'nearly kills me', but journal editing is, of course, a superb way to keep abreast of other work in the field. 'If you are trying to clone a gene for a particular disease, as we are for example in spinal muscular atrophy, I know what is going on in every other neuromuscular disease. If you are reviewing papers in related fields, they review the literature for you, so it's very easy to spot whether there's anything really significant coming through – there's an enormous benefit from editing that journal at the moment.'

Finding the gene for spinal muscular atrophy, by what is called 'positional cloning' will be her last such project, she declares. What was once a triumph for any gene is now boring, because the techniques are well-proven – 'it's just a turning of the wheel'. Once, it was far from boring, of course. The famous early successes, like the identification of the gene which carries the mutations for cystic fibrosis which Williamson worked on, or muscular dystrophy, Davies' special study, are among the most remarkable developments in biology of the last thirty years.

That work, always stretching the limits of technique, has the curious double aspect – of appearing inspiring, but already a little quaint – which defines landmarks in very fast-moving fields. Along with the expansion of knowledge has come a fantastic proliferation of techniques, molecular tricks for doing almost anything the geneticists can think of. Davies' science has been transformed in just a few years.

'When I did a PhD you really had to make sure that you had the basic techniques at your fingertips. I don't think that's the case any more in molecular biology. The techniques come so thick and fast these days that you couldn't possibly keep up with them. There is a completely different way of looking at things.'

One consequence is that the researchers work in larger teams, so that the full range of techniques is available. If the ultimate goal is clinical, the team has to be larger still. But their concerns are now no longer mainly with identifying genes. The new battery of techniques means that the initial gene tagging – known as 'reverse genetics' because it inverts the traditional logic of finding which protein does a particular job and then looking for its gene – is becoming routine. That, after all, is the purpose of the human genome programme.

But, extraordinary though this ability is, it creates a much harder job: working out what each gene does. For because this is reverse genetics, when most genes are found no one has any idea what proteins they code for, let alone what those proteins are used for in the cell. 'Of all the genes that have been cloned, there are still very few where we have a full understanding of the functions now. So there's a tremendous amount of biology doing the rest of the reverse genetics.'

This, in a way, takes her back to her earlier research concerns, with proteins and how they work, and to an older research style. 'There will be a gradual shift in my group, I expect, from using the reverse human genetics approach to more classical genetics, and using classical genetics means you have to use other organisms, to understand the function of genes by looking at mutations. So it's still genetics, but genetics of a very different, more basic type if you like.'

The best current example is muscular dystrophy, a wholly mysterious disease until a few years ago. In 1987, after a seven-year effort by Davies' group and many others, the enormous gene which was linked to this progressive wasting disease was finally tracked down on the short arm of the X-chromosome. That was the key to a rush of discovery. The gene identified a (very large) protein, dystrophin, which is defective in those who have the disease. Not suprisingly, this protein normally appears in muscle cells. Less predictably, it is also made, in a slightly modified form, in the brain, which is presumably linked to the mental retardation which afflicts a proportion of patients.

Even more suprisingly, Davies discovered that human cells carry another, almost identical gene on a different chromosome. This gene, which codes for a protein dubbed utrophin, is active in most parts of the body. The different roles played by the two proteins have yet to be disentangled, but it is already clear that utrophin appears in fetal muscle, but disappears from some parts of muscle cells after dystrophin manufacture is turned on.

So the existence of utrophin, whose description in 1989 Davies reckons is her most important paper, immediately raises speculation about treatment. This might be the simplest form of gene therapy. No need to fix a gene, or substitute new for old; simply turn one back on which is already there in the patient's cells. 'We have thought, well if you look at it theoretically, utrophin could replace dystrophin in DMD patients. There are also lots of reasons why it might not, but the best thing to do is to try and find something that will upregulate utrophin and then see if it works.'

From this point of view, the prospects for therapy look more promising than before. 'There's an awful lot of redundancy in the genome that we never realised before. You knock something out and you find that the animal is perfectly OK. So there is a complexity which we didn't know about; there are ways in which different genes can compensate, in certain circumstances, for the absence of others.'

Fast as all this is moving, she would still like to see progress speed up, for the sake of patients. 'It is just a little disappointing that we are not moving to the therapy phase quite as fast as some of the families hoped we might.' She deals regularly with families coping with muscular dystrophy, or with spinal muscular atrophy – known as 'floppy baby syndrome'.

Many babies with this condition die very early on, but unlike muscular dystrophy, it is not progressive, and some survive. 'They tend to be incredibly bright, so when you go to their meetings, and see them speeding around in their motorised wheelchairs, you don't feel any sort of real depression. The families know that what they're contributing to is unlikely to help their particular children, and they're quite happy to accept that.'

Nevertheless, it is a constant reminder of the need to move beyond pre-natal diagnosis. 'That's an enormous advance, but the next advance is therapy. It will come within the next decade, but that's still a long time compared to how long it took to get the linkages to these genes.'

Most often, pre-natal tests give the all-clear, as she knows from personal experience. Married to an Oxford chemist, she has one son and she admits that at times, working in this field, 'you begin to wonder whether they are ever born normal. I certainly tested myself for everything I was working on, so you check that you aren't a cystic fibrosis carrier or a muscular dystrophy carrier as a matter of course'.

She was not, and the risks, she emphasises are still pretty low. But when you work with the people who have fallen foul of the risk, the motivation for pressing on with the research is always clear. 'Particularly now, as we discover more genes that have nothing to do with disease at all, the whole area is going to have an enormous impact on developmental biology. But my own specific interest has always been in muscular disease – we always have been part of the group concentrating on the applications.'

Publications include:

Molecular Analysis of Inherited Diseases, 1988, with A. P. Read, IRL Press.

(Ed.) *Human Genetics Diseases. A Practical Approach*, 1988, IRL Press.

(Ed.) *Genome Analysis. A Practical Approach*, 1988, IRL Press.

(Ed.) *The Fragile X Syndrome*, 1989, Oxford University Press.

(Ed.) *Application of Molecular Genetics to the Diagnosis of Inherited Disease*, 1989, Royal College of Physicians of London.

(Ed.) *Genome Analysis Review* series on genome mapping, 1990–94, with Shirley Tilghman, Cold Spring Harbor Press.

(© Jon Turney)

Natalie Zemon Davis, born 1928, is Henry Charles Lea professor of history, Princeton University. Regarded as one of the leading female historians in the United States, her work includes the book which was the source for the film *The Return of Martin Guerre*. Her protests against McCarthyism in the 1950s resulted in her passport being taken away for six years.

Photograph © Rob Judges

Natalie Zemon Davis chooses to begin her story with her great grandparents. 'I am from a typically American immigrant family. In my case Eastern Europe Jews who came from Lithuania and White Russia in the nineteenth century. My parents were typical second generation Americans – they would never talk about the old country.'

Her desire to understand her own history led her first to Europe and then to France. Today she is one of the most respected historians in the United States, holding the Henry Charles Lea chair of history at Princeton. In 1994–95 she became the first woman to occupy Oxford University's prestigious visiting professorship, the Eastman Chair. She is not only a first-rate scholar, but also a wonderful story-teller, and her work bubbles with her irrepressible interest in people's tales – and how they choose to tell them.

Meeting her right at the end of her year-long stay in Oxford is not easy. The panic in her voice at how to fit in an interview, and a session with the photographer, is tempered by what can only be called a consideration to be helpful and generous. It is an instinct that becomes more and more identifiable as the conversation develops – throughout she has a desire to be generous about the work of others, forever break-ing off halfway through a criticism to add a qualification. This is not based on a wish to please – it is based on a desire to communicate. As she says: 'I think it is interesting to define periods not so much in terms of what people believed, but what they chose to debate, to argue about. Positions should never become too rigid.'

In recent years Davis has become associated with a school of history often called the 'narrative school' or 'micronarrative'. Her book *The Return of Martin Guerre*, the story of an imposter in a sixteenth-century French village, which served as the source for a film of the same name, is often quoted as an example of how historians have used narrative, or an individual's story, as a way of illuminating wider aspects of a particular society. As Davis says in her introduction to the book, she wanted to describe the 'peasants' hopes and feelings; the ways in which they experienced the relation between husband and wife, parent and child; the ways in which they experienced the constraints and possibilities in their lives'.

She further explains: 'I . . . chose to advance my arguments . . . as much by the ordering of narrative, choice of detail, literary voice and metaphor as by topical analysis'. But as she makes clear, as she tells her own story, a conscious interest in narrative as a historical tool only appeared in her work in the 1970s. It was present in some form before then, but her path towards narrative has incorporated a number of approaches – all of which are still present in her work today. 'There is often this contrast between what is loosely termed old and new history,' she says. 'I think this contrast is sometimes exaggerated, it is more that you ask new questions as well as the old ones.'

Davis's development can very much be seen in these terms, forever adding new questions to her existing repertoire. She charts her interest in history back to her high school days. 'Within my family there was no historical depth, everything was oriented towards becoming American. I went to a girls high school and I fell in love with history. I liked it so', she recalls with enthusiasm. Looking back at her interest in European history, which also developed early on, she says: 'I have often thought that at that moment in my life it was easier for me to have a historical connection with European things than with American things, since my family were not old WASPs'. Then she adds, in her now familiar spirit of reconciliation: 'But I married a man from an old WASP family'.

By the time she went to college, which was the prestigious but conservative, all-women Smith College, she knew that she wanted to study history. But what has informed her study of history throughout has been a love of literature, of stories and of drama. And her parents' influence was more direct. 'My father was an amateur playwright and actor. That sort of glamour of the theatre, that was part of my family background to be sure. And I was really happy that my father lived long enough to see the Martin Guerre film.'

Combined with these intellectual interests came a politial activism that both informed and fed off her work. 'I think my political involvement strengthened my sense that history is deeply meaningful to the present. I have always taken the Marxist idea that men, or humankind, make their own history. This is a notion I have always taken very seriously, much more seriously than the more deterministic side of Marxist history.'

Davis's political involvement was not, however, to be without a price. Her protests against McCarthyism, in particular the publication of a pamphlet called 'Operation Mind', meant that she had her passport taken away for six years – a tragedy for a young academic building a reputation as a historian of France. But it was an adversity that she turned to her advantage. Denied access to French archives, she looked instead at what she could lay her hands on. 'They are not going to keep me down', she says, recalling her sentiments of the time and clenching her fists. Her consequent use of printed as well as archive matter, has marked her out ever since.

It was while at Smith College that Davis married Chandler Davis, a graduate student in mathematics at Harvard. As Smith College forbade marriages she had to elope, but did go on to graduate. The marriage, which has lasted, led to the birth of three children in the 1950s and was a profound influence on her life. 'Most of my decisions in life have been life choices. I had to balance my many different roles as a mother, as a wife and as an academic. There were no role models for me at that time. Most of the teachers at Smith were single women living alone.'

Chandler Davis was an equally active opponent of McCarthyism. In 1954 he was called before the House Un-American Activities Committee, partly because he had signed the printer's bill for 'Operation Mind'. He refused to answer the committee's questions, taking the First Amendment. He lost his job, and five years later the Supreme Court ruled against him and he went to jail for six months in 1960, leaving behind his wife and three young children. Davis dwells very little on those days. 'This is maybe not very interesting,' she says, pausing in her tale, with typical modesty. 'But just in terms of source material it had a big influence on me.'

She began her graduate training at Harvard, where she really began to develop her interest in social history. She recalls the influence of Wilbert K Jordan, a social historian whose major work was on the philanthropy of early modern England. Not only did he fully introduce her to archival sources and social history, but he encouraged her. 'He really wanted his women to succeed. And that was in a place where most of the graduate students were men', she says. Her original work was on

English social history, and it was only when she and her husband moved to Michigan that she switched to France. 'I'm actually rather glad that I did, although maybe I shouldn't say that,' she says, before clarifying. 'I would rather know about English history but be based on the continent so that I can do cross-referencing. So many people do English history and don't pay attention to other places.'

Her book *Society and Culture in Early Modern France* is really a product of these years. Its concern with social issues, with class, with Protestantism and its relation to class is clear. But what also emerges in this work is her interest in rituals, in festival occasions. In a piece called 'Rites of Violence' she looks at the behaviour of religious crowds, at why Catholic and Protestant crowds behaved as they did, what motivated and formed their seemingly irrational behaviour. She concludes: 'Even in the extreme case of religious violence, crowds do not act in a mindless way . . . if we try to increase safety and trust within a community, try to guarantee that the violence it generates will take less destructive and cruel forms, then we must think less about pacifying "deviants" and more about changing central values.'

It was this fascination with rituals, with festivals, that was to set Davis apart from the *annales* school of history, so dominant in France at the time, and from more traditional social historians. The *annales* school, with its interest in structures, and deeper currents of history, appears at first sight to have little in common with a historian like Davis, who probes into the smallest affairs of a village community, and listens to the individual stories of its people. But it would be wrong to see her too much at variance with this *annales* school. Davis was fascinated by its work, and did much to popularise it in the States. 'It is not so much that I felt in opposition to the *annales* school,' she says. 'It was more that we were doing different things, I did not feel I could draw on their work particularly.'

To some extent it was the same with more traditional social historians, particularly those preoccupied with social movements in terms of what they showed about class conflict. 'When I studied printing organisations, for example, I felt out on a limb because I was interested in their rituals, while other social historians looked more to the strike actions and demands of such organisations', says Davis. Instead she turned to the work of anthropologists. While the *annales* school drew on the structuralist work of the anthropologist Claude Lévi-Strauss, Davis looked to the work of anthropologists on ritual and performance. And here once again her interest in narrative, drama and film, re-emerged.

'Anthropologists were able to talk to their subjects, to converse with them,' she says. 'And it was only through making a historical film that I felt that I could get anywhere near this.' She describes working on the film, *The Return of Martin Guerre*, as the nearest she has got to an anthropologist's experience. 'The actors came to me and discussed their roles, and said how they thought the characters would have behaved and why. I found that fascinating. Gerard Depardieu, who starred in the film, really did think what it was like to be a sixteenth-century French peasant – as well as perhaps drawing on a more universal sense of human experience.'

What is so fascinating about the Martin Guerre story is how Arnaud de Tilh manages to persuade a whole village and his wife that he is indeed the long-lost Martin Guerre. Equally fascinating is the role of the wife Bertrande de Rols, who chose to believe the imposter – a charming and intelligent man by all accounts when contrasted to her true husband – and who betrayed him in the end. But although Bertrande comes to say that she has been duped – the cost of complicity being death – she relates only those details of her marriage that Arnaud de Tilh can confirm. As a result it is not until the real Martin Guerre returns that the truth becomes apparent and the imposter is sentenced to death. Sadly the film version chose to simplify Bertrande, portraying her as a woman who stands by Martin Guerre to the end, instead of the fascinating mix she was.

The appeal of the story is in part the universal appeal of a story about an imposter, but takes its strength from the fact that it was so grounded in sixteenth-century France. 'It is a plot embedded in issues of property, heirship, and bastardy, enacted in a society without ample frontiers for new village lives, and where memory is the main guarantee of identity', says Davis. This concern with stories and their place of telling is again apparent in Davis's book *Fiction in the Archives: Pardon Tales and their Tellers in Sixteenth Century France*. In this book, published in 1987, Davis argues that she wants the 'fictional' aspects of the documents to be the centre of the analysis. She explains: 'By "fictional" I do not mean their feigned elements, but rather, using the other and broader sense of the root word *fingere*, their forming, shaping, and moulding elements: the crafting of a narrative.' What she is after is how 'sixteenth century people told stories'. Last year, *Women on the Margins: Three Seventeenth Century Lives* was published. It is the story of three women's lives – one a Jew, one a Catholic and one a Protestant. At the beginning Davis gets as near to a dialogue with her subjects as she can, crafting a fictional dialogue with them in which they criticise her work, in particular, her decision to put all three in the same book.

Merchant and mother of 12, Glikl bas Judah Leib, the Jew, living in seventeenth-century Europe, mystic Marie de l'Incarnation, the Catholic in North America, and painter and naturalist Maria Sibylla Merian, who joined a radical Protestant sect in the Netherlands – women with different lives, yet facing common challenges. It is one of her first books to specifically give vent to her feminist leanings, although she has always been interested in women's history. 'When I had my babies in the 1950s I began a dossier on sixteenth-century women's pregnancies,' she says. 'And I have always been particularly interested in women's voices. In this new book they come to the fore.'

It is hard to find a disparaging critique of Davis's work. Peter Burke, reader in cultural history at the University of Cambridge and a fellow of Emmanuel, describes her as 'the leading female historian in the United States'. And even Richard Cobb, who wrote a critical review of her work in *The Spectator* in 1975, accusing her of intervening too heavily to interpret the thoughts of her subjects, describes her today as 'a very good example of someone whose conclusions have all been strictly based on very sustained research in French urban archives'. Struggling to the phone, despite a severe illness, Cobb, who has since died, added: 'I couldn't speak too highly of her'.

Davis's interest in film, narrative and history has not ended. She plans to retire from academe so that she can work on films – not documentaries but works of fiction in the mould of *Martin Guerre*. As a young graduate in the 1950s she sought work as a film assistant in New York, – but was unsuccessful. Today, thirty-five years on, she has been able to bring her interest in history and drama together, to produce the perfect happy ending.

Publications include:

Society and Culture in Early Modern France, 1975, Stanford University Press.
The Return of Martin Guerre, 1983, Harvard University Press.
Fiction in the Archives: Pardon Tales and their Tellers in Sixteenth Century France, 1987, Stanford University Press.
Women on the Margins: Three Seventeenth Century Lives, 1995, Harvard University Press.

(Claire Sanders, © Times Higher Education Supplement)

Acclaimed novelist **Anita Desai**, born 1937, the leading woman writer about India, is professor of writing at Massachusetts Institute of Technology.

Photograph © Paul Salmon

Anita Desai has a complicated relationship with academe. Fellow of Girton College, Cambridge, member of the American Academy and Institute of Arts and Letters, professor of English literature at Smith and Mount Holyoke Colleges in Massachusetts over several years, for the past few years she has been the first professor of writing in the creative writing course at the Massachusetts Institute of Technology. At the same time she is a widely respected novelist read in several languages besides English, twice short-listed for the Booker Prize in Britain, and a speaker much in demand at literary conferences: in other words, one of India's leading writers, the leading woman writer about India – and a favourite subject for articles and books by academics working in comparative literature.

Of course it is nothing unusual for a major novelist or poet to mix writing with academic work, particularly in the United States. Think of, say, Professor Saul Bellow or Professor Seamus Heaney. But Professor Desai is quite a late incarnation, born when she was already 50 with an established literary reputation (she has written ten published novels as well as short stories). Apart from having taken a degree at Delhi University in the 1950s, her previous contact with university life was small, her experience of teaching nil; for some thirty years, while writing fiction, she was a housewife living in Calcutta, Delhi and Bombay, bringing up two sons and two daughters. To start teaching writing, especially to non-Indians, was a jolt.

'It is a conflict, of course it is,' she admits. 'When I'm working on a book I find myself completely torn in two really. I find the only thing to do is put aside the writing when one's teaching. Think about it, make notes, read, but put aside the writing.' Writing literature and teaching how to write are opposed processes, she feels; and there is also the fact that when teaching one is immersed in reading 'some very bad stuff' written by students. 'That's quite fatal. I think it's terribly important when you're writing to read well.'

Nevertheless she is grateful for her American academic position. Besides enjoying her contact with science students (female as well as male) at MIT ('ever so much more interesting than the girls I taught in liberal arts colleges'), she has been able to educate two of her children in the USA. And the financial security has kept her free from the pressures of the literary market-place. She has never churned out writing to order: 'If I didn't earn my living this way, I would be writing differently, I would need to make money from my writing – and that's something I've just never thought about. In that I am awfully fortunate.'

But Desai's ambivalent feelings about academe lie much deeper than these comparatively familiar conflicts. Her best-known novel (filmed by Ismail Merchant in 1994), *In Custody*, published in 1984, some years before her decision to leave India, encapsulates them. Its central character, Deven, is an ineffectual, penurious literature lecturer in an undistinguished, dusty private college outside Delhi, whose subject is Hindi but whose passion (despite his being a Hindu) is for Urdu, the court language of the Mughals. 'He had never found a way to reconcile the meanness of his physical existence with the purity and immensity of his literary yearnings.' In post-Independence India, Hindi, the language of commerce, politics and hundreds of millions of Hindus, has expanded, while Urdu, the language of poetry, music and the minority Muslim community, has decayed.

Deven is given the unique opportunity of interviewing for a literary magazine his boyhood hero, the greatest living Urdu poet, Nur Shahjehanabadi, who is ill, probably dying. He muffs it. Faced by an unsuspected Byronic gulf between the poetry of Nur and the poet's squalid private life (something here of the frisson over Philip Larkin's poetry and life), Deven cannot cope. He attempts to tape-record Nur in full poetic flow – but obtains chiefly the poet's reminiscences about the pleasures of the flesh.

At one point he desperately nudges Nur 'with the earnestness of an interviewer': '"And, sir, were you writing any poetry at the time? Do you have any verse belonging to that period?" The effect was disastrous. Nur, in the act of reaching out for a drink, froze. "Poetry?" he shot at

Deven, harshly. "Poetry of the period? Do you think a poet can be ground between stones, and bled, in order to produce poetry – for you? You think you can switch on that mincing machine, and I will instantly produce for you a length of raw, red minced meat that you can carry off to your professors to eat?"' But though the recording is an absolute failure, and Deven's hopes of academic glory are utterly crushed, something less tangible has emerged from the encounter: a kind of friendship and trust. Deven's love of Nur's poetry is genuine, and Nur has perceived this: poet and reader have become bound together, willy-nilly. Hence the ironic title of the novel, *In Custody*. Deven 'had imagined he was taking Nur's poetry into safe custody, and not realized that if he was to be custodian of Nur's genius, then Nur would become his custodian and place him in custody too. This alliance could be considered an unendurable burden – or else a shining honour. Both demanded an equal strength.'

Such feelings, and their delicate exploration in literature, are far removed from the professionalised pursuit of literary criticism in the majority of academic institutions. While Anita Desai is keenly interested in the work of other writers – she was perhaps the first reviewer to recognise and welcome Salman Rushdie's novel *Midnight's Children*, and in 1995 wrote an introduction to its Everyman edition at Rushdie's insistence – she has little interest in literary critical theory.

Her latest novel, the most complex so far, *Journey to Ithaca* (a title taken from Cavafy's poem *Ithaca*) – which was written, for the first time in her life, out of India (mainly in Italy and Cambridge, England) – moves even further away from the academic literary mainstream. But, once again, she has created a tortured alliance. This time it is a man and a woman, and they are not Indians but Europeans, an Italian man married to a German woman, who set off for India in the mid-1970s. They begin as hippies but gradually their search deepens into a spiritual journey, or rather journeys, since they violently disagree. He becomes obsessed with 'the Mother', an enigmatic guru who runs an ashram – she cannot share his faith. When children arrive, she eventually decides to take them home to Europe; but once there, she feels compelled to return.

Their frequent exchanges keep the story in constant tension:

> Sophie: 'And what is she, this Mother – a hypnotist, a magician? It sounds as if she gets up on a stage and hypnotises you all like some magician.'

He groaned, 'Must you have a scientific explanation? You remind me of the child who pulls a butterfly to bits so it can see what makes it fly.' And again later: 'The Absolute, the Soul, the Supreme. Supra this and supra that. Don't use those words, I am sick of them. They are non-words.'

'And what words do you like? Don't tell me, I can guess. Food. Bed. Baby. House. Are those your words?'

'Yes. Yes! They are good words and I like them. Say them again. I didn't know you knew them. I thought you had forgotten them.'

. . . 'What do you want, Sophie?'

'I want to know why we are here.'

'I told you – to find India, to understand India, and the mystery that is at the heart of India.'

'I have found it. At its heart is a dead child. A dead child, Matteo!'

'Don't shout, Sophie, I can hear,' he hissed. 'And why is it the dead child? Why not the temple? Or the people climbing up the hill, singing when they reach their god? Why not their journey, our journey?'

'Because at the end of that journey is a dead child,' she repeated.'

'Matteo covered his ears with his hands. 'Don't people die elsewhere?' he cried. 'Haven't children ever died in your own country?'

'Then why,' she breathed, lowering her knees and coming closer to him, 'couldn't we stay in our own country? To die there?'

In writing the novel, Desai was influenced by her knowledge of Krishnamurti, of the famous Mother at the Aurobindo ashram in Pondicherry, and by two post-war books about India often regarded as classics of spiritual autobiography. Both were written by non-Indians of a scholarly bent: *The Ochre Robe* by Aghenanda Bharati (born Leopold Fischer, a Viennese), and *The Thousand-Petalled Lotus* by Sangharakshita (born D. P. E. Lingwood, an English Buddhist). There was also a third book of this type, more dubious, published in 1991, *A Hidden Journey* by Andrew Harvey, a part-Indian Fellow of All Souls College, Oxford, who described with hallucinatory vividness his consuming fascination for his guru, Mother Meera. Iris Murdoch admires the book, as does the *New York Times*, which dubbed Harvey 'The Merry Mystic' in a celebrity profile. Desai is more circumspect, though amused by the fact that Americans have happily labelled Harvey 'mystic' almost like a job description, such as professor or postman.

She herself experiences no such easy assimilation into American society. After living in the USA on and off for more than nine years, she still feels a 'total outsider', except when she is in the classroom: 'then one is included'. A few of her MIT students have been of Indian origin, though American-born. 'I find it quite unsettling because they're so absolutely like the American students in my class. And yet they look Indian, and I know they're Indian.' She cannot write about the contemporary American scene as a brown American, as Bharati Mukherjee has. 'I've tried it and I can't write about America the way I see it and experience it.' Instead, in the last part of *Journey to Ithaca*, she tackles a past America (New York and New England) of the 1920s. It appears as a land totally, ludicrously ignorant of India. 'That would be wholly accurate, even today,' she says with a quiet laugh. 'Either uninformed or misinformed.'

But India, too, is in some respects a foreign land for Desai. Only one of her parents, her father, was Indian; he was a Bengali from what is now Bangladesh. Her mother was German. Anita Majumdar was born in Delhi in 1937, and spent the first twenty-one years of her life in the city until her marriage to a businessman, Ashvin Desai. She grew up speaking English, with an admixture of German and Hindi, conscious too of Bengali (her father's mother tongue) and Urdu, the language of Old Delhi. Indian, English and German culture – literature primarily, but also music and the other arts – were fused together in her mind. 'I was not aware of it as a child, when I took my home and parents for granted, but I realize now that they created for me a synthesis that is the base of all my work and that I didn't have to strive for, was not even conscious of ever, but quite naturally inherited from them. I am sure this is what makes my writing whatever it is. I see India through my mother's eyes, as an outsider, but my feelings for India are my father's, of someone born here', she wrote in a letter from India some ten years ago.

Today – after writing two novels about foreigners in India, and herself living outside the subcontinent – she is less certain of her point of view. 'I'm really glad I spent all those years in India, that I left it so late. I think it matters that I spent my childhood there. I find it matters enormously to my children that they spent their childhood in India. If one doesn't have that, I think one has nothing really. I'm sure I shall be an Indian to the day I die, no matter where I am. I'm not being patriotic or nationalistic – I don't even know India very well – it is simply that of the choices I have, this is the only one. But I know I don't fit into the Indian box any more. And in my writing I'm drifting further and further away from it. I can't really write of it with the same intensity and familiarity that I once had. If I feel at home in any society, it is such a society where nobody really belongs, everyone is in some way uprooted.'

Clear Light of Day, Desai's 1980 novel, probes these emotions beautifully, though it was written years before its author left India: she calls it 'the most autobiographical of all my books'. Weaving together pre-Partition and post-Partition Delhi, childhood and adulthood, Hindu, Muslim and British cultures, it scrutinises the relationship of two sisters, one of whom has stayed in the old family house, unmarried, a college teacher of history, while the other, married young and with children, has spent years abroad as the wife of a diplomat. Neither has achieved all that she was capable of, both are to a great extent prisoners of their time. 'I would think that women who read the novel now in India would reject it completely,' says Desai. 'Women think I am doing a disservice to the feminist movement by writing about women who have no control over their lives. But I was trying, as every writer tries to do, even in fiction, to get at the truth, write the truth. It would have been really fanciful if I had made Bim and Tara modern-day feminists.'

When she herself returns to India now on visits, as she quite often does, she finds gaps in her experience. In certain respects, India has changed more in the past decade or two than at any time in its history. There are cars, television sets with satellite dishes, newspapers and magazines to rival Western models; and there is a concomitant increase in the pace of urban life. Since 1992, the government has been publicly committed to reducing the economic protectionism put in place by Nehru; and to encouraging foreign investment, Western and other outside influences. V.S. Naipaul, noticing change, changed his view about India and published a book in 1990, *India: A Million Mutinies Now*, to the effect that middle-class Indians are at last learning to take charge of their lives. Desai is not convinced. 'I don't notice any change. That is what really frightens me when I go back. People talk of it but the only change is in the scale of things. There was always a small class of people who were well-to-do. There are more of them now and far more wealthy, but the poor . . .' She leaves the sentence incomplete.

What about an increase in skills, in professionalism? 'Not at all. I'd say the opposite. For instance, when I was a student at university, at least students did study, and professors did teach. But that hardly happens any more, as far as I can make out, except in the IITs (Indian Institutes of Technology) and in business management.'

In Custody, set in the 1960s, shows the earlier stages of this decline. With characteristic, if painful, honesty and with an equally characteristic undertow of bleak humour, Desai draws us into Deven's entrapping and disillusionment. And yet, as we know, she does not abandon

[81]

him there: the conclusion of the novel is one of 'high exaltation', according to Salman Rushdie. In the end, out of apparent failure Deven derives strength of spirit – or is it fatalism? 'Western readers seem to expect a story to end in triumph, in a conquest of some kind,' says Anita Desai. 'I don't believe in conquests; I think that the human condition being what it is – and in India you see it at its most extreme – one can only hope for the strength to endure. You might call it fatalism but I don't think it is as passive as all that. What my characters strive for is to cease to be victims of philosophy and become its masters instead. As I see it, that is the only kind of triumph available to man.'

Publications include:

Cry, The Peacock, 1963, Peter Owen.
Voices in the City, 1965, Peter Owen.
Bye-Bye, Blackbird, 1971, Interculture.
Where Shall We Go This Summer?, 1975, Vikas.
Fire on the Mountain, 1977, Heinemann.
Clear Light of Day, 1980, Heinemann.
In Custody, 1984, Heinemann.
Baumgartner's Bombay, 1988, Heinemann.
Journey to Ithaca, 1995, Heinemann.

Fiction for children
The Peacock Garden, 1979, Heinemann.
The Village by the Sea, 1982, Heinemann.

(Andrew Robinson, © Times Higher Education Supplement)

Anthropologist **Mary Douglas**, born 1921, is professor emeritus at Northwestern University, where, from 1981 to 1985, she was Avalon Foundation professor in the humanities. Before that she taught at University College London for twenty-five years, raising her family the while. A pioneer in the relatively new field of risk assessment, her invention of grid/group structures to map different kinds of society has been applied by academics in a wide range of disciplines. She remarks that her own willingness to cross disciplinary boundaries is something she has noticed in the careers of other women.

When misfortune strikes, explanation and blame are inseparable. Environmental calamity offers the clearest examples: dead seals; dying trees; floods in Bangladesh – holes in the ozone layer. Debate about causes is inextricably bound up with responsibility, even when the argument is that no one is responsible. As Peregrine Worsthorne once put it in a *Sunday Telegraph* critique of the environmental movement: 'There can be no natural catastrophe without someone being to blame – a proposition which is nonsensical'.

Mary Douglas invites her readers to move a pace back from this debate, to a point where natural always appears in quotation marks. Of course there is blame for a selection of catastrophes. What is interesting is not whether the implied causal chain is in our sense rational, but what it reveals about the social structure of perception.

In a tribal society, where does the finger of suspicion point if cattle sicken, crops wither, or children die? In our world, how are our more varied misfortunes used to underscore moral imperatives? How are they related to an underlying cosmology, in the sense of justifications of last resort, invocations of the natural order? Mary Douglas's sustained inquiry into the ties between cosmology and social context is the most provocative attempt around to link understanding of the widest possible range of cultures – to bring anthropology back home.

Over twenty years after *Purity and Danger* first presented her characteristic approach to a wide audience, she pursues the same project. But its roots go back much further, to her religious schooling and early years at Oxford. The first strands in her thought were laid by a Catholic schooling, at a Sacred Heart convent school in Roehampton. Study for diocesal exams, on top of the regular curriculum, took in Catholic social thought, 'a matter of going over the Papal encyclicals of the nineteenth century', and theology. A taste for fine distinctions endures.

Then on to read politics, philosophy and economics at Oxford (the nuns cautioning against sociology at the London School of Economics). The adjectives adhering to this time are still strong: immensely satisfying; terribly difficult; a very great strain, given her earlier background. It remained important to be a Catholic, but she became preoccupied with crucial questions as a result of her Oxford studies. The main new strand was the problem of explaining where the individual is free – to choose, to act, to believe. 'I've been trying to put those pieces together for the rest of my life.'

The vehicle for thinking things through was anthropology, discovered during an otherwise dull wartime sojourn in the Colonial Office, keeping the files tidy for peacetime. There she met real anthropologists, which was wonderful: 'To read their books and see this was what one should be doing, getting the authentic understanding through ethnography'.

Rather little ethnography of her own, as it turned out. She went back to Oxford after the war to read anthropology under the newly-installed Evans-Pritchard, and wanted to do fieldwork in Italy. But Africa was the place in those days; the anthropology of other places was not yet regarded as a subject.

So she turned to Zaire, then still the Belgian Congo, for a first ethnographic foray. It made a tremendous personal impact. The monograph *The Lele of the Kasai,* which emerged many years later, is virtually unread, she maintains – the price of writing about the tribal culture of a French-speaking colony for English readers. But the Lele, with their classifications of the natural world, and rules about who can eat what, their complex of sexual rituals and prohibitions, their ideas of pollution and sorcery, are a constant presence in her later, more general work. They remain a central plank in the bridge Douglas has tried to build between 'traditional' and modern cultures.

They were also her first and last field study. Independence struggles and their aftermath meant the field was closed to her, an inducement to thinking, as she now sees it. The thinking was done at University College London, where she taught for over twenty-five years, raising her family the while.

She resisted a temptation to leave academic life, in her self-deprecating account, because of a sense of obligation to the sponsors of her fieldwork. And although family life delayed completion of the ethnographic monograph, it also meant her characteristic general concerns were maturing over the same period – from the early 1950s to the early 1960s. Her first book on more general themes, *Purity and Danger: An Analysis of the Concepts of Pollution and Taboo*, was also waiting to be written, and appeared quickly after the account of the Lele.

That book, on a topic 'in the very anthropological theory of magic and taboo', is a compellingly written reflection on principles of classification and the drawing of boundaries, on rituals, on categories, and above all on the selection of significant dangers. 'We should start any cosmological inquiry by seeking the principles of power and danger', she wrote.

Like the Lele, she is concerned with pollution, a special class of dangers 'which are not powers vested in humans, but which can be released by human action'. (The introduction reveals that one reason for her initial attraction to the subject was her husband's distaste for household dirt.) Then, as now, she writes out of the Durkheimian tradition. But her work also bears the clear imprint of her mentor Evans-Pritchard. Indeed, her own later verdict on him in a book-length account of his work is also a rubric for Douglas's own project. She judged that Evans-Pritchard justified the distinctive claims of anthropology by 'systematically attending to people's response to misfortune'.

Anthropology, though, was not the most comfortable home for her project. Already in *Purity and Danger* there is a sense of straining the bounds of the discipline, and the strain has grown over the years. There is an urge to distil the accumulating mass of ethnography and wrest some workable generalisations from the collected exotica of reports from the field, a feeling that one product of studying many societies should be clues toward a better sociology.

It is an ambitious project, pursued with a disarming combination of apparent diffidence and single-mindedness, and with a sharpness which breaks through more often in print than in person. You see it in comments like her wry prefatory observation in a book on the new scholarly analysis of risk perception that she set out to review the state of the art but found that 'art is in no state at all'.

The reason she found the risk analysts wanting was their persistent focus on risk assessment as an individual and not a social matter. They show how far her basic assumptions are from penetrating fields where she thinks they are needed, and give the lie to her hopeful assurance in interview that the social construction of reality is such a commonplace it hardly needs discussion. Her view in *Risk Acceptability According to the Social Sciences* that 'the neglect of culture is so systematic and so entrenched that nothing less than a large upheaval in the social sciences would bring about a change' seems nearer the mark.

The wish to take social influence on perception as read comes from the force of her desire to go further. The key Douglas question is how to understand variations in cognition. If cognition is sustained and underpinned by social relations, it ought to be possible to move on from there to some kind of typology, 'kinds of societies that give you kinds of consciousness; that's the project'.

Her scheme for mapping kinds of societies is worlds away from grand theory, though its simplicity has a grandeur of its own. In *Natural Symbols* she first put forward a notion of the key dimensions of varia-tion, building on earlier work on language use by Basil Bernstein. She has remained faithful to these dimensions ever since – 'grid', or the strength of the rules which govern how people relate to one another, and 'group', or the clarity of the boundaries around the groups which people belong to.

This was all methodologically pretty hair-raising, as Alan Ryan, now warden-elect of New College, Oxford, put it at the time. How, exactly, did location in the space defined by twin axes of grid and group deter-mine cosmology? Unless the links are spelled out, there's no way of testing the theory properly.

Her answer is twofold. She responds to general objections by demanding to know the alternative to this kind of theorising. 'If you don't try a synthesis of this kind, what are you left with?' Again, there is the presentation of a bold claim as merely a codification of what we already know, gently pushing existing ideas into an explicit typology. She is contemptuous of the mass of anthropologists, disabled by a conviction that any attempt at a typology is merely a product of its times, and who retreat into *belles lettres*.

The more elaborate response is her work since then, which demon-strates uses of the approach, and refines it, and encourages others to use it. Her work on consumption, on food, and on risk perception, all pursues the analysis. And there is now a small band of others doing grid and group studies in contexts as varied as occupational crime, poverty relief, and student evaluation in university departments.

The analysis of the public perception of risk offers some of the clearest connections with her earlier work. She was prodded into the area by the political scientist, the late Aaron Wildavsky, encountered when she was research director for the Russell Sage Foundation at the start of a ten-year post-UCL stay in the US. 'He kept saying to me, "All this anthropology on purity and danger – here are people seeing new kinds of danger, has it got anything to do with us?"'

Douglas thinks it does. All societies attend to some dangers and not others, and the selection is shaped by moral judgements: 'The well advertised risk generally turns out to be connected with legitimating moral principles'. The next step is to describe the kinds of judgements, and kinds of blame, likely to fit particular types of society. A hierarchical society with a strong community bond (strong grid and group, in Douglas's terms) needs to minimise conflict and political discussion. This is best served, she argues, by belief in a morally sensitive cosmos. Loss is blamed on the victim. The need for expiation to limit the load of guilt induced by all this blame creates its own machinery, typically within religion.

The starkest contrast is with the 'enterprise culture' (low grid, low group), which values individual competition. Absurd to believe that nature hands down punishments for internal conflict here; conflict is the stuff of life. Better to have a morally neutral cosmos, which is driven by forces the individual can harness, through luck or good judgement, and increase their chances of advantage over others contending for power or influence.

The detailed analysis is richer and often more persuasive than this, but it gives the idea. Douglas is convinced that the repeated application of grid and group is making it a better instrument. 'I keep finding it only plays a very few tunes, and only certain kinds of music.' These tunes come through more strongly as extraneous elements are pared away. 'The more we shed, the less it can do, but the more powerful it becomes for doing these things.' What she feels most deeply it is good at is giving a new light on choices in life and society. Her powerful opposition to the individualism of conventional rational choice theory in economics is rooted in a conviction that 'we make our choices in choosing the kinds of social relations we have'. And she thinks *these* are individual choices.

People have a constitutional 'map' in their minds of the kind of society they can bear to live in, judging their chances of survival. 'If we make no rules, who is going to look after me, or who is going to blow the whistle when I get attacked?' Everything is being processed through this kind of constitutional monitoring. It is part of everyone's sociality.

Her overall vision is often open to politically radical readings, most obviously in a dense mid-1970s essay on 'environments at risk'. Here she conveys the exhilaration of peering over the relativist abyss, becoming fully conscious of each environment as a mask and support for a certain kind of society. Yet she now seems less inclined to take things so far – and professes no interest in conventional politics.

What she does still maintain is that the grid-group analysis has the value that 'there are certain illusions of our own culture which can be examined through this model which you can't really examine otherwise'. They include the illusion that less structure yields more choice, which she thinks is quite wrong.

The argument over how inclusive her scheme is will go on. Can so many groups, from sports clubs to social movements, all be fitted into this framework? And how much freedom do people really have to choose, either within what is in some lights a deterministic scheme, or within a real society where some have power to constrain others? But her view, with its stress on choice between imperfect alternatives, appeals to people from a range of disciplines. There are no utopias here, no unflawed models. But there are options, and the possibility of moving to a position where one feels more comfortable.

Her influence continues to penetrate corners of social science. She has a visiting professorship now at Lancaster in the department of religious studies, an appointment in a direct line with her earlier work. But a seminar on her ideas at the University of East Anglia a few years ago was organised by the 'Centre for Public Choice Studies', and drew participants from departments of environmental studies, politics, philosophy, business studies, and economics, not to mention anthropology. All of these people work in fields where understanding the social basis of cognition is of use. Whatever their views on grid and group, they all on occasion assent to Douglas's most general contention about social problem-solving. As she puts it in her last book, *How Institutions Think*, 'An answer is only seen to be the right one if it sustains the institutional thinking that is already in the minds of individuals as they try to decide'.

Asked about her own experience of being a woman in academe

[88]

Douglas is fascinating. She was offered, she says, opportunities to serve on college committees, stand for office in the Royal Anthropological Institute, organise conferences – all of which would have helped her secure the head of department at UCL on the retirement of Daryll Forde in 1970. She 'vehemently refused'. 'It was partly a problem of time – with three small children at home, there was certainly good reason for not taking on extra responsibilities.'

But, she adds, she was also anxious and inefficient and disparagingly attributes any gender-based problems in her own career to very subtle influences, some stemming from her sheltered childhood.

'It was not just that the nuns at school had rules to protect us from clashing with each other or with them. I had never heard a swear word or an adult voice raised in anger until I was seventeen. I remember my horrified embarrassment when at that age I visited a French family where during the first half of the midday meal the father regularly baited the teenage children, and in the second half always rushed out of the dining-room yelling that he was treated like a dog, the mother running behind to propitiate him, and the children sullenly going on eating. Our grandparents raised us in a kindly, predictable, formal environment. My sister and I never heard them disagree; in front of us they never talked about money, passed adverse judgements on people, or proposed rival plans. Even when my grandmother felt agitated (as when she entered a jar of honey in the Women's Institute competition, or captured a swarm of bees, or sold poppies on Remembrance Day), the stresses she underwent had nothing to do with us. "Drat!" was her only expletive.'

'To this calm upbringing I attribute my unreadiness for the confrontations and subtle rivalries of academia. Signs of suppressed fury still agitate me. I never learnt cajolery, or how to gain my point by stealth; instead of the conciliatory phrase I could only blurt, weep, or flounce red-faced out of meetings.'

She is interesting too, both on why she felt it necessary to take leave of her institutional origins and 'poach on other academic preserves' and on the dangers inherent in such an approach. 'Did the work spill out because it was not easy to innovate within professional structures? Were there invisible constraints on my professional expectations?' she wonders.

A willingness to cross disciplinary boundaries is something she has noticed 'in the careers of other women. Sometimes the professional structures do not exert a strong enough grip, and in consequence they enjoy a freedom which others may envy, but pay a price of isolation which they may themselves regret . . . a move from being original to being bizarre which Margaret Mead's writings exemplified.'

The wheels have come full circle in Douglas's recent work, which marries her earlier anthropological research on purity and uncleanness with biblical study. Using the discoveries of French sociologists that in our own urban society 'people invoke quite fanciful dangers of contagion to reinforce their own separatist wishes', Douglas embarked on a study of the doctrine of uncleanness in Leviticus.

'As I see it, theories of contagion, sacred or secular, are used as means of social control,' she writes. 'When I first tried to apply this idea to the Bible, and found that it does not work, I thought that a more careful reading would produce the evidence.' That did not happen and so Douglas 'made a U-turn, not about the general uses of contagion, but about biblical uncleanness which seems to be quite different from that encountered in world-wide ethnography.' How to account for the difference called, she decided, for study. So once again the disciplinary boundaries were breached.

Douglas felt 'embarrassingly unqualified' to lecture about the Bible when she gave the Gifford lectures in Edinburgh 1989, but chose to give them on the Book of Numbers, thinking that the priestly books of the Pentateuch would yield rewards if read through cultural theory. 'As I studied Numbers I got the impression that it deserves much more esteem among Bible scholars, partly as a theological statement of greater universality and openness than is generally credited to it.

'In the course of trying to make sense of what has been regarded only too often as incoherent repetition I discovered that the Book of Numbers had been composed by the editors according to an archaic literary convention. Interlocking ring composition is well known to classics scholars, especially in the work of Homer, Herodotus, and Hesiod. In the Bible small pieces written as chiastic rings are also recognised, but the evidence (to my mind compelling) that the whole of Numbers has been cast in this form calls for a new reading.' *In the Wilderness, the Doctrine of Defilement in the Book of Numbers* applies her argument to the Book of Numbers.

The next question Douglas intends to tackle is whether other books of the Pentateuch have been written according to this convention. And if her revisionist ideas about ritual cleanness are accepted the priestly books of the Pentateuch will no longer be read as if they equated godliness with cleanliness. Their message will be reconciled with that of the narratives and the prophetic books, not separated as they have tended to be since Wellhausen.

Accordingly she is now working on Leviticus, learning Hebrew to facilitate the research. 'After three years I am even more convinced that these two books have been gravely underestimated as literary creations and their theology misread. Such heterodox views ought to make me lonely in Bible studies but such is the diversity among Hebrew scholars that there are enough like-minded souls and enough who are so passionately devoted to these books that they allow me to join their conversation,' she says. 'So I am very happy with this latest phase of my work.'

Publications include:

The Lele of the Kasai, 1963, International African Institute, Oxford University Press.

Purity and Danger: An Analysis of the Concepts of Pollution and Taboo, 1966, Routledge & Kegan Paul.

Natural Symbols, 1970, Barrie and Rockliff.

Implicit Meanings, 1975, Routledge & Kegan Paul.

Evans-Pritchard, 1980, Harvester Press.

Risk and Culture: Essays in the Selection of Technological and Environmental Dangers, 1982, with Aaron Wildavasky, University of California Press.

In the Active Voice, 1982, Routledge.

Risk Acceptability According to the Social Sciences, 1986, Routledge.

How Institutions Think, 1987, Routledge.

Risk and Blame: Essays in Cultural Theory, 1992, Routledge.

In the Wilderness, 1993, Sheffield Academic Press.

(© Jon Turney)

Mildred Dresselhaus, born 1930, was the first tenured woman in the department of engineering at Massachusetts Institute of Technology. Now an Institute professor, she successfully argued for equal admission standards for women at MIT and has watched the proportion of women entering the freshman class grow from 4 per cent in the 1960s to 45 per cent today.

Photograph © 1995, Peter Serling

Two qualities leap out from any encounter with Mildred Dresselhaus – generosity and modesty, born of comfortable self-confidence, remarkable accomplishment, recognised brilliance, and a sunny disposition. Wearing lightly Massachusetts Institute of Technology's most prestigious academic title, institute professor, Dresselhaus, who gained the chair for her distinguished leadership in education, service, and scholarly research, continues to contribute new findings in her field almost four decades after beginning her career in solid state physics. An authority on solid state physics, she has explored the electronic properties of graphite, graphite intercalation compounds and other solids.

In recent years she has continued to focus on a broad array of topics – the modification of the properties of electronic materials by intercalation and implantation, high temperature superconductors, and the structure and properties of carbon fibres and carbon nanotubes. But her greatest current interest, as captured in the title of her book-in-press, is the *Physical Properties of Fullerenes*, a work that integrates much of her and her collaborators' recent research on fullerenes and carbon nanotubes, and advances these topics to new levels of understanding.

Fullerenes are cage-like carbon molecules that are rapidly gaining attention from several branches of science. Several decades ago, they were named fullerenes, by the chemists Kroto and Smalley, for the architect R. Buckminster Fuller, whose design of the geodesic-dome house in 1952 mimicked the structure of carbon 60. The geodesic house combines light, weight and strength, and is supported by a triangular arrangement of aluminium tubes in much the same arrangement that the carbon 60 atoms are attached to each other. While the design structure of Fuller's house may not have proven to be as useful as initially anticipated, the jury is still out for fullerenes. Once they became widely available in 1990, fullerenes became more interesting scientifically. Researchers are now looking to their potential industrial applications.

'Fullerenes' were quickly familiarised to 'buckyballs'. More precisely, a 'buckyball' refers to the C60 molecule, while the generic term, 'fullerene,' includes the carbon molecules (Cn cage molecules) that are built from a collection of hexagonal and pentagonal faces. Dresselhaus has written that the formal structure of C60 is called a 'truncated icosahedron', drawings of which can be traced back as far as Leonardo da Vinci and Albrecht Dürer's precise depictions in the sixteenth century. More familiarly, buckyballs have the same structure as a soccer ball. Most familiarly, they can be found in soot.

I first learned about buckyballs when I spotted Dresselhaus, seated serenely, writing with intense concentration, amidst loud noise and harried travellers on a crowded flight between Chicago and Boston. On learning that I wanted to write about her career, she immediately responded: 'You should interview someone younger'. She proposed another woman physicist insisting that 'Her work is exciting and less well known' – the first of many references to the work of others I would hear from her. Finally she put aside her writing – the last chapter of the 900-page book – and enthusiastically launched into a vivid description of why, scientifically, fullerenes were exciting and gaining attention.

Her uncomplicated overview of the importance of the field exemplified her reputation as a gifted teacher. Without assuming that I might not understand the physics or the mathematics, Dresselhaus swept me along in a lucid account of this cage-like structure of hexagons and pentagons, whose sixty vertices hold the carbon atoms of this truncated icosahedron.

In a 1993 article, the precursor to their book, Dresselhaus and her colleagues, Dr Gene F. Dresselhaus (her husband and a scientist at MIT's Francis Bitter National Magnet Laboratory, who contributed to the first theory of cyclotron resonance in solids), and Dr. P. C. Eklund of the Department of Physics and Astronomy at the University of Kentucky, reported their work on the structure and properties of fullerenes, particularly their behaviour as molecular solids.

Collaborating with scientists from Japan, Belgium and others in the US, and also drawing on the research of scientists in several different disciplines, they were able to integrate the findings so as to contribute significantly to what has become a burgeoning new field. Because of their unique properties and structure, fullerenes have attracted attention from astrophysicists and spectroscopists interested in examining the infrared emissions 'streaming out of red giant carbon stars'.

The advancement of fullerenes to prominence was made possible by ever-more sophisticated spectroscopic and surface-science technologies such as nuclear magnetic resonance, which early on revealed that the assumed structure of C_{60} was correct. Electron paramagnetic resonance provided additional information about the structure and electronic properties of fullerenes. Scanning tunnel microscopy helped to identify surface crystal structures, while experiments in photoemissions helped to provide systematic information about the electronic structure.

Fullerenes may have the potential to contribute to the fabrication of industrial diamonds; to function as optical limiters – a process that protects materials from damage by high light intensities; and to enhance photoconducting devices. And as Dresselhaus pointed out, they make for very exciting science.

Throughout Dresselhaus's discourse on her early work 'on this carbon science business', ideas for which she credited EXXON scientists and other scientists around her, she unself-consciously wove the fabric of her life, rarely separating family and home, and her several decades of work on issues of women in science, from life in the laboratory. In fact, she credits her early interest in the field of physics of carbon solids not only to the intrinsic science itself, but also to her need to work in an area in which there was little interest and consequently, little pressure to achieve results quickly. 'I was comfortable in this field because it was a research backwater, and I had four small children at home. If you missed a day, you didn't care.'

Raising four children, now in their thirties, who like herself, are accomplished chamber-music players (she read music before she read script), demanded that she cultivate her research at a slower than traditional pace. There is little to indicate that the pace was, in fact, anywhere behind that of her male colleagues. Over the five years during which the children were born, she was a staff member of the MIT Lincoln Laboratory. Rather than bemoaning the conflict between child care and the laboratory, Professor Dresselhaus enjoyed doing her conceptual work at home. 'While nursing babies and changing diapers, you get a lot of good ideas. The distance was very good, and there was a nice supportive environment at MIT.'

Both of these statements reveal an amazingly sanguine disposition. MIT in the 1960s provided little emotional support to the few women in its classrooms and laboratories. There were few women faculty or students. Bringing up four children under any circumstances would tax the patience of the proverbial saint. Dresselhaus's description of their child-care regimen reinforced the distinct impression of her (and undoubtedly her husband's) uniqueness – their baby-sitter had five children of her own and many grandchildren, several of whom she even brought with her to work on occasion. Where there was stringent need for elegance and order in their intellectual lives, they obviously were able to forgo it at home.

Dresselhaus's childhood held few clues of what might lie ahead. She was born in 1930 to struggling parents in Brooklyn. As she explained to a Harvard magazine journalist, Georgia Litwack, some years ago, her mother did hard physical work in an orphanage from 7p.m. until it was time to return home to get her own children off to school. In addition to housework, her days were filled with piecework, assembling costume jewellery for small manufacturers. Unlike the images of simpler times past, Professor Dresselhaus's reality in her junior high school was terrifying. 'I never once went to the bathroom there. Everybody knew it was unsafe – that's where the girls would get attacked. You learned not to go there.'

Her older brother, whom she described as a child prodigy in music and science, had attended the Bronx High School of Science, long an incubator for promising scientific talent, but in the 1940s not open to female students. On her own, Dresselhaus wrote away for information about Hunter High School (a school for gifted young women under the aegis of Hunter College), and persisted in applying despite the contrary advice from her teachers. College, she anticipated, would prepare her for a job in elementary school teaching.

However, by the time she was a sophomore at Hunter College, a tuition-free city college, she knew she wanted to be a scientist. Her teacher, Rosalyn Yalow, who was to be awarded a Nobel Prize in 1977, took an interest in her which extended over many years. With typical Dresselhaus candour, she observed that until many years later she had never thought Yalow was very successful. Anyone who gave so much time to a student and was so interested in helping her to further her career obviously was not very busy.

Innumerable young women at MIT and elsewhere have reaped the benefits of the guidance and nurture provided by Yalow. Dresselhaus, in time, became the first tenured woman in the department of engineering, occupying the Abby Rockefeller Mauze Chair first as a visiting professor in 1967, and as a permanent appointee from 1973 until 1985, when she was named an Institute professor. Established to support the scholarship of women, the Mauze chair enabled Dresselhaus not only to further her research in solid state physics, but to work with the then dean of women, Emily Wick, to reform the admissions policies for women students at MIT. Dresselhaus reports happily that the post of dean of women students has been abandoned as an anachronism. Women have become the norm at MIT today.

Before arriving at MIT and before going to graduate school, Dresselhaus spent a year as a Fulbright scholar at the Cavendish Laboratory at Cambridge University where, she believed, her musical education 'kind of disguised my humble background'. The broad education gained at Hunter High School and College also proved to be an asset. She added, England was very class-conscious in the 1950s.

Following the Fulbright year in England, Dresselhaus received a master's degree from Radcliffe College (actually from an education gained at Harvard's department of physics; Radcliffe has neither faculty nor department. After 1965 all graduate degrees were granted by Harvard University). A PhD from the University of Chicago was followed by a postdoctoral fellowship at Cornell University. By 1960 she was a staff member of MIT's Lincoln Laboratory and has remained at the Institute since then. The Mauze chair recognised her academic talents; concurrently held professorships in the department of electrical engineering and computer science, and the department of physics have attested to her research accomplishments as well as teaching skills.

Not surprisingly, she was the only woman during the early stages of her career at MIT's Francis Bitter National Magnet Laboratory, where her research continues today, as well as at the Institute's Centre for materials science and engineering, which she formerly directed. Her interest in the career development of women scientists grew rapidly and continues undiminished.

In the 1960s, Dresselhaus had become 'outraged' upon learning of MIT's discriminatory admissions policies. In effect, women applicants had to be significantly better than their male counterparts, which resulted in such small numbers of admittees that the young women found themselves isolated and routinely 'being put down by the men in their classes' as well as by the male faculty, who for the most part did not take them seriously. Their drop-out rate was high, which reinforced the male admission committee's bias against admitting women. Dresselhaus (and Wick) argued successfully for equal admission standards and for increasing the numbers to 'a critical mass.'

In the 1960s the percentage of women grew slowly from 4 per cent of the incoming class to 10 per cent. Wick and Dresselhaus began 'to dream of 25 per cent'. The changes have been dramatic. This year the incoming freshman class boasts 45 per cent women. As the numbers have increased, so has the rate of retention; more than 90 per cent of women students graduate and maintain a slightly higher gradepoint average than their male classmates.

During the past three decades, Dresselhaus has produced about 55 PhD students, some 12 of whom are women, and as she notes proudly, 'Almost all of the women are professors in universities and have tenure'. She added that today there are more than 100 women on the MIT faculty, 30 of whom are on the engineering faculty.

When asked about the possibilities for today's young women in science to emulate her having been able to juggle family and career in the 1960s and 1970s, she pointed to the numbers as a positive sign. However, she noted that career women today have fewer children. Sadly, she added, there are fewer jobs available overall, and this complicates the lives of two-career families. 'Having couples separated in space is very difficult.' Nevertheless, her enthusiasm for a career in academic science is unabated.

She is using her elected role as treasurer of the National Academy of Sciences, her prominence as a recipient of the National Medal of Science (1990), and the prestige accumulated from more than a dozen honorary degrees to convey her belief in the need to support effective teaching and research worldwide and to make opportunities greater for women and all science students.

Her genuine interest in others and the spontaneity of her response to anyone who seeks her counsel, or who in my case was about to take away time from a demanding task, accounts for her affectionately being referred to as 'Millie' by one and all.

But science is a tough business, and Millie does not escape her share of criticism. Several academic scientists in other universities gave her full credit for being 'extremely effective as an organiser who could be depended on to follow through any commitments'. Nevertheless, it was clear the attention she has received rankles some. 'Pushy' women (as one described her), set the molars grinding among their peers. In the nineteenth century, Hawthorne's Scarlet Letter, A, emblazoned on the bodice of Hesther Prynne's dress, branded her an adulteress. Today the letter could well stand for Aggressive – a quality not unattractive in men, but still sinful in women.

Not wanting to appear too harsh, one colleague who criticised Dresselhaus for 'liking to be the centre of attention', conceded that 'She is rock solid in what she has done'. But he added quickly, 'There is nothing in it that's a moonshot. No Nobel Prize'. 'Rock solid', which I assume was not intended as a pun, is pretty good praise from a critic.

I came away from my time with 'Millie' realising that under that sunny exterior and beguiling smile, lay a ferocious determination to excel. Her early childhood deprivations have been taken in stride as she purposefully marches through life. In fact, I thought, had science been outlawed, Millie would have taken herself to a secure hiding-place and continued to churn out her buckyball findings. As she said some years ago, 'If you go into science and engineering, you go in to succeed.'

Publications include:

Graphite Fibers and Filaments, 1988, with G. Dresselhaus, K. Sugihara, I. Spain and H. Goldberg, Springer Series in Materials Science, 5, Springer-Verlag.

Ion Implantation in Diamond, Graphite and Related Materials, 1992, with R. Kalish, Springer Series in Materials Science, 22, Springer-Verlag

Science of Fullerenes and Carbon Nanotubes, 1995, with G. Dresselhaus and P. C. Eklund, Academic Press.

(© Dorothy Zinberg)

Professor **Uta Frith**, born in 1941, is a senior scientist in the Medical Research Council's Cognitive Development Unit. Her research on dyslexia and, in particular, autism, is ground-breaking. Frith has suggested that these disorders may be due to specific cognitive deficits, deficits which, in the future, she and others may be able to map within the brain.

Photograph by Simon Grosset © Insight

Think of the brain as the last unexplored continent, the final frontier. During that thought, the electrical activity in your own brain travels through the semi-charted territory of sight, language processing and memory. (You see the words; you decode them, you remember their meaning.) But it also crosses the shadowy lands of still more subtle mental processes. (You imagine, you are aware of metaphor, perhaps of irony.)

But what if your mind's map had an unexplained blank? Or a sea where there should be land? Or 'Here Be Dragons'? Your cognitive development would seem disorientated. Often your mental journeys could move along well-established routes. But then you would reach this missing area.

You might avoid it. You might fear it. You might be totally unaware it appears differently on other people's mental maps. Or, like one autistic young man Uta Frith studied, you might poignantly perceive that there was a void on your map. 'People talk to each other with their eyes,' he remarked. 'What is it that they are saying?'

The idea that specific cognitive deficits, tiny missing continents in the mind, could explain the seemingly inexplicable and intractable difficulties of people with autism and with dyslexia, is the idea that Professor Frith has made central to current understanding of both those disabilities. And her exploration of what and where the absent territories might be, has led to a filling in of some of the sketchy landscape on the map of the normal mind.

'Here Be Dragons' certainly never seemed much of an explanation.

When in 1964 she arrived at London University's Institute of Psychiatry to do a postgraduate clinical psychology diploma, psychodynamic explanations of autism were in the ascendant: 'People would obscure things just for the sake of covering up their ignorance, using a kind of story-telling form with wonderful words and phrases about parents and children and childhood and being psychotic or being cocooned. It was quite clear that certain things were completely unscientific, like the claim that autistic children avoided people. It just didn't ring true.'

In fact her own background was in storytelling. Her father was an artist in the small German town of Kaiserslautern, his work often exploiting geometrical patterns; her mother was a housewife who also wrote stories. She herself has written science fiction. But an unusual education meant she was equipped to move easily between arts and sciences: 'My parents sent me to a girls' school, but I demanded at the age of 12 to be put into the boys' school. I just discovered that I liked academic work and I wanted to go to what was considered to be the most demanding school in the town, where you did nine years Latin and five years Greek and maths and physics and chemistry up to A-level standard. My parents have always been completely and utterly supportive in whatever I wanted to do, and so they sent me there.'

Even now she is slightly awed by her temerity: 'My mother tells me that on my first day at school when I was six I insisted on going alone – I wouldn't let her come with me like all the other mothers. On that first day there was a school inspector there, and he asked this silly question about who was the best in your class, and I said "Me". I lost this confidence completely in adolescence, I should say. Occasionally I remember it, but I have never regained it.'

Her two-cultures education meant she could comfortably combine courses in psychology and anatomy with history of art at university in Saarbrucken. But she already knew where she was heading: 'Even when I was an undergraduate student I knew I didn't want to do clinical work. I knew the thing would be to ask questions and answer questions that are all around. It seemed like gold-mining. There was all this gold around you, all you needed to do was bend down and pick it up.'

In London, she discovered, there were other psychologists who felt the same. Under the guidance of Beate Hermelin and Neil O'Connor, she did a PhD at the Institute, gained a post at the newly-formed Medical Research Council's Developmental Psychology Unit and has stayed with it, and its successor Cognitive Development Unit, ever since. All the time the intention was to try and chart the mind in a different way.

'It was a very hard-edged, tough-minded approach. We talked about subjects, we talked about multi-retarded and sub-normal. It was almost surgical, and it got round the problem of one's whole emotions becoming engaged in these beautiful children, the empathy with the parents, the distress at what happens to them later on.

'I can imagine that some people could be repulsed by this. People would say, how could you? That you were being a scientist, not caring about children, just finding things out. But I have been always very paradoxically attracted both to the romantic and the classic, and here you have both the romance of the developmental problems and the tools that are just so sharp . . . It seemed like there was such a thing as truth, and we could get at it. And that through looking at learning difficulties we might also find a key, get a glimpse of the normal process.'

It has been the pattern of her work ever since: moving between adults and children, autistic and dyslexic, piecing together tiny squares of the mental map with 'the scalpel approach: very small, very elegant little experiments, that would tell you quite a lot about that particular problem'.

She was one of the first to point out, for example, that the ability to spell must be determined by a discrete bit of the brain, separate from general 'intelligence'. She still quotes this to critics who say conclusions from the abnormal – people with dyslexia or autism – may not be relevant to understanding the 'normal' brain: 'The point is that if spelling is working well, you can't see that it is separate. You see it in dyslexia because it isn't working well. If we hadn't studied the abnormal mind, we would never have found that out'.

Often she drew on experiments from outside her own field of developmental psychology. One, by Premack and Woodruff in 1978, particularly appealed to her as it defined a previously unexplored area of the mind. These two animal psychologists argued that because chimpanzees use deception to play tricks on their keepers, they must have at least a rudimentary understanding of what was in their keepers' minds. They called this perception the 'theory of mind', meaning the ability to understand that other people have minds, and therefore thoughts and emotions, which are different from one's own.

Could this idea shed light on the minds of autistic people, already known to be confused by deception, jokes or lies? It was immediately obvious that this would be a fruitful line of exploration, says Uta Frith, but it was only in 1986 that she had the time and the PhD student – Simon Baron-Cohen – to do it. She used a classic experiment, devised by Wimmer and Perner. It is known as the Sally-Anne experiment, and it works like this: Sally and Anne are dolls. They play together. Sally puts a marble into a basket and then leaves the room. While Sally is out, Anne moves the marble into a box. When Sally comes back, where will she look for her marble?

Show normal four-year-olds this scenario, and they will promptly reply that of course poor old Sally will look for her marble in the basket because she doesn't know that Anne has moved it. Tell a child with general delayed development the same story, and they will answer the same. (Frith and Baron-Cohen checked this, by including children with Down's Syndrome in their study. These children had no trouble getting inside Sally's mind.)

But show the same playlet to autistic teenagers with normal to high intelligence, and almost all of them get the answer wrong. The marble is in the box and that is where Sally will look, they insist. They seem unable to differentiate what Sally knows from what they know themselves.

No one was more surprised by these results than Frith herself. 'I thought they would be able to do it,' she recalls. 'I thought we would have to do something much more sophisticated, along the lines of deception and double bluff, before we really saw the problem in autism.'

She and Baron-Cohen tried various other experiments, to make sure the autistic children weren't simply confused by the scenario. They gave them picture-stories involving a child not knowing he had a hole in his bag of sweets. They couldn't make sense of the pictures. They surprised them with a pencil inside a Smarties tube and asked what another child would expect to find in the tube. A pencil, was the almost inevitable reply.

Meanwhile, psychiatrist Dr Lorna Wing at the Institute of Psychiatry had come up with a definition of autism rather more precise than earlier ones of the child in the bell-jar or the idiot-savant (as played by Dustin Hoffman in the film *Rain Man*). Autistic people were characterised by three main failures, she argued: in imaginative activities, in two-way social interaction, and in verbal and non-verbal communication. (Not the same thing as language.)

What would be the implications of a missing theory of mind, wondered Frith with colleagues at the CDU. You couldn't lie, or flatter; you couldn't pretend or imagine; you wouldn't understand the subtle code of social relationships, the body language, the intentions behind the words. In fact you would fail in the entire Wing triad: in imaginative activities, in two-way social interaction, and in verbal and non-verbal communication.

'We have suddenly found a window through which we can glimpse a new view of autism', Frith wrote soon afterwards. 'It . . . is not demonstrating yet another deficit in autistic children, however interesting, but rather it consists of providing a link between previously unconnected impairments and in suggesting a specific dysfunction in a single mechanism . . . The concept of theory of mind enables us to see autism as a kind of blindness, a mindblindness.' This was the blank on the autistic map, the missing theory of mind.

To some it seemed an elegant but pessimistic explanation. A traumatised child might be healed, a shut-off child might be reached, but mindsight – like real sight – would rarely be restored to the blind. 'Isn't there a bit of the autistic in all of us?', people would sometimes saccharinely inquire of Frith. No, she would reply. There isn't.

'If you have autism it pervades your whole life. That's why I think blindness is the metaphor that's right for autism. It's a major step to understand how they are so different, to really challenge people to imagine what it's like.'

She presses the argument when others question the usefulness of knowing whether or not autistic people have a theory of mind. 'As a scientist I have a different point of view from the day-to-day practitioner. But thinking these ideas through has practical benefits for teachers, for parents, for carers. It explains the inexplicable. And it means you can adjust their environment to them, to suit their needs.'

She cites numerous examples. The apparently irrational frustration of children who are trying to communicate using Maketon sign language, while failing to realise that the reason no one is taking any notice is because they are signing underneath the dinner table. The child whose unprovoked tantrums were explained once his father realised that he pointed at the sweet cupboard and expected to be given sweets even when no one else was in the room to see him pointing.

Some of her time these days is spent writing and lecturing to teachers, parents and carers about autism and dyslexia. More is spent supervising PhD students: she has a knack of picking and nurturing high-fliers, some of whom are now prominent names themselves. In 1990 she was the first woman to receive the British Psychological Society's prestigious President's Award. She only lacks the research team-leader's job that she agrees an equally successful male academic at her age might have: 'If I hadn't had children I could have moved about and worked longer hours. But possibly my whole age and generation and background would have never allowed me to bid for those jobs. I'm not a feminist, but I now see my role as to encourage younger women to do that.'

Ironically, her husband, fellow-psychologist Chris Frith – 'a marvellous husband: my work totally depends on being able to discuss with him all the time, and his influence is absolutely major. But I think he would also say the same about his work' – took considerably longer to get promotion and tenure than she did. But he has now got one of those jobs: head of the MRC's brain-imaging centre at Hammersmith Hospital. He and nannies took equal shares with her in looking after their two sons, to no visible ill-effect except once, says Uta Frith: 'When my younger son was at primary school they were asked to write stories about their mothers, and he wrote "I love my mum because she fetches me from school every day and gives me tea and is there for me". And every little bit of it was not true! But I did ask him recently if he wished I had always been there, and he said no.'

Although she and Chris Frith have collaborated in the past – his work has been mainly on schizophrenia – they are likely to work together even more in the future. For brain-imaging is the newest tool in mental cartography. If Uta Frith can design an experiment that exercises the theory of mind, while Chris Frith simultaneously plots electronically the precise bit of the brain that is being exercised, the results will show exactly where the theory of mind bit of the brain lies.

But they may do more: 'The thing I am most fascinated about is why some people with dyslexia manage to become good readers and other people just don't'. The same is true of the minority of autistic people who successfully pass theory of mind tests. The answer, she thinks, is that - often by an heroic struggle – they manage to call into play pathways in the brain which are designed for other purposes. Brain-imaging may prove that too. But it could never have done so if mind-mapping had not led the way.

Publications include:

Autism: Explaining the Enigma, 1989, Blackwell (translated into French, Spanish, German, Danish, Hungarian, Japanese, Swedish, Greek).

(Ed.) *Autism and Asperger Syndrome*, 1991, Cambridge University Press (translated into Japanese).

(© Karen Gold)

Carol Gilligan, born 1936, is professor of education in the graduate school of education, Harvard University. A psychologist, she argues that women's sense of morality is different to that of men.

Photograph by Neil Turner

'Lies make you sick,' says feminist psychologist, Carol Gilligan. The lies she is concerned about are 'the lie in psychological theories which have taken men as representing all humans', and the lie that girls and women tell when they speak in 'false feminine voices'.

Her first book, *In A Different Voice*, which was reissued with a new preface in 1993, was enormously influential in exposing the masculinist bias of psychology. As a new assistant professor at Harvard, she was working with Erik Erikson, a leading expert on self and identity, and Lawrence Kohlberg, famed for his research on moral development. Interested in how people deal with moral decision-making in real life (Kohlberg's work was based on hypothetical examples), she began a research project on Harvard students facing the Vietnam war, which came to an abrupt end when Nixon ended the draft.

'There went my study. I was back at square one . . . Then, in 1973, the Supreme Court legalised abortion, and I started to interview women. See, I was still interested in the difference between the way psychologists talked about the self and morality, and the way people actually experienced it. I was completely blind to the fact that my first sample was only male and my second sample was all female. But when I listened to what women were saying, it just didn't fit the theories: these women constructed self and constructed moral problems differently. And it was then I realised that Erikson's work on identity was done with an all male sample; that Freud's work had a male voice, a male point of view, all through it; that Piaget had all boys in his *Moral Judgement of the Child*; and that Kohlberg's 20-year longitudinal research was done with an all-male sample. I hadn't noticed it! So when I wrote "In a different voice: women's conceptions of self and morality" (an article published in the *Harvard Educational Review*), I was saying here's a different way of conceiving the self and talking about morality, and I'm hearing it in women.'

After the publication of her article 'it was like a public confessional – person after person said they'd used only male samples, and a lot of them said they didn't put the women's data in their published work because "it didn't fit their categories" so "we left out the women, and I don't think we mentioned it". This includes the studies of creativity, *all* the motivational research, studies of social perspective taking, the literature on adult development – I mean this was absolutely across the field. Leaving women out of psychological samples is an enormous design flaw.'

This realisation led to the publication of the book, *In a Different Voice*, which, unlike traditional writing in the social sciences, is accessible, inspirational and eloquent, weaving together quotations from interviews, fictional examples, myth, drama, and psychoanalytic insight. The book was read by feminists and non-feminists across a wide range of disciplines – philosophy, history and law as well as the social sciences – and was widely interpreted as endorsing the idea of an authentic female moral perspective, based not on abstract principles of 'justice' or 'rights' but on an ethic of care and responsibility. This idea resonated with what many feminists have long believed – that differences between men and women are not just the unfortunate outcome of patriarchal oppression, but that women's practices and ways of knowing might also be a source of empowerment. While some feminists celebrate this as a positive identity for women, others are suspicious of a message which seems to enshrine those very characteristics – nurturing and caring – which are used to keep women subordinate.

I met Carol Gilligan at her temporary home in Cambridge, where she was visiting professorial fellow in the faculty of social and political sciences. Others have described her as 'warm', 'vibrant' and 'charismatic'. I found her distant and reserved; courteous but cool, intense but not animated, intellectually engaged but emotionally detached. Conversation was guarded, cautious, circumspect. It was a difficult interview. Both of us are feminist psychologists, and she was sufficiently aware of my academic work to know that there are major theoretical differences between us. Given the hostility her ideas have provoked from some of her opponents, it is perhaps not surprising that she seemed tense and wary.

Although she is well-established as a leading feminist theorist, and is the recipient of both academic awards and feminist accolades (including the nomination 'Woman of the Year' in 1982 by the American feminist magazine, *Ms*, her work has also been severely criticised. The elegance and seductiveness of her writing is no substitute, say her critics, for 'the slow, painful and sometimes dull accumulation of quantitative data'. If women's identity and morality are different from men's this should be open to empirical proof, using reliable and objective scoring systems, matched samples, and all the apparatus of objective science. The impressionistic lyricism of her writing makes it intuitively appealing to many women, but, says feminist psychologist Carol Tavris, 'we must be wary of the pitfalls of relying on intuition or personal experience as the major way of understanding the world'. Other criticisms include the failure to contextualise her work in relation to feminist and other psychological research, her perpetuation of individualistic concepts of self, her failure to deal adequately with structural power, mother-blaming, heterosexism, cultural imperialism, and essentialism.

In direct proportion to her fame, she has been subjected to that special animosity and vituperation that feminists have (alas!) reserved for each other. As Kathy Davis, a feminist psychologist from the Netherlands, says: 'It is a peculiar feature of political debates that those who are the closest to us tend to be attacked most vigorously. Thus Gilligan is allowed into the feminist fold only to be severely chastised once there for not conducting herself properly.'

I asked Carol Gilligan about the criticisms of her work: 'The people who say my work isn't science: I just totally disagree with that, and I find it insulting, and I don't say that about their work. I myself don't write about somebody's work unless I find it interesting. The critics of my work that I most respect are those people who have shown me things that I didn't see or hear in my own work, and first and foremost among those were black people, who showed me that I wasn't hearing the silence of race in my own writing.' She calls for 'respectful disagreement and serious discussion of our differences that isn't about name-calling'. Describing herself as 'on the edge of the academic world' rather than fully part of it, she is profoundly uncomfortable with its competitive and adversarial nature ('the idea that you have to say "I have invalidated everything you do, and so you're down and I'm up"').

Since publishing *In A Different Voice*, she has worked on joint projects with other women as part of the Harvard Project on Women's Psychology and Girls' Development. 'I think I have modelled, with my colleagues, the creation of a feminist collaborative in the midst of a patriarchal institution. We worked very hard at collaborating together for nine years in Harvard, across hierarchy – faculty and students, male and female, lesbian and heterosexual, black and white.'

Her book, *Meeting at the Crossroads: Women's Psychology and Girls' Development*, is a product of that collaboration, and like her earlier writing, eschews technical language and mechanistic images in favour of metaphors from literature and music. Co-authored with Lyn Mikel Brown, and based on work with nearly 100 girls between the ages of seven and eighteen, the book exposes the lie of 'false femininity', by describing the 'psychological foot-binding' which girls undergo at adolescence. In place of the openness and directness of childhood, say Brown and Gilligan, girls learn to keep silent, to replace honesty (now called 'rudeness', 'meanness' or 'selfishness') with social lies, and to disconnect from their own experiences and desires 'so that they can better approximate what others want and desire, or look more like some ideal image of what a woman should be'.

Together with other women in the Harvard group, Carol Gilligan has developed a voice-centred relational approach to psychology. The dominant voice of psychology, which purports to be disembodied, objective, and dispassionate truth, 'has presumed, at least implicitly, a male body, a story about relationship that is, at its centre, a story about separation, and a society that men govern within the framework of Western civilisation. By listening to women and to girls and bringing their voices into the centre of psychological theory and research, we are changing the voice, the body, and also the story about relationships'.

What does she mean by 'voice': 'People keep talking about the *metaphor* of voice or the *concept* of voice, and I mean the *instrument* of voice. I didn't really have a language for that until I was introduced to Kristin Linklater, author of *Freeing the Natural Voice*, which shows how you can hear when a person's voice is connected with thoughts and feelings, and you can hear when those connections are blocked. Her analysis of the human voice has given me a physics for my psychology – a way of understanding how the voice works in the body, in language, and also psychologically. For girls at adolescence, voice no longer carries feelings, because of the danger that voice would carry sexuality, or other feelings that would upset people.' In her new preface to *In a Different Voice*, Carol Gilligan claims, 'Voice is a new key for understanding the psychological, social and cultural order – a litmus test of relationships and a measure of psychological health'.

The 'different voice' which has not been represented adequately in psychological theory is a relational voice, 'a voice that insists on staying in connection so that the psychological separations which have long been justified in the name of autonomy, selfhood and freedom, no longer appear as the *sine qua non* of human development, but as a human problem.' The aim of Carol Gilligan's work is 'to restore the missing text of women's development to life cycle theories' and doing this implies not simple addition, or a 'separate-but-equal' perspective, but a transformation in thinking. In one of her published lectures she illustrates what she means, using as an example two four-year-olds who were playing together and wanted to play different games: 'The girl said: "Let's play next-door neighbours." The boy said: "I want to play pirates." "Okay," said the girl, "then you can be the pirate who lives next door." She has reached what I would call *an inclusive solution* rather than *a fair solution* – the fair solution would be to take turns and play each game for an equal period . . . [But] neither game would change . . . It is what is called "androgyny". Now look what happens in the other solution . . . By bringing a pirate into the neighbourhood, both the pirate game and the neighbour game change . . . a new game arises through the relationship. That is basically my point: The inclusion of two voices in moral discourse, in thinking about conflicts and in making choices, transforms the discourse. It is no longer either simply about justice or simply about caring . . . We are into a new game.' Listening to the voices of women and girls will create new maps of development, new visions of maturity and lead to the transformation of scholarship.

It is a bold vision, and one that is hotly contested, as witnessed by a 1994 debate in the journal *Feminism & Psychology* between Carol Gilligan, Lyn Mikel Brown and their critics. Carol Gilligan's greatest achievement lies, not so much in her empirical research, but rather in having recast the terms of psychological discourse and forged a powerful new image of women's lives.

Publications include:

In a Different Voice: Psychological Theory and Women's Development, 1993, Harvard University Press, 2nd edition, with a new preface.

(Ed.) *Mapping the Moral Domain: A Contribution of Women's Thinking to Psychological Theory and Education*, 1988, with J. Ward, J. Taylor and B. Bardige, Harvard University Press.

(Ed.) *Women, Girls and Psychotherapy: Reframing Resistance*, 1991, Haworth Press.

Meeting at the Crossroads: Women's Psychology and Girls' Development, 1992, with Lyn Mikel Brown, Harvard University Press.

Between Voice and Silence: Women and Girls, Race and Relationship, 1996, with Jill McLean Taylor and Amy M. Sullivan, Harvard University Press.

(© Celia Kitzinger)

Jean Berko Gleason, born 1931, is professor of psychology at Boston University. Her pioneering work supports the theory, first expressed by Noam Chomsky, that children have an innate capacity for grammar.

Jean Berko Gleason is famous for working with wugs. Look in any text-book about child language development, and you'll probably find a reference to the seminal experiments she did with children in the late 1950s, in which the nonsense word 'wug' (as well as other nonsense words such as 'zib' and 'rick' – used as a verb) figured.

'Without making it sound like discovering the atom bomb, it was in a sense the first experimental psycholinguistic study done in the modern era,' she says of the work she did then. (It was published in 1958.) By showing that young children were able to form plurals, past tenses and add other 'bound morphemes' (syllables such as 'ing' and 'ness') to nonsense words, the wugs study was a support for the contention that children do not learn language simply by imitation, but have the ability to infer the rules of language and apply them.

The contention is, of course, originally that of the American guru of linguistics, Noam Chomsky, who has argued that children's brains contain a template for language – a 'universal grammar' – which enables them to infer the syntactic patterns of parental speech and apply them for themselves to make original sentences, i.e., sentences which the children have never heard before. Chomsky's first major work, *Syntactic Structures,* was published in 1957.

Gleason's study was, in the words of Steven Pinker, professor at the Massachusetts Institute of Technology, 'seminal'. It remains, as she says, 'some of the strongest empirical evidence we have that children are not simply learning bits and pieces of the adult linguistic system, but are constructing generative systems of their own, and that this results not from adult instruction, but from the children's inborn grammatical capacity'. The wugs experiment, which has been repeated many times since, and in many languages, shows that young children's systems for acquiring language 'are beautifully regular, productive, and rule-governed'.

As befits a pioneer, Gleason came to the subject by a roundabout route. 'I'm one of those combination creatures,' she explains. 'I have a degree in literature and history from Harvard-Radcliffe, and wrote my undergraduate thesis on the image of the gypsy in nineteenth-century English literature.' Then after some time out in New York and Europe, she returned to Harvard to take a master's degree in linguistics and a joint doctorate in linguistics and psychology. 'Most people now take a degree in psychology and specialise in language, or do a degree in linguistics and take some psychology. But I fulfilled the requirements of two departments – I took clinical psychology, Sanskrit, Old French . . . It was a very broad programme.'

At Harvard, Gleason was the first doctoral student to be supervised by Roger Brown, author of *A First Language* – in her words 'in many respects the father of modern child language studies'. His psychology of language course proved to be inspirational, she recalls.

Since the wugs study, Gleason says that she has become increasingly interested in 'what Dell Hymes called communicative competence' in children. 'I'm a developmental psychologist who's been worrying about language for thirty-five years or more.' Now a professor of psychology at Boston University, where her subject is the most popular choice of undergraduate majors, Gleason is often to be found behind a door marked 'Child Language Laboratory', of which she is the co-ordinator.

She turns from the computer on her desk. 'I was just playing with this CD-ROM before you came in. It's packed full of data,' she says. 'It's all too easy for people to talk off the top of their heads. But you really have to go out and get the data, and we have. Before this room was re-done it used to be a toddler lab; we brought a lot of parents in here with their children and recorded them. Also, we sent those families home with tape-recorders and got dinner table conversations from them . . . All of this is on computer now.'

The CD-ROM is part of CHILDES, the Child Language Data Exchange System. Set up in 1984 under the leadership of Brian MacWhinney, professor of psychology at Carnegie Mellon University in Pittsburgh, the system is a global undertaking that enables developmental linguistics researchers everywhere to share their studies. 'For instance I got a message on e-mail the other day that some newly submitted Portuguese data are now available,' Gleason notes.

'The child language research community is only a few thousand worldwide,' says MacWhinney, co-editor of the recently published *Handbook of Child Language*, 'but over half use the CHILDES system in some way or other. Probably something in the order of eighty people in Britain use the data.' Gleason was involved in the project right from the start, and helped develop accurate ways of notating children's conversation, says MacWhinney. He himself was one of the earliest people to replicate the wugs experiment in another language: 'I actually did a wugs study in Hungarian in 1971. I modified the technique, and gave the kids toys to play with . . . It worked with children as young as one-and-a-half years, which I found remarkable.' The eighty subjects of the original wugs experiments were four- and five-year-olds.

Gleason eagerly demonstrates the capabilities of her database. 'Here are transcripts of twenty-three families at dinner, just like the script for a play. And now here is every word that is used, in alphabetical order, with how many times it's spoken . . . I could ask for all the instances of "stupid" said by a father, and by a mother, and see what the differences are.'

Because, as she says, 'everywhere you go in the world, adults have special ways of talking to young children', Gleason is interested in both sides of the dialogue between children and adults. 'Kids aren't learning language by listening to their parents talk about, for instance, Bill Clinton at the dinner table,' she says. 'I think it's true that you could not learn a first language from watching television: somebody has to talk to you.' It is observations such as these that are doubtless the reason America's child-care writers call her up: 'I must talk several times a month to magazines like *Parenting*. They are forever writing about talking to babies, that kind of thing.'

She feels she is in a minority among her American colleagues in regarding class as important. 'Working-class people talk not nearly as much to their children as middle-class people; when they get to school, working-class kids have smaller vocabularies, and they never catch up. That has immense implications for our society.'

'You learn your vocabulary from people talking to you, but you need exposures. If your mother doesn't talk very much, and your dad doesn't talk so much, it will take a lot longer before you get those exposures.'

The study of twins, too, seems to back this up. 'Twins are wonderful companions, but they can't teach one another language,' she says. 'Typically they fall behind unless somebody else older talks to them.'

As a paper that she recently published with one of her colleagues (entitled 'The Neglected Role of Fathers in Children's Communicative Development') indicates, 'father-speech' has been the focus of some of Gleason's most recent work. 'Nobody wants to say fathers talk in a particular way because it's in their genes – they may play a different role from mothers. They do different things with their children,' she says. 'But they do speak differently to their children.'

In conversation, for instance, mothers are more likely than fathers to talk about what someone else has said; and when fathers do, they are more likely to use indirect speech. (She told me not to do it.) Mothers on the other hand prefer direct quotes (So she said to me 'Don't do it'): 'You can see these patterns in girls' and boys' speech as well.'

What's more, both mothers and fathers have different ways of talking to their children according to whether they are boys or girls, she adds, but 'men are much more polar than women – they seem to speak much more gently to little girls, and much more roughly to little boys'.

As it happens, this is not a contrast that Jean Berko Gleason has been able to observe at first hand in her own role as a parent. All three children from her long-lasting marriage to Harvard mathematics professor Andrew Gleason are girls – or rather women, now pursuing their own careers in publishing, writing and business. Because of their father, she thinks the three 'have better right brains than I do. I have a lot of trouble with certain kinds of things that require visualisation, but I think they have acquired a better balanced brain because of him'. She describes her husband, the younger brother of pioneering linguist Henry Allan Gleason, as 'an abstract analyst . . . famous for having solved Hilbert's fifth problem'. He has also been active in the movement for reforming maths teaching in the United States.

When her children were young, did she study their language? 'I made lots of observations of them, but it always struck me as inappropriate to allow any project to interfere with communication between us. I think children are wonderful to get ideas from, but only Piaget was able to make a major theory out of his own children. My daughters ended up in a few articles here and there, though.'

While the Gleason daughters were young, their mother only worked part-time on various Harvard research projects – but did manage to write and publish. 'This helped quite a bit when I did finally go back to work full-time,' she says. 'I had a nice list of publications out there.' While engaged in one project, in the Harvard Medical School's psychiatry department, she had her first brush with fame: a talk she gave, about parents' speech to children, to the Linguistic Society of America in the summer of 1971, happened to be attended by a *New York Times* reporter who made it the subject of a column, which was syndicated. 'We were simply inundated with calls and letters from publishers and television shows – including the David Frost show – as a result of the column,' she recalls. 'Probably that was the precipitating event that got me out of the supposedly quiet research and into the more public arena of the university.' When she joined the psychology department of Boston University in 1972 her daughters were nine, ten and eleven.

Although she is the daughter of Hungarian immigrants – she was born in Cleveland, Ohio – Jean Berko did not grow up speaking Hungarian. But she did learn the language later, when, curiously, she returned to the subject of her undergraduate dissertation, gypsies. But it was not George Borrow's literary insights but the real-life gypsies of Hungary that she began to study a decade ago. Sent as an exchange scholar to the then Communist country in 1981, Gleason met the linguist Zita Reger, 'working pretty much in isolation', and began collaborating with her. They have written papers together, and a book 'on growing up gypsy' is planned in the not too distant future.

'Zita started out looking at how gypsy children were acquiring Hungarian – the Hungarian government is interested in what can be done to help them stay in school. But she discovered that of course nobody was doing anything. There would be monolingual children speaking a gypsy language arriving in Hungarian schools, and they didn't have anybody to translate for them.'

Now Gleason sees the pair's focus as on 'language and socialisation' among Hungary's gypsies. 'You know how we say children are learning from the media. But gypsies have an oral culture; they are not spending a lot of time watching television or reading, so you have to look to the language to see what is going on. How can we explain the incredible cohesiveness of gypsy society – how is it that they are still there, in the face of death camps and discrimination by almost every country? How do you get to be a good gypsy? You don't read the book.'

This may seem some distance from her other research – which as well as child language covers such fields as the speech of adult sufferers of Broca's aphasia, and the 'tip-of-the-tongue' phenomenon – but Gleason sees it all as a part of one discipline. 'Psycholinguistics has traditionally been concerned with how people comprehend language, how people produce language, and how children acquire language . . . These are still the bedrock questions.'

Jean Berko Gleason is now preparing the fourth edition of her text-book, *The Development of Language*, 'so people must be using it'. And the early nineties saw the publication of *Psycholinguistics*, a comprehensive survey of the field, which she co-edited and partly wrote with Nan Bernstein Ratner, a former student who is now professor of hearing and speech science at the University of Maryland. 'One's students become one's friends,' Gleason observes. 'That is why one has to be nice to them . . . you get to be a mom in many ways in this world.'

Does she have any advice to the young female academic ? 'No matter what anyone tells you about the relative importance of academic activities, there is nothing like publishing in refereed journals. I also think it's a good idea to regard the university as your employer – if someone asks you to serve on a committee or meet the parents of prospective students, that's part of the job. Unfortunately, it's hard to teach, serve on committees, write papers and be a mother all at the same time.'

Even working part-time, she adds, 'is not easy'. With help from an au pair before her daughters were at school, and later 'a variety of baby-sitters', she was able 'to cobble together the time to work when I could – it helps that I am a middle-of-the-night person.

'But alas, the common wisdom is correct: one minute your children are babies and poof! the next they are grown up. So you had better find a way to spend time with them when they're little. Take pictures; you'll forget otherwise.'

Publications include:

'Language and Socialisation', 1988, in F. Kessel (ed.) *The Development of Language and Language Researchers*, Erlbaum.

(Ed.)*The Development of Language*, 1993, 3rd edition, Macmillan.

(Ed.) *Psycholinguistics*, 1993, with Nan Bernstein Ratner, Harcourt, Brace, Jovanovich.

(© John Davies)

Now director of the Jane Goodall Institute for Wildlife Research, Education and Conservation, zoologist **Jane Goodall**, born 1934, has been the recipient of international awards and honours. Goodall opened the public's eyes to the complexity of chimpanzee society, with its mass of human-like relationships.

The dramatic moment when chimpanzees were first spotted using tools: 'Evered, as he climbed through a tree, suddenly stopped and, with his face close to the bark, peered into what looked like a small hollow. He picked a handful of leaves, chewed them for a moment, took them out of his mouth, and pushed them down into the hollow. As he withdrew them we saw the gleam of water. Quickly Evered sucked the liquid from his homemade sponge . . .'

Jane Goodall's discovery that chimpanzees make and use tools distorted the line drawn by humans to separate themselves from other animals. It was the second of a series of dramatic discoveries she made over decades, by watching and watching, deep in the forests of the Gombe chimpanzee reserve in Tanzania. She watched from up in trees, down in bushes and perched on mountain tops overlooking the reserve.

Now she sits in a deckchair, in the sunny gardens of London's Royal Overseas League. A delicate figure with an open face and very dark eyes, at 62 she is growing old gracefully. She is wearing – unusually, one assumes – a smart dress, suitable garb for receiving a CBE. She soon kicks her shoes off, saying they are uncomfortable.

The CBE, nine honorary degrees and a mass of other awards, such as the National Geographic Society's Hubbard medal, its highest accolade, marks the admiration with which Goodall is regarded by the establishment. She opened our eyes to the complexity of chimpanzee society, with its variety of personalities, its mass of human-like relationships. Eminent biologist Robert Hinde, former master of St John's College, Cambridge says of the woman who is eleven years his junior and whom he once supervised: 'She changed the way I worked. She saw the animals as individuals. She taught me that you couldn't add the data on a lot of animals together in a simple way.'

Now the academic world admires her too: 'She is regarded as an aberrant person but academics always respect this,' says Hinde. But she was not always accepted. When she first came across universities, they were full of zoologists who, she says, 'chopped animals up to see how they worked'. This was anathema to a keen and patient observer of primate behaviour who seems always to have had an emotional independence from the world of universities and scientific laboratories. She single-mindedly followed her goal of studying chimpanzees, a route which sometimes converged with traditional academia but often did not.

It did not converge at the start, when she left her Bournemouth home, with an A level in biology and a dream she had had from the age of eight, inspired by Dr Doolittle, of living in Africa and writing about wild animals. She had saved for a holiday in Tanzania. There she found a job as assistant secretary to Louis Leakey, the famous palaeontologist, who was curator at the National Museum of Natural History in Nairobi and who became her mentor.

Why did Leakey choose this girl, in her mid-20s, with no degree (she couldn't afford it), to fulfil his ambitious plan of sending someone to observe the wild chimpanzees on the shores of Lake Tanganyika? Because, as well as being a keen observer, she was simple in habits, patient, degree-less, independent of mind and female. 'He realised that I didn't care about clothes, hairdressing and parties,' she says, perched on the edge of her deckchair. Her simple way of living, which included eating only once a day, was essential for studying chimpanzees. (The simplicity persists – she celebrated her CBE, of which she is proud, with a sandwich.)

Goodall jumped at Leakey's idea and soon she, and her amazingly supportive mother, were living in a tent by the lake. She would leave at dawn with nothing but a kettle for coffee to sustain her through the day. She had scant money for her supplies.

Leakey's choice of a patient and persistent researcher was wise. It took six months before she was able to get nearer than 500 yards to any chimpanzee. And a sense of persistence exudes from her descriptions: 'For three hours I watched the chimps feeding'; 'I was not only weary but soaking wet from crawling through dense undergrowth'; 'sitting in one place for a week waiting for something to happen'.

Her first six months of frustration were rewarded with two discoveries which excited Leakey, and via him, the wider world. She demolished the idea that chimpanzees were primarily vegetarians with her discovery of chimps eating baby pigs and baby baboons. Later, she would see them hunt. Then, after 'a frustrating morning, tramping up and down three valleys with never a sign or sound of a chimpanzee', she saw the chimp she was to love most, David Graybeard, using a grass stem to poke into a termite mound and withdraw insects to eat. Not only did she see chimps using tools, but making them as well, by stripping down twigs.

Leakey also chose Goodall because she did not have a degree. 'He wanted someone with a mind uncluttered and unbiased by theory who would make the study for no other reason than a real desire for knowledge,' she writes in her book, *In the Shadow of Man*. At the time the study of animals was full of taboos: animals were not credited with having emotions, minds, personalities.

Without a degree she had not learned about the sin of anthropomorphism: shockingly, she gave the chimps names; she recorded anecdotes as if they might be scientifically useful; when they appeared to be jealous, happy or afraid, she recorded that they were jealous, happy or afraid.

Hinde understands Leakey's antagonism towards graduates but disagrees with it. It was vital, he says, for Goodall's keen observations to be moulded by scientific discipline. This she acquired when she started her PhD at Cambridge at twenty-eight – placing Hinde in a strange position, which included having to persuade the Cambridge authorities that Goodall needed £3000 a year for bananas and that a Tanzanian thumbprint was sufficient as proof of receipt.

Exceptionally, Cambridge allowed her in without a first degree because of the work she had done. But she was very different from the other students. She was older; she had been in the field; her direct knowledge enabled her to contradict many of their beliefs. Above all she hated their assumptions and their methods. 'I wasn't happy,' she says. 'They couldn't accept how like us chimps were.' In addition, she did not care passionately about getting her PhD: for her it was only a means to her beloved end of immersing herself in Gombe. But the exposure to Hinde and his scientific rigour worked. Goodall appreciated scientific discipline, which she says is the same as self-discipline.

But it was her independence of mind which really enabled Goodall to wreak such a change in the way many academic disciplines consider primates. She did not, for example, give in to *Nature* when she received the proofs of her first paper for that journal, in 1964. The editors had replaced the words 'he', 'her' and 'who' with 'it' and 'which': she scrawled them out and reinstated their anthropomorphic alternatives. *Nature* demurred.

In fact, Goodall could not avoid using unacceptable words such as 'adolescence', 'childhood', 'social excitement' to describe the complexity of what she saw. She watched, for example, the mother-infant relationship. Mothers often form the head of a family group of females and infants who will stick together and support each other throughout their lives. Chimps remain dependent on their mothers for years: even at three years old they may die if their mothers disappear. It would appear that they can die of depression since, by three, they should be physically able to cope alone. Some chimps adopt their orphaned infant siblings. Goodall wrote: 'Who would have guessed that at five years of age a child might still be suckling and sleeping with his mother at night? Who would have dreamed that a socially mature male of about eighteen years of age would still spend much time in the company of his old mother?'

Leakey was responsible for directing three women towards the study of primates: Dian Fossey, whose work with gorillas is legendary, Goodall and Biruté Galdikas, who worked with orangutans. Between them they set in motion an ethological revolution. 'Leakey thought women were more patient, better observers,' says Goodall. They could also move more easily amongst native Africans. 'In Africa a white female is much less threatening. Males were seen as so arrogant.'

But her sex led to problems while she was at Cambridge. It was during the period when the *National Geographic* magazine put her on their cover. 'It was a picture of me in shorts with my chimps,' says

Goodall, sure that she would not have been a 'cover girl' if she had been a man. Cambridge wanted her to wait until she had her PhD before the exposure. But she wanted to please the National Geographic Society, which had faithfully been funding her work. 'That was horrific for Cambridge. But I didn't have loyalty to Cambridge at that time.'

Similarly, her first book, rather unacademically titled *My Friends the Wild Chimpanzees,* was also for the National Geographic Society. Popular science writing was not seemly at the time. 'I had to do that work,' she says. 'And I'm glad I was a woman because I got the money.'

The National Geographic Society had also funded a photographer to document the chimpanzees: Hugo van Lawick arrived and the two fell in love. They married in 1964. The wedding cake carried a clay model of David Graybeard. Their relationship is described, along with the rest of her experiences in Gombe, with refreshing simplicity, honesty and idealism. They had one son, in 1967, and again Goodall broke the rules, this time with his early upbringing.

Goodall believes that there is little difference between chimpanzee and human infants before they reach the stage of talking. Over the years she had observed that the most socially successful chimps were the ones whose mothers paid them lots of attention when they were young: plenty of touching; keeping the infant constantly nearby; suckling on request and toleration of misbehaviour when the infant is too young to grasp the difference between right and wrong. So Goodall gave the young Hugo absolute security, diverting him rather than punishing him when he misbehaved and exposing him to two or three trustworthy adults. 'Everybody said he would never be able to go out in the world if I treated him like that,' she says. 'In fact he is now supremely self-confident.' She likes to attribute this to his early experience, in which case it must also have helped him through an early start in prep school away from home and his parents' divorce in the early 1970s. (In 1975 she re-married, the MP Derek Bryceson, now deceased.)

But infants are not always cocooned at Gombe. If Goodall had stopped her work after the first ten years she would never have witnessed the four-year reign of terror by Passion and her daugher, Pom. They stalked the mothers in the community, killing and eating their new infants. Similarly, she would never have witnessed a four-year war, in which one chimpanzee community systematically exterminated another.

Until this infanticide, the only cannibalism Goodall had witnessed was the result of an attack by a group of males, while they were protecting their territory, on an alien female. During this attack the stranger's baby, possibly accidentally, was killed. The males ate a small bit of the baby.

'In contrast,' wrote Goodall, 'Passion's attack on Gilka seemed to have been directed to one end only – the capture of her baby. And the carcass was consumed in the way that normal prey is consumed, slowly and with relish.'

Gilka lost three babies to Passion, who would kill them by biting them in the neck, and then had no more. Passion stopped when she had her own baby. 'Those events changed for ever my view of chimpanzee nature,' Goodall wrote in her second book, *Through a Window*. 'For so many years I had believed that chimpanzees, while showing uncanny similarities to humans in many ways were, by and large, "nicer" than us. Suddenly I found that under certain circumstances they could be just as brutal.'

'Often when I woke in the night, horrific pictures sprang unbidden to my mind – Satan, cupping his hand below Sniff's chin to drink the blood that welled from a great wound on his face; old Rudolf, usually so benign, standing upright to hurl a four-pound rock at Godi's prostrate body; Jomeo tearing a strip of skin from Dé's thigh.'

Goodall's understanding of chimpanzees has made it inevitable that she should tackle their abuse by humans. They languish as tourist attractions on beaches, they suffer grotesquely as pets; they have miserable lives when kept for scientific experimentation. Goodall has built up a reputation as an animal welfare campaigner and the welfarists she works with seem to worship her. She says her lecturing work is a mission: 'It's as though someone takes over when I speak. I can almost stand aside'. She has also set up a scheme called *Roots and Shoots*, which aims to enlighten children about environmental and humanitarian ideas.

She argues that if chimpanzees are to be used to study human illnesses then they should be treated as 'honoured guests in the lab' – given space, things to do, the comfort of physical contact with other chimps and a comfortable retirement.

Despite her horror of the conditions in laboratories she visits, she is controlled in her reaction to those scientists who allow such conditions to persist. 'Most people are not evil,' she explains, with a calm look on her clear face. 'People mostly do bad things because they haven't understood or haven't bothered to think through what they are doing. It's when people begin to understand in their own hearts that they will do something.'

As a result, her lectures, which draw the crowds, concentrate on revealing the fascinating society of chimpanzees. She believes that condemnation of the atrocities committed against them will follow automatically.

One famous Aids researcher, when he discovered her work, told her: 'I had absolutely no idea about chimpanzee behaviour'. He revealed that his work on chimpanzees involved receiving specimens: he had never been to see how they were kept.

Goodall believes in gradual change and compromise. As a result, she has alienated some animal rights groups, including the World Society for the Protection of Animals, which has run high-profile campaigns to seize dancing bears and maltreated apes. She resigned as an advisor to the charity in 1995, arguing that aggressive campaigns alienate established activists and governments. Also, a charity which saves a chimp must be sure it has raised enough money to pay for its well-being for the rest of its long life.

Back at Gombe there is a flourishing research centre, where she now spends only five weeks a year. She says: 'I miss it but I have it inside me so that just ten minutes in the forest fills me up.'

There is still a lot to find out. There is now the first opportunity to watch healthy twins growing up; she wants to find out why some females stay with their mothers all their lives and others move to new communities, braving as strangers the murder of their infants.

But above all, one senses that she wants to watch, in a grandmotherly way, her beloved characters produce the next generation and the next.

Publications include:

My Friends the Wild Chimpanzees, 1967, National Geographic Society.
Innocent Killers, 1970, with H.von Lawick, Collins.
In the Shadow of Man, 1971, Houghton Mifflin.
The Chimpanzees of Gombe: Patterns of Behaviour, 1986, Bellknap Press.
Through a Window: Thirty Years observing the Gombe chimpanzees, 1990, Weidenfeld and Nicolson.
Visions of Caliban, 1993, co-authored with Dale Peterson, Houghton Mifflin.

(Aisling Irwin, © Times Higher Education Supplement)

Susan Greenfield, born 1950, is lecturer in synaptic pharmacology at Oxford University and fellow and tutor in medicine at Lincoln College, Oxford. She is a leading researcher on Parkinson's disease and one of the band of academics from a variety of disciplines who are trying to unravel the mystery of consciousness.

Photograph © Rob Judges

A woman in a startling pink satin suit, and a more soberly dressed man, are waiting in the Royal Institution lecture hall to begin a discussion on 'consciousness', the problem of how our awareness of everything – colours, smells, scenes, pain . . . is actually formed. The hall is packed, with the kind of disparate crowd of academics, journalists and lay-people that such a subject always pulls.

The woman is Susan Greenfield and she is launching her book on consciousness, which explores what she has framed as a question: 'How do our personalities and mental processes, our "states of conscious-ness", derive from a gray mass of tissue with the consistency of a soft-boiled egg?' The man, Roger Penrose, Rouse Ball professor of mathematics at Oxford University, is following her talk with a blast of ideas taken from his book, *Shadows of the Mind*. The two look odd together – and they talk very differently too. Penrose's talk is massive. Like a mad genius he rushes us through quantum mechanics, round the brain, leaping over hundreds of unintelligible concepts and bits of mathematics: he can't stop for one second to explain them because he wants to sweep us up into his overall vision of consciousness.

Greenfield is the opposite: breezy but slower and painstaking. She explains every word; she meticulously obeys the rules about talking science to the public. She leaves her audience with a little neurology and the solid foundations of a theory. Perhaps it is Penrose who should have been in the glitzy outfit.

And this is how Greenfield's ideas fit in amongst the wild speculations about, and ambitious 'solutions' to, the mystery of consciousness, many published over the last few years. Compare the ambition of her claim, for example, with that of the American philosopher Daniel Dennett. Greenfield would have been as unlikely to use Dennett's confident title, *Consciousness Explained*, for her slim book as he would have been to use her modest subtitle: *Toward a Science of Consciousness*. Grand solutions are not her business – yet.

Instead, her business is threefold. First, she is a lecturer in synaptic pharmacology at Oxford University (and fellow of Lincoln College), where her work includes piecing together the minutiae of Parkinson's Disease, an illness of which she is a leading researcher. Second, she is pursuing her lifelong passion for tackling consciousness, believing that other thinkers have set their sights 'almost at the impossible' in trying to explain how it is generated by brain tissue. 'We don't even know how to frame the questions,' she says. Third, she seems to have become a bit of a television darling. She is a high-calibre scientist who is not just articulate and lively but also female, a characteristic much sought after by those who want to show they are not sexist in their choice of scientists. She was the first woman to give the prestigious, 165-year-old Royal Institution Christmas Lectures for young people, in December 1994.

Before the RI lectures began she seemed slightly uncomfortable about her status: 'I'd like to be judged on my own worth but it would be stupid to say that I want the fact that I am female to be ignored. I am very excited but I am conscious of what it means. Another bastion has fallen'.

And after the first lecture, given to schools, she realised the importance of her gender when lots of girls came up afterwards to ask questions. 'I'd hate to be a role model,' she says. Greenfield, married to Oxford chemist Peter Atkin, is not a mother: 'Some of my friends seem to manage a career and children all very well but I personally wouldn't have been able to. Also, it wasn't an ambition of mine to have children'. But she has never made a 'policy decision' about it, she says.

At the children's lectures she talked about brains, Prozac, dreams and how the brain develops. But at the launch of her book she was pursuing a more intangible animal. Consciousness, she writes in *Journey to the Centres of the Mind*, is 'an absolute and inviolate individuality, a personal inner privacy of cascades of thoughts and feelings to which no one else has automatic access'. Throughout its ups and downs we retain an unbroken sense of individuality. Yet it apparently emanates from 'a grey mass of tissue'.

The pursuit of this magical question is a theme that unifies

Greenfield's apparently disparate biography. She became interested in consciousness at fifteen, stimulated, she says, by her mother telling her that neither of them would ever know what the other felt when they saw the colour red. At her school, Godolphin and Latymer, she did A levels in Greek, Latin, ancient history and mathematics ('I enjoyed the rigour of maths. That for me was a nice counterbalance'). She wanted to spend her time at university searching the thought of the ancients, where she thought she would find the best insights into consciousness. Science seemed unexciting compared to the wealth of human behaviour and thought available from the classics. 'That may be why girls don't go into science,' she says.

That interest in philosophy has been useful throughout her life. 'Unlike many of my science colleagues outside Oxford, I have had to serve on fellowship election panels. I'm only too aware of just how technical the subject of philosophy is. I'm very in awe of philosophers. I wish there were more dialogue between them and neuroscientists.

'The philosophers ask big questions such as "what is consciousness?". The scientists still find this really embarrassing. They know so much about the brain that they are daunted by the big questions.'

But philosophers have their own problems, she says. 'They are confined to the tools of metaphor, unable to translate their ideas into physiological reality.'

Her frustration with the lack of communication between the disciplines spilled over several years ago at a dinner with the philosopher Susan Hurley. 'Rapidly it became clear that a debate between philosophers and neuroscientists would be enormously revealing and valuable, not only in clarifying areas of formerly esoteric mystery but also perhaps in enabling us to make more progress together than we could ever achieve in isolation,' she wrote in her book.

The result was a series of debates between philosophers and neuroscientists, which she organised with physiologist Colin Blakemore. They were eventually edited into the book *Mindwaves*.

Back doing philosophy at university in the 1970s, the realisation had come slowly to Greenfield that science could have something to offer in exploring consciousness. At Oxford she had chosen PPP (Philosophy, Politics and Psychology). But she wasn't interested in politics and found the 1970s philosophy too mired in linguistic theory. So she ended up with a degree in experimental psychology.

Greenfield says: 'Although I didn't know it at the time I've always had the same line of inquiry and at different times of my life things have come up to fill it.' The next 'thing' she found was physiology. She was stunned to discover how much work physiologists had done on the brain: 'I didn't know that so much was known about the brain'.

As this interest was growing, she was dithering about what to do after her degree. She was applying for biophysics and wondering about a career in computer programming.

It was at this weak moment that a far-sighted tutor and the flexible Oxford system came to her rescue, propelling her towards neurology and a career in neurochemistry, despite the fact that she couldn't then tell her synapse from her subthalamic nucleus.

'Oxford puts a lot of standing on how motivated you are rather than what you know,' she says. 'If you really want to know something you'll spend three hours in the library trying to work it out.' As a result of this environment, she says 'I can't be bothered with arrogant people who saunter in thinking they know it all.'

Clutching a mug of coffee on a sofa in her office, Greenfield herself appears not the slightest bit arrogant. Instead, she is approachable, interested in anything new, intellectually excited about life. 'I'm never frightened to admit that I am an amateur. There were times when I was very sensitive to criticism. But if someone says "this is not possible" then I don't go and cry in a corner, I try to prove them wrong.' Proving the sceptic to be wrong has sometimes been the force that has driven her further: 'In a way I am grateful to those who predicted doom and gloom'.

It is probably this multidisciplinarity which has allowed her confidently to explore what has been said about consciousness and to devise her own theory. She is a sufficiently flexible scientist to say that consciousness may not, ultimately, be completely explicable in terms of brain cells. In the preface to *Journey to the Centres of the Mind*, she writes: 'the more I heard, read and thought about it, the more it seemed incredible that mere molecules could in some way constitute an inner vision, idea, or emotion, or – even more astounding – that they could generate the subjectivity of an emotion. Yet consciousness is continuous with the brain's activity and must emerge from it.'

She has investigated many disciplines in order to work on consciousness – philosophy, cognitive psychology, basic neuroscience, computation, brain damage studies, animal behaviour and developmental psychology. She thinks that any method that could give insight about our subjective experiences is a method worth adding to the repertoire.

'At the moment people are setting their sights almost on the impossible – on how the brain tissue generates consciousness. We don't even know how to frame the questions. We need to look at how brain events match up with subjective events, not at how they "cause" them.'

So Greenfield is trying to match the phenomena of consciousness with the physiology of neurons. She has tracked how consciousness grows as we mature, how it varies in depth as we vary our interaction with the outside world. Studies show that there is no centre for consciousness in the brain; and there is no uniform distribution of consciousness in every neuron. 'Rather,' she writes, 'it is far more plausible to consider different groups of noncommitted brain cells each taking over the job temporarily from one moment to the next.'

Think of a puddle, into which drops of rain sporadically fall. Greenfield's image of consciousness can be likened to the constantly changing surface of that puddle. Say, says Greenfield, you pause to contemplate an orange. It is the focus of your consciousness and, in your brain, a group of neurons has been stimulated. This stimulation is like a single raindrop falling on the puddle. For a little while your consciousness is taken up with the idea of this orange. It sets off many associations – the idea of slaking your thirst, of a holiday in Morocco, of an orange dress. These associations spread out from the group of neurons to other neurons, in much the same way as the ripples emanate from the epicentre of a raindrop.

Eventually some powerful association with the orange occurs, such as a plan to return to Morocco. This might be sufficiently powerful to act as a trigger for further, new associations. If this happens then the trigger becomes the new epicentre (just as another raindrop will hit the puddle and its ripples override the fading ripples of the previous one). This epicentre will take over as the 'seat' of your consciousness.

New epicentres can be formed either as a consequence of what is happening internally, as with the Morocco idea, or from some external source, such as a car screeching round the corner, making you forget the orange.

Consciousness is, then, an emergent property of groups of neurons, says Greenfield. It always involves a stimulated epicentre. The size of the stimulated group of neurons can be equated with the depth of the prevailing consciousness and is a product of two factors: the power, or 'recruiting strength' of the epicentre and the person's degree of arousal.

This explanation preserves our sense of individuality because the repertoire of possible connections between neurons, and the size and shape of each grouping, will be idiosyncratic.

The theory also allows Greenfield to account for our experience that we have a continuing identity throughout all our conscious experiences. At any given moment when we are conscious, we use 'meta-habits' that we have developed, which decide which bit of the brain activity should be in charge.

Greenfield delves deep into the neurology of the brain to find the science to put underneath this theory. But she stresses that she has just set the framework. She wants her theory to be falsifiable, which is a defining requirement of a scientific theory, according to the philosopher Karl Popper. She suggests ways in which it could be tested. She says we await the technological developments necessary for imaging the neuronal groupings as they change.

Her work is full of hard science. Brian Josephson, professor of physics at Cambridge University, who praises her for not trying to fit her ideas into an ideology, says in a review of her book: 'Her detailed proposals for fitting together the psychological aspects of consciousness and the neurophysiological ones will doubtless be seized upon by the experts keen on uncovering both their faults and their merits'.

At work in her laboratory, one of Greenfield's big interests is Parkinson's disease. The cells that are vulnerable to Parkinson's disease have an unusual feature: most brain cells secrete only little molecules, but these cells secrete a big one.

The scientists' theory is that a brain cell somehow becomes damaged; it then secretes this unusual protein in order to mend the damage, but unfortunately the protein has some other effect as well which leads to the symptoms of Parkinson's disease. 'We're trying to work out exactly how this protein does what it does and study the receptor it works on.'

Parkinson's is a particularly horrible disease, says Greenfield, because the sufferers are fully conscious of what is happening to them. There is a link with consciousness: 'The person wants to move but they can't. It's thought into deed. Thought and action.'

Working on this disease and on other studies is her fifteen-strong team – a variety of people including psychologists, pharmacologists, biochemists and cell biologists. 'There's a cross-fertilisation of ideas,' she says. 'It's much richer.'

The work is done in Oxford's department of pharmacology, a new building which opened in 1991 and was funded in bulk by £10 million from the Squibb Research Institute. At the time it was the biggest grant given by industry to academia. Greenfield was there at the start of it and directed the layout of her labs. She is proud of them. Perhaps their layout demonstrates her more female theories about how to run a team. 'It's not open-plan – everyone has their own space, which defuses arguments and stops friction. And I sacrificed an area that could have been a lab to make a general office where people can read or talk.'

This set-up is deliberately anti-authoritarian. The ideas came partly from her experiences working in a laboratory in Paris in the late 70s. 'That lab had the feel of the family, partly because there were more women in it. They all met for coffee in the morning. I'd much rather have this than be authoritarian in style.'

Her support for female academics involved taking part in the successful 1993 campaign to persuade Oxford University not to create fifteen new professorships, which would go to men, but instead to create a host of new readerships, to which women were more likely to be appointed.

If she thinks that attitudes towards female academics are a little primitive, she certainly thinks the same about attitudes towards consciousness. 'This is really the dark ages of consciousness,' she says. 'At the moment, everyone could have a theory of consciousness. Consciousness is seductive and deceptive. Everyone wants to be the person with the ultimate withering comment on everyone else.'

Publications include:

(Ed.) *Mindwaves: Thoughts on Intelligence, Identity and Consciousness*, 1987, with C. B. Blakemore, Blackwell.

Journey to the Centres of the Brain, 1994, with G. Ferry, BBC Education.

Journey to the Centres of the Mind: Towards a Science of Consciousness, 1995, W. H. Freeman and Co.

Concepts in Cellular Neuroscience, 1996, Prentice-Hall (in draft).

A Glimpse of the Brain, 1996, Orion/Basic Books (in draft).

(Aisling Irwin, © Times Higher Education Supplement)

Gloria Watkins, aka **bell hooks**, born 1952, is professor of English, City University New York. She has been described as one of a handful of America's 'black public intellectuals'.

'I have borne five children and I seen 'em mos all sold off into slavery, and when I cried out with a mother's grief, none but Jesus hear – and ain't I a woman ?'

Thus Sojourner Truth, an emancipated former slave, in 1852, at the convention of the women's rights movement in Akron, Ohio. Truth was answering a white man who argued that women's physical inferiority would always prevent them from enjoying the same opportunities as men. 'Look at me, look at my arm . . .' railed Truth. 'I have plowed and planted and gathered into barns . . . and ain't I a woman? I could work as much as any man (when I could get it) and bear de lash as well – and ain't I a woman?'

Truth's passionate vernacular gave the black American academic bell hooks the title to her first book, written when she was just nineteen and still an undergraduate at Stanford – though it took eight long years to be published. A controversial polemic, *Ain't I a Woman?* attacked the racism of the predominantly white, middle-class, feminist movement of the mid-seventies and demanded that the very different interests of black, often working-class, women be aired and represented in the struggle for equal rights with men.

Instead of the simplistic binary divide 'blacks' and 'women' (the former usually meaning black men, the latter white women), hooks, now a professor of English at City University New York, examined power play across a far more complicated framework, one fractured by race and class as well as by sex. Women complained of being discriminated against by men, but black American men were often in more vulnerable positions than their white female counterparts. So who was the oppresser and who the oppressed?

'When a baby is born,' says hooks, 'the feminists argued that the first thing you notice is what gender it is. When a black baby is born, the first thing the parents notice is what colour it is; because that's going to have an impact on its class mobility.'

hooks herself was born Gloria Watkins, one of seven children, father a Post Office janitor, mother, later, a maid 'in white folks' homes', in 1952 in Hopkinsville, Kentucky. In Britain to speak at a conference, staying in a musty hired room in the heart of Bloomsbury, she looks exhausted as she fills in the bones of a childhood to which she often – and deliberately – makes reference in her work.

She has written joyously of the sense of security she imbued from attending the black schools Booker and Washington and Crispus Attucks before the desegregation of American education, and of her unhappiness when they were closed and she bussed to a mixed school, 'where there was mostly contempt for us, a long tradition of hating'. She has told how her father occasionally hit her mother, of the family's poverty and of being punished by her parents for her childish curiosity and forthrightness. But she has written too, more positively, of her great-grandmother's gift for quilting, of her Kentucky clan-like family, five sisters, one brother, and its communal critiquing of early TV's crass black stereotyped characters, of a mother who also wanted to be a writer and who provided a sense of 'homeplace' for her rebellious young daughter.

Her raw and painful autobiographical asides, together with the use of vernacular black speech ('dissed', 'folks', 'say shit like') have drawn criticism from academic peers, but hooks believes that they provide a means both of keeping in touch with her roots and of reaching a wider public, an aim she, as a 'revolutionary', holds close to her heart.

She took her great-grandmother's name as a pen name because she 'wanted to show that women could trace their lineage through the matrilineal line'. She lower-cased it because, at the outset of American feminism, activists wanted to 'move away from the notion of iconic figures'; the message, they thought, should be more important than the person espousing it.

'Unfortunately,' she remarks drily, 'bell hooks has become an iconic figure in her own right – but the lower case still makes people question how we name. I see it as a useful intervention even now.'

Even in accounts of her childhood the germ of her later demons, sexism and racism, is visible. In a family where the majority was female hooks started early to question the dominance of her father's word. *Ain't I a Woman?* argued that both sexism and racism had to be countered; both were spawned of a 'white supremacist patriarchal system' (a favourite hooks phrase) which must be overturned. So black American women no longer had to choose between two liberation movements; between supporting either feminism (and white women) or black activism (and their often sexist black menfolk). The two activist movements were indissolubly entwined.

'Racism and sexism are interlocking systems of domination which uphold and sustain one another,' hooks writes in the essay 'Race and sex'. 'Since black liberation struggle is so often framed in terms that affirm and support sexism, it is not surprising that white women are uncertain about whether women's rights struggle will be diminished if there is too much focus on resisting racism, or that many black women continue to fear that they will be betraying black men if they support feminist movement.'

Women's studies classes across America have by now accepted hooks' central idea – that women's social status is not determined solely by gender but by an interplay of factors including class, race and – a more recent addition – sexual preference. Working-class women, straight women, Hispanic women have different preoccupations to those of middle-class women, lesbians, WASPS. But in 1982 when *Ain't I a Woman?* was published, such notions were seen as a betrayal of feminist solidarity. 'I remember,' hooks says in *Outlaw Culture*, 'people being enraged because the book challenged the whole construction of white woman as victim, or white woman as the symbol of the most oppressed . . .'

A corpus of books now into double figures has propelled hooks to iconic status in America. As a 'black public intellectual', one of the few women in that category alongside outspoken male academics such as professor of religion at Harvard, Cornel West, and head of the Afro-American Studies department at Harvard, Henry Louis Gates Jnr, hooks' opinion is sought by the media on issues ranging from the representation of black women in Spike Lee's films to misogynist pop music lyrics. She has voiced her viewpoint on recent court cases involving fallen black stars, such as the baseball player O. J. Simpson, acquitted in 1995 on charges of allegedly murdering his (white) wife and her companion, and the boxer Mike Tyson, who was convicted of rape. She has interviewed the rap singer Ice Cube and written a self-help book,

Sisters of the Yam, for black American women dissatisfied with their tight curls, size, the colour of their skins. (She counsels against chemical processing and wigs and urges them to 'love their bodies'.)

An America fractured by ethnic differences (where, as Professor Gates has stated, in 1994 African-Americans accounted for nearly a third of AIDS cases and nearly half of all murder victims were black), is particularly likely to heed the message of people like hooks. But one of the most powerful elements in her revolutionary message comes, not from the present, but the past. It is her sense of what she calls 'the holocaust of slavery'.

Ain't I a Woman? contains stories of terrifying brutality – such as that in which a nine-month-old child was flogged on a slave ship for refusing to eat. 'When beating failed to force the child to eat, the captain ordered that the child be placed feet first into a pot of boiling water . . . the captain dropped the child and caused its death . . . then commanded the mother to throw the body of the child overboard.'

Or the memory of Solomon Bradley, an ex-slave, who recalled seeing a female slave punished for burning the breakfast waffles by being staked out, face down, on the ground, and whipped with a leather belt. 'Sometimes when the poor thing cried out too loud from the pain Farrarby would kick her in the mouth. After he exhausted himself whipping her he sent to his house for sealing wax and a lighted candle and, melting the wax, dropped it on the woman's lacerated back. He then got a riding whip and . . . picked off the hardened wax by switching at it.'

hooks believes that 'the suffering many black people experience today' is linked to the suffering of the past, to 'historical memory', and that black people's attempts to 'understand that suffering' have created a hunger for literature which tackles the emotional, what hooks calls the 'psycho-social', reality of slavery. Hence, she argues, the acclaim and attention accorded Toni Morrison's *Beloved*, a nightmarish novel from the Nobel-prize-winning academic about Sethe, a black female slave who kills her own baby daughter Beloved rather than have her taken into servitude.

Mental health, argues hooks, is the next field which needs to be tackled by black Americans. 'Politicised mental care is the next revolutionary frontier,' she writes in one of her essays, arguing that psychoanalysis holds out a promise of redemption from the horrors of history, but, as ever, its practice needs to be re-thought and its theoretical assumptions altered to take in the different experiences of African

Americans. 'There have yet,' she says in an essay on black women intellectuals, 'to be extensive psychoanalytic studies discussing the fate of gifted black children raised in homes where their brilliance of mind was not valued but made them "freaks" who were persecuted and punished.'

A scholarship to Stanford took hooks away from her own 'dysfunctional' family. She completed her doctoral thesis at the University of California Santa Cruz, but not without difficulty. She has written of being told she was not 'really graduate school material' by one white male professor and of her own fantasies of entering his office with a loaded gun and making him 'experience the fear, the humiliation'. But she got her doctorate, subsequently gaining the post of assistant professor of African-American studies and English at Yale, followed by that of professor of women's studies at Oberlin College. In 1994 CUNY offered her her current position.

Despite such a successful academic career she is ambivalent about academe. From childhood she wanted to be a writer rather than a teacher – indeed she was single-minded about her ambition, developing a fifteen-year relationship with Nate, a black intellectual older than herself in which both saw writing as their life's project. She imagines herself in the tradition of Elizabeth Barrett Browning, Simone de Beauvoir – childless women with partners who are their intellectual equals engaged in a common struggle for expression. Nate and bell had their work-spaces, they went to them daily for a set number of hours. She still reads a book a day.

As she points out, publishing the amount she has requires time – 'part of that is not having children'. It is, she adds, ' a mythic feminist notion that imagined women could have it all.' Yet she admits wanting a child, wanting too a partner who is her age and her intellectual equal instead of the younger men who are attracted to her, she thinks, partly because of her fame. In *Breaking Bread*, a dialogue between bell hooks and Cornel West, there is a question about 'the price one has to pay as a prophetic intellectual'. hooks responds: 'We've had many black women academics but, to some extent, we are a new generation. We represent the first generation of black women thinkers who don't have to have children, or manage a household, if we choose . . . I think one of the costs we pay for uncompromised intellectual pursuit is certain forms of isolation, which, if one does not take care to find community, can be very disenabling and debilitating.'

Recognising the problem, she has been 'inventive' in circumventing it, informally adopting a 'play daughter', Tanya Mckinnon, a young black graduate, and overseeing her intellectual and emotional development and nurturing a network of close black women friends. Exposure of her personal life is part of her revolutionary project. There is almost a sense of 'the talking cure' being put to work when she describes her love for a black British film-maker, who has both child and partner already.

By drawing a distinction between academics and intellectuals and developing an informal personal style of teaching hooks has resolved the tension she felt between writing and teaching. She is more of a mentor then an intellectual superior to her graduates, encouraging them to question ideas emotionally as well as rationally, drawing on their own experiences. This teaching style she sees as subversive. 'Academics and intellectuals are not the same thing. I do not feel my success is due to how much I have played the good game of academe. It is more due to the strength of the contribution outside academe – how my work has transformed people's lives in a meaningful way.'

She waves a card from a young South African woman who came to hear her speak. 'Your work has changed my life' is inscribed on it. She gets many such cards. 'That to me is what being a public intellectual is all about.'

There are criticisms of her work and its style. One *Village Voice* article described it as a mixture of psychobabble and guilt tripping. An American historian has said that she would not want her graduate students to think they could do work without footnotes, as hooks does. 'She,' says hooks rather bitterly, 'is not saying that about white men like Roland Barthes, who has written all sorts of books which are not footnoted according to the Modern Languages Association style sheet . . . In general when folks make that sort of critique it is to do with discomfort with the ideas in the books. Documentation does not legitimate your work. Look at the books which are well-documented which are inane.'

It is not, she adds, as though she has not done that kind of scholarly, meticulously referenced work. Check out her thesis. But then she made a choice – to write for the largest possible audience, to change the greatest number of lives. It is an idiosyncratic solution to a widespread dilemma in America. If you are successful as a black American, do you 'assimilate', accept the culture and customs of the mainly white middle-class banding in which you find yourself; step, as hooks herself puts it, with their 'decorum'? Or do you find ways to stay close to your roots, to keep in touch with the different problems and aspirations of the majority of black Americans, who remain lower class? For an intellectual working in the field of African-American studies the dilemma is even more acute, for how can you speak and interpret the culture of this other black America if your own life has diverged from their daily reality?

hooks seems to belong to an older, more radical America. Her emphasis on class politics and her denigration of black capitalism, which has been part of the conservative agenda from the seventies onwards, have a distinctly sixties flavour. The Black Panthers, Malcolm X – yes, she criticises them for sexism. But there is a sense too of revelling in their power, in the message of revolutionary action they proposed.

One of her latest books, *Killing Rage: Ending Racism*, takes issue with the sense of hopelessness rampant in black America. 'A lot of the new books by men – cross-race, cross-class – are all cynical, all say racism is never going to end. I was struck by the difference between that and the writings of revolutionary feminism, which is more optimistic. I felt really distressed by the message that racism is here to stay and there is nothing we can do about it. That is a disempowering message,' says hooks.

Publications include:

Ain't I a Woman: Black Women and Feminism, 1982, South End Press.
Feminist Theory: From Margin to Center, 1984, South End Press.
Breaking Bread: Insurgent Black Intellectual Life, 1991, with Cornel West, South End Press.
Black Looks: Race and Representation, 1992, South End Press.
Sisters of the Yam: Black Women and Self-recovery, 1993, South End Press.
Teaching To Transgress: Education as the Practice of Freedom, 1994, Routledge.
Outlaw Culture: Resisting Representations, 1994, Routledge.
Killing Rage: Ending Racism, 1995, Henry Holt.

(Sian Griffiths, © Times Higher Education Supplement)

Sarah Hrdy, born 1946, is
professor of anthropology,
University of California, Davis.
Her pioneering work on female
langur monkeys in India changed
our benevolent view of how
primates behave, replacing it with
a study of sexuality, competition
and dominance.

Photograph © Catherine B. Hrdy

When Sarah Hrdy set out as a postgraduate student to study the sacred
langur monkeys in Rajasthan, India, a project which brought her fame
and changed the way biologists interpreted the behaviour of primates,
she found she was identifying with the plight of the female langurs.

Why, she wondered, did they put up with strange predatory males
coming along and attempting to kill their offspring every two years or
so? More to the point, why did the wretched females go and mate with
said infanticidal males afterwards?

The answer is pure Darwin: sexual selection. The invading males
killed the infants of the vanquished to get the females to mate with them
more quickly, and thereby produce their own offspring. The females
tolerated the deaths of their babies and mated with the killers because
that way they ensured the survival of their sons. 'It would be to her
progeny's detriment that a female refused to breed with an infanticide,'
she wrote in what has become a classic text and was her PhD thesis, *The
Langurs of Abu: Female and Male Strategies of Reproduction*. 'If
possession of that trait is indeed advantageous, her sons would suffer in
competition with the offspring of less discriminating mothers.'

That empathy of one female animal for another forced a reassessment of old assumptions and came at a time when Sarah Hrdy – whose
name is Czech – was becoming aware of the power relations between
men and women in her own life. A research project which had begun as
a simple attempt to test the Malthusian theory that infanticide by male
langurs was brought about by overcrowding grew into an ambitious
study of sexuality, competition, and dominance among that species.

[137]

Hrdy's book received terrific reviews, though her new ideas also caused a furore among eminent anthropologists because they overturned the prevailing ideology – laid down by the British academic, Alfred Radcliffe-Brown – that primates behaved in ways that promoted peace and happiness and the interests of the group. Clearly, something was amiss with this dogma if male langurs were busily biting to death the offspring of male competitors.

It did not take long for anthropologists to realize that langurs were not alone in this respect. A host of species, including lions, hippos, bears and wolves, are driven to kill babies for motives other than eating them. By patient observation, year after year, in the blazing heat of the Indian sun, Hrdy saw what previous researchers had ignored – that life for the langurs is nasty, brutish and short.

At the same time, she pioneered a whole new branch of feminist primatology, highlighting how male-biased early animal behaviour studies were. 'No one will will ever again be permitted to make pronouncements about primate breeding systems after having studied only one sex or after watching only the conspicuous animals,' she wrote in a contribution to the book, *Feminist Approaches to Science*. In that same chapter, she asks whether women are better observers than men, quoting Louis Leakey, the Kenyan primatologist, who liked to use women researchers: 'You can send a man and a woman to church, but it is the woman who will be able to tell you what everyone had on'. Or perhaps women are temperamentally more pragmatic or more empirical, less open to theoretical bias, she wonders.

Today, at the age of forty-nine, Sarah Hrdy is a highly regarded professor at the University of California at Davis, where she teaches anthropology. She has four books and numerous articles behind her, and travels widely, giving papers and talks. Her latest interest is motherhood – how much time, money and energy parents invest in their offspring. And her ideas about infanticide – heterodox when they were published in the 1970s – are the new orthodoxy.

Scrupulously, Hrdy devoted equal space to both sexes of langur monkey. She was not only interested in the male infanticide – so seized upon by reviewers at the time – but also the behaviour of the female. The latter, however, was virtually ignored. Female langurs, Hrdy discovered, were nymphomaniacs, forever stealing away from their harem to copulate with outsiders, even when they were pregnant. In almost every case of copulation she found the females soliciting males by sticking their behinds in the air and shaking their heads. What were they up to? Hrdy speculated that they were often trying to fool the invading males. By showing estrus (on heat) behaviour to the new master of the troop, they might deceive him into thinking the unborn child was his and should not be killed, she suggested. It was only when the new male made clear he was determined to kill the infant that the females gave up and abandoned their child.

From there Hrdy embarked on an altogether bigger canvas in her book *The Woman That Never Evolved*, which tried to dispel some long-held myths about female primates. That work gave Hrdy a much bigger readership – beyond the confines of animal behaviour majors – because it looked at human female sexuality from the viewpoint of a feminist sociobiologist schooled in primatology. Hrdy suggested that the female orgasm might be on its way out. Her theory is that the female orgasm is adaptive, a hangover from our pre-hominoid past, connected to the fact that our ancestors mated with a bunch of males, a bit like the langur monkeys of Abu. That way our female ancestors could gain access to good genes (the 'let the best sperm prevail' theory) and cast their nets wide to bring in care for their offspring from a number of males. Many case-studies show male primates helping out with children, according to the likelihood that they are the fathers. As Hrdy found with the langurs, males who were possibly the father were less likely to kill an infant too.

Underpinning such rampant sexual behaviour was a psycho-physiological reward – the female orgasm. It worked best after a female had mated with a number of males, which is why the human female is left with a 'cumulative' orgasm, according to Hrdy. 'If humans are no longer living in breeding systems where females are mating simulataneously with multiple males – and I have to tell you I don't know of any evidence that they are – then you have to say this is a legacy,' says Hrdy. 'This was something that was adaptive in our pre-hominoid past and it's there as a vestige.'

These ideas were all the more radical coming from someone who fell into primatology by accident. A fifth-generation Texan who grew up in Houston, the heiress to an oil fortune, Hrdy found herself out of place in that state because of her intellectual leanings. 'Growing up in Houston was a bit like growing up in South Africa,' she says. She was happy to be sent away to an all-girls boarding-school in Maryland at the age of sixteen, to an academically superior establishment which nurtured her love of reading and writing. 'It was the first time in my life when the things I loved were valued and vindicated,' she explains. 'I loved books. I always wanted to be a writer, and all of a sudden it was all right, and that was a tremendous blessing for me.'

It helped that her mother and grandmother were right behind her in her intellectual endeavours. She followed in their footsteps to Wellesley, the élite all-female liberal arts college outside Boston, overlapping with Hillary Clinton, who was the year above her. But she didn't stay. 'I was a philosophy major but I was taking a lot of creative writing,' she explains. 'I was writing a novel about the Mayans, based on old Mayan folklore . . . so I went to talk to Evan Vogt, the great Mayanist at Harvard, and I said, "I want to be a writer and I'm interested in learning more about the Mayans to write about them". And he arranged for me to transfer from Wellesley to Harvard, which was virtually impossible in those days. Still, I try to reconstruct how it happened. For me it was a miracle.'

Radcliffe, the female part of Harvard, was heaven to someone like Hrdy. 'It was the best thing that ever happened,' she enthuses. 'To have so much scope dumped in your lap. Anything you wanted to do, they assumed you could do it. And that you were serious. And that you had the skill to do it. And that you would do it.' She loved anthropology and ended up writing her undergraduate thesis on Mayan mythology – a structural analysis on the lines of Lévi-Strauss. This thesis became her first book, *The Black-man of Zinacantan: A Central American Legend.* Based partly on stories Hrdy was told by women in Guatemala and Honduras, where she had been spending her summers working in medical clinics, the book looked at the Mayan myth of the bat-demon H'ik'al, a fiend who wreaks vengeance on women who misbehave.

After graduation, Hrdy enrolled to do a course in film-making at Stanford. She decided she wanted to do something useful, like making educational films for people in developing countries, but she soon realized this was not Stanford's strongest programme. Instead she began to attend Paul Ehrlich's classes on population biology. She remembered from an undergraduate course at Harvard that the langur monkeys in India, supposedly because of overcrowding, had been driven to kill babies. 'I thought, you know, I'll go study these monkeys and I will document the effects of crowding on behaviour and how it's detrimental.'

Because she had done very well at Harvard, she was able to return in the middle of the year and enter the graduate programme in human biology. After that, graduate school was a less happy experience. As a postgraduate at Harvard, Hrdy encountered sex discrimination, and found life much more of a struggle. She moved closer to biology, which may have explained the sexism, she thinks, because male biology graduates were so aggressive. She met people who were expecting her to fail, hoping she would fail, she says.

Her first summer in graduate school saw her in India searching for the langurs. It was a heady period in evolutionary biology at that university. Robert Trivers was beginning what was to be an important transformation of evolutionary perspectives on behaviour and Professor E. O. Wilson was putting together his ideas on sociobiology. 'It was an incredibly exciting time,' she says. 'The intellectual excitement was paired with a lot of emotional distress and tension as I encountered a view of women on many fronts . . . All my life I had felt a little embarrassed because I was so overprivileged. It never occurred to me that anyone would ever discriminate against me. I was encountering incredible things.' Pressed for an example, she recalls a seminar where the conversation turned to the topic of women being traded between groups as wives. 'It was done with just no thought at all about these people,' she explains.

Hrdy decided that was what it must have been like to be a black person listening to a lecture on niggers and the Klu Klux Klan. For the first time in her life she understood the anger that drives people to want to be revolutionaries and throw bombs.

The one man she remembers with gratitude and fondness is E. O. Wilson, the great American biologist. He appreciated her work, without making any great fuss about it, arranging to have a paper which particularly impressed him published in a prestigious scholarly journal. He also helped her to get *The Langurs of Abu* into print. Sarah Hrdy agrees that she has been a kind of Trojan horse among anthropologists, infiltrating the profession with feminist ideas. But it has been accomplished only with considerable grief. 'It hurt me,' she explains. 'It caused me great anxiety and stress, and undue misery. I have written letters to the president of Harvard complaining about sexism and then burned them and flushed them in the toilet to be sure no one would see them. And I have seen what's happened to the women who have complained and paid big prices.' But the agony helped in one way. It propelled her to write *The Woman That Never Evolved*, she says. 'I feel I was so polarized by what I saw that it actually tapped some creative juices that wouldn't have been tapped otherwise.'

And later on, when Hrdy was made a full professor at the University of California at Davis at the age of thirty-eight, and elected to the

National Academy of Sciences in 1990, six years later, at what was considered a young age for such an honour, she felt the advantages of being a woman. By then affirmative action had taken hold on American university campuses. 'I knew at the time that there were men who deserved it more,' she says of the National Academy of Sciences election. 'They wanted women.' She concludes with a typically thoughtful summation: 'I've suffered because I was a woman but it's helped me in my career.'

She was also helped at crucial moments by her family money, though she says it was a handicap as well. Her mother funded the early trips to India, and she was accompanied by the man who was to become her husband, Daniel Hrdy, who was then an anthropologist and is now an infectious diseases doctor. But it was gruelling research nonetheless. She makes light of it now, talking about the 'soap opera' or the 'high drama' of the langurs' lives, as if she were watching something on network TV. Each night she would have to note in which trees the monkeys chose to sleep. Next day she was up at the crack of dawn to catch the monkeys before they left the trees. Otherwise she would have to spend hours hunting them down.

The hard part was in the middle of the day, she says. The monkeys would take their naps, but Hrdy couldn't afford to. She read novels. All in all, she spent ten years flying back and forth to India to research the monkeys. The part of the work she was most anxious about was the part on female dominance hierarchies in langurs. 'We thought we had discovered a new type of structuring of a dominance hierarchy, and it seemed kind of odd at the time,' she explains. 'The young females just about the time they were reaching reproductive maturity were starting to move up the hierarchy and then they would have a stable period near the top during their prime years and then fall again with age. So, you had a dominance hierarchy where the bottom was populated by the very old and the very young, and the prime females were at the top. And it was fluctuating, from three-month period to three-month period, from year to year.' Not unlike Hollywood today, points out Hrdy.

That pattern was quite different from the one seen in other types of monkey where rank is inherited and fixed for life, with offspring playing strict roles. Hrdy worried about what she had found. Was it really right, she wondered. But a young German at Jodphur, in India, had found the same thing, which made her realize her observation was being replicated. She and her husband had been hoping to continue in India doing further research to nail down Hrdy's findings, but they ran into trouble with the Indian government.

They had money from the Smithsonian and the National Science Foundation to go in on a much bigger scale to take blood samples from the monkeys to determine paternity and to research langur epidemiology. But the enterprise fell apart amid nefarious suggestions that the Hrdys were working for a non-existent body called the Defence Pathology Organization. There were objections too about blood being taken from sacred monkeys. Research permission was cancelled. Hrdy is wistful about not having conclusively proved her findings with modern technology such as DNA analysis. During the 1970s she was flying by the seat of her pants, making shrewd observations on the basis of not very much evidence and hypothesizing about them. She would not accept such standards of evidence today from her PhD students.

Had she been able to take those all-important blood samples she would have avoided some of the criticism to which her research has been subjected since. The criticism has resurfaced again recently in magazines like *American Anthropologist* and *Evolutionary Anthropologist*, much to her chagrin. She finds it irritating that the critics are still picking over her research when she freely acknowledged she was taking some big risks. 'The data were not all nailed down,' she says. 'We didn't know for sure that the males who were killing the infants were then siring the subsequent infants.' It was an informed guess. 'Some of the criticism I am getting now is what right did this woman have to take these risks,' says Hrdy. 'I feel that scientists take risks all the time. What matters is whether the research can be replicated and whether it is supported by subsequent research.' Hrdy's findings have been borne out again and again.

Today she lives with her husband and three children, daughters of seventeen and twelve, and a son aged eight, on a farm outside Davis. They are engaged in a wonderfully idealistic California experiment – trying to restore their land to its native California condition. Eighty acres has been sown with native grass seed, and a wetlands area created. This year sheep arrived to engage in intensive grazing. 'It's a way of giving back something,' she explains, with her Texan drawl. 'You tread heavily on the world but you can leave something behind.' To this end, the Hrdys are growing tomatoes, rape seed, sunflowers, wheat and picking nuts in their almond and walnut groves. Roaming their land are wild turkeys, mule deer, guinea-fowl and rattlesnakes. The family have taken their crusade to Washington. They are lobbying for a group to be set up – a national institute of the environment – to feed into policy.

It is difficult to see how Sarah Hrdy has much time for her academic work. Running throughout our conversation were the themes of compromise and balance in life – her desire for work and travel against the need for a spouse and family. 'I would think for any woman scientist this has got to be one of the major issues: these compromises you make,' she says. 'As an anthropologist, I was acutely aware of the needs of children. They need to be attached to stable figures.' The way she has resolved the conundrum is to hire long-term help. Her eight-year-old son is looked after by a woman who has worked for Hrdy for seven years. As a result he has two mothers. 'That has helped me tremendously to continue my work,' she says. 'But it doesn't take you off the hook.'

Publications include:

The Black-man of Zinacantan: A Central American Legend, 1972, The Texas Pan American Series, University of Texas Press.

The Langurs of Abu: Female and Male Strategies of Reproduction, 1977, Harvard University Press.

The Woman that Never Evolved, 1981, Harvard University Press.

(Ed.) *Infanticide: Comparative and Evolutionary Perspectives*, 1984, with G. Hausfater, Aldine Publishing Co.

(© Lucy Hodges)

Carole Jordan, born in 1941, is Britain's most senior woman astronomer. Yet despite this, she had not, by the end of 1995, been awarded a professorship at Oxford University, where she is, at the time of writing, a reader in the physics department.

Carole Jordan is Britain's most senior woman astronomer, with a position in the theoretical physics department at the University of Oxford and the distinction of having been the first woman president of the Royal Astronomical Society – over 170 years after its establishment. She says that, like many women scientists, she has succeeded despite being 'the odd one out' numerically in a male-dominated field. Supporting women physics students at Oxford is important to her.

But Jordan is quick to stress that she is 'wary of institutions' and as an undergraduate, would never have lived in a women's hall of residence. Her career has been an unusual one, via the British Civil Service as well as academe, and until her arrival at Somerville she knew few women scientists.

Jordan comes from Pinner, a north-western suburb of London, and was born in 1941, long before astronomy entered the school curriculum. She went to Harrow County Girls' grammar school, where high academic achievement was expected. Her own interest in the subject was stimulated by reading classic astronomy books found in the school and public libraries. By contrast, she says, it was not until years later that she found physics equally fascinating. The result was an undergraduate career at University College, London, where she read astronomy with maths and physics, one of a year with just three astronomers, and took a first. She stayed there to do her PhD with C. W. Allen, author of the classic reference work *Astrophysical Quantities*.

It was Allen, Jordan says, who offered her a choice of three PhD ideas. One, a statistical study of a particular class of star, sounded too dull.

Another was highly experimental, and in that era workshop staff were none too liberated about women messing with their lathes. The third is the foundation of her career. It involved looking at spectra of the atmosphere of the Sun in ultraviolet light.

These were new to science at the time because they cannot be observed from the surface of the Earth. But in the 1960s, US and UK rockets took up instruments to allow them to be observed and today, satellites allow extended observation of the ultraviolet sky.

Spectra are made up of lines at particular wavelengths, each characteristic of a particular atom or – more to the point in this case – a particular state in which an atom can exist. In these new spectra were many mysterious ones, and Allen said: 'If you can identify them you could make a name for yourself'. The resulting investigation took her into the world of practical physics as well as astronomy. Lines like those seen in the atmosphere of the Sun were also detected in readings from Zeta, an early machine for studying nuclear fusion at the Harwell laboratory in Oxfordshire. She thought that the lines in the spectra of the Sun's atmosphere were from highly ionised atoms of iron from which up to fourteen electrons had been stripped by the high energies there. Allen saw the Zeta spectra at an open day and realised that they were very similar to those of the Sun.

This was the beginning of a collaboration between Jordan and the spectroscopy group at Culham laboratory, to which fusion research was moved when it was declassified. Jordan says that Allen was a 'very good, honest and nice' man and a fine supervisor. In retrospect, she feels that when the paper describing the line identifications was published in *Nature* in 1965 she received less credit than she deserved, probably because she was younger than her collaborators at Culham. To this day, she is keen to push for more credit to go to young researchers.

This work, however, led to a paper which by 1984 was the most cited in the *Monthly Notices of the Royal Astronomical Society*, Europe's most important astronomy journal. It set out the relationships between different atomic species in the solar atmosphere and their temperature; a godsend, she says, for folk too lazy to do their own calculations.

After getting her PhD and spending most of 1966 at the Joint Institute for Laboratory Astrophysics in Colorado, Jordan went to Culham, where the UK budget for developing fusion power was paying for a rocket programme to examine the Sun's atmosphere. For three years she was funded by the UK Atomic Energy Authority, which she describes as 'a good time with good data'. In 1969 the spectroscopy group was transferred to the Science Research Council as the astrophysics research unit, and she remained there until 1976 when she moved to Oxford.

In retrospect, she says that in spite of her rarity as a female scientist, she has few complaints about SRC, whose annual reviews and promotions boards were probably fairer than the university promotions system.

Jordan arrived at Oxford with a specific type of lectureship (CUF), a college rather than university post, an apparently arcane distinction that meant a larger teaching load and less status. Her appointment was funded mainly by Somerville College to provide tutorial teaching, with a relatively light lecturing load for the university. In fact, such appointments required an excellent research record. (Before 1976 Jordan's only previous teaching experience was lecturing for the Workers' Educational Association and the University of Maryland. She taught US Air Force staff at Upper Heyford, an air base in Oxfordshire. The group there was fascinating, she says, because they were mostly from a background which could not afford higher education in the US, but could obtain it in the forces. They had also worked out that volunteering put them in a position to avoid the Vietnam war zone.)

Jordan says that she did not immediately understand the complicated interplay between the collegiate and university system at Oxford. At the time, there were five women's colleges and about twenty-three for men. University lectureships were associated with a college, so that if a position traditionally associated with a men's college became vacant and a woman was appointed, the men's college involved lost that post. This may be one reason why so few women obtained these positions. The distinction between the university and college appointments seemed to her artificial since in physics most of the CUF lecturers, including herself, ran active research groups.

She says: 'I thought I was good at physics but it emerged that there was more to it than that, and not being an Oxford graduate it took me a while to appreciate that.'

In 1990 she finally became a university lecturer. In the same year came her election to the Royal Society, Britain's highest scientific honour – the day after a letter from the university turning down her application for a readership, the next stage on the university career ladder.

In 1992 there was concern in the university at the small number of women being promoted to professor, and since it appeared that only current readers were being considered, and few women were readers, many female academics claimed that this was tantamount to discrimination against women. Jordan herself was not promoted in 1992, despite her Royal Society fellowship.

Taking account of the strength of feeling about the lack of women professors, the university's legislative body, Congregation, voted to concentrate the next promotion round on creating readerships, giving more women a chance to compete for professorships in the future. Jordan was duly appointed as a reader in 1994. In 1995 her professorship was still awaited.

The whole process has led to the constant irritation of having to explain outside the university why she is not a professor, an anomalous situation for someone serving on senior bodies such as the Science and Engineering Research Council, the Particle Physics and Astronomy Research Council (PPARC), and not least as president of the RAS.

The progress of the space age has led to remarkable advances in Jordan's area of research. Having started with the first crude spectra of the Sun's atmosphere, gathered from short flights of US rockets, her work now involves data from telescopes on satellites capable of obtaining similar data about a wide range of other stars, as well as far more detailed information about the Sun. To some extent, she says, the name of the game is still the same: finding out what heats up stellar atmospheres to perhaps ten million degrees while their surfaces are at only thousands of degrees.

The answer has to do with the transmission of energy via magnetic fields, whose strength can be measured by the appearance of spectral lines. In the case of the Sun, bright active areas where huge amounts of energy are transported are visible. For other stars, models with a lot of data exist for a few while for some types, only broad trends can be discerned with today's observations. The iron lines that started Jordan's research career have now been observed in about six other stars as well as the Sun.

It turns out that like the Earth, stars have magnetic fields whose strength is related to their internal rotation. With stars, a fast-rotating convection area means more magnetism and a hotter atmosphere.

Keeping a group of two research assistants and three to four research students busy on this work means getting money, mainly from PPARC, and getting access to data. This in turn means bidding for time on instruments in space on satellites like the International Ultraviolet Explorer: at the time of writing, she was about to get her first time on the Hubble Space Telescope.

This work makes Jordan a leading light of a research community numbering a few hundred around the world. The biggest group is at the Joint Institute for Laboratory Astrophysics in Boulder, Colorado, and others are in England, Ireland, Scotland and elsewhere.

Although life in Oxford has had its frustrations, Jordan is careful to praise Somerville for its work in encouraging women students and academics, and for its patient dealings with the university, and thought that the college's recent move to mixed status was 'premature'. The result in physics has been a dominantly male entry instead of the seven or eight, mostly very capable, women of old.

Despite her present distinction, Jordan adds that the science she does today resembles the activity she took an interest in as a Harrow schoolgirl of the 1950s. 'Then I was fascinated by the way astronomers used observations to understand what happens in stars. Now I can make my own observations, even though much remains to be understood.'

Publications include:

'Classification of iron VIII to XII and XIV lines in the solar EUV spectrum and their isoelectronic sequences from argon to nickel', 1966, with A. H. Gabriel and B. C. Fawcett, *Proceedings of the Physical Society*, 87, pp. 825–39.

'The Ionization equilibrium of elements between carbon and nickel', 1969, *Monthly Notices of the Royal Astronomical Society*, 142, pp. 501–21.

'Ultraviolet spectroscopy of cool stars', 1988, *Journal of the Optical Society America*, B, 5, pp. 2252–63.

'Modelling of solar coronal loops', 1992, *Memoirs of the Italian Astronomical Society*, 63, pp. 605–20.

'On magnetic fields, stellar coronae and dynamo action in late-type dwarfs', 1993, with B. Montesinos, *Monthly Notices of the Royal Astronomical Society*, 264, pp. 900–18.

(Martin Ince, © Times Higher Education Supplement)

Catharine MacKinnon, born 1946, is professor of law at the University of Michigan Law School. She is perhaps best known for her campaign, with feminist Andrea Dworkin, for laws giving women the right to sue if they can prove pornography has harmed them.

Photograph © The Guardian/David Sillitoe

It is difficult to imagine Catharine MacKinnon achieving the kind of success in British life that she has across the Atlantic, Britain being so much less litigious a country, with a far slighter regard for individual rights, particularly those of women.

In America, MacKinnon is *the* anti-pornography advocate, a tenured professor at the University of Michigan Law School and darling of the campus lecture circuit. Students flock to hear her radical feminist ideas, her advocacy of legal sanctions against pornographers whose works produce sexual abuse and her forceful language.

How about this for the first paragraph of one of her books, *Only Words*: 'You grow up with your father holding you down and covering your mouth so another man can make a horrible searing pain between your legs. When you are older, your husband ties you to the bed and drips hot wax on your nipples and brings in other men to watch and makes you smile through it'.

As if that were not enough, she adds: 'Your doctor will not give you drugs he has addicted you to unless you suck his penis'. Get the message? Pornography is not just words and pictures. Acts like these are what it takes to make pornography and sooner or later men want to live out, through violent sexual activity, the pornography they have consumed. Pornography, she says, pointing out that the opening description of *Only Words* carries the footnote 'two published cases and years of research', is a practice of the power of men over women 'expressed through unequal sex' and effectively sanctioned through state power.

[150]

None of this – neither the politics nor the language – endears Professor MacKinnon to the chattering classes. In fact, she is one of the few people whom many intellectuals of the left and right, wedded as they are to their interpretation of the role of the Constitution's First Amendment in American life, agree is dangerous. Not surprisingly, some women are rather more enthusiastic. She inspires the same sort of strong feelings as does someone like Salman Rushdie. You either love her ideas or you hate them.

'It is her view that pornography is so dangerous that we ought to be prepared to sacrifice principles we would not comprehend in other situations', says Professor Robert O'Neill, who runs the Thomas Jefferson Centre for the Protection of Free Expression at the University of Virginia. 'That seems to me a very dangerous notion in a society which has protected free expression consistently for 200 years.'

Reviews of her latest book, *Only Words*, have been almost uniformly hostile. 'Much of it is one long scream about sex and men', said a reviewer in US News and World Report. 'This professor. . . . is a leader of the most radical assault on free speech in American history', said conservative columnist George Will in *The Washington Post*. Carlin Romano, in his review in the magazine *The Nation*, even proposed a hypothetical rape of MacKinnon – to make his point that there is a difference between the verbal description of rape and the actual physical act; that those who depict rape and those who violate women are not equally guilty. This review angered MacKinnon, who has never argued that pornographers and rapists do the same thing.

Only Words is three lectures which MacKinnon gave as the Christian Gauss lectures in criticism at Princeton, a prestigious and well-known lecture series. Asked how she would respond to critics of the book, she says: 'Critics should read it. Then they might think for themselves about what it says.'

Catharine MacKinnon has a long history of holding up two fingers to the establishment. Although she is a child of relative economic privilege, the daughter of George E. MacKinnon, a judge and adviser to Eisenhower's and Nixon's presidential campaigns, she has taken up legal cudgels on behalf of victims of inequality. These include pornography's female subjects, most famously Linda 'Lovelace', who featured in the porn movie *Deep Throat* and later said she was coerced into participating; more recently, the Muslim and Croat women raped by Serb soldiers in Bosnia.

During the 1960s MacKinnon worked with the Black Panthers and opposed the Vietnam war, in the 1980s she came to oppose pornography after inviting the internationally known radical feminist author, Andrea Dworkin, to teach a class with her at the University of Minnesota School of Law, where she was an assistant professor. A famous partnership ensued.

The two women concluded that pornography was not an example of freedom of expression because women are silenced. Second, they said that because pornography harms women it does not extend civil liberties. Rather, it violates civil rights. Together they drafted ordinances in Minneapolis and Indianapolis – the first such proposals in law anywhere – that allowed a woman to sue if she could prove that pornography had harmed her. (Pornography is defined as 'graphic sexually explicit subordination of women through pictures and/or words'.) Mitigating circumstances such as pleas for artistic merit are not allowed.

MacKinnon says that the ordinances drew a clear line between equal rights and freedom of expression. 'Acts in connection with pornography that violate this law – coercion into pornography, forcing pornography onto a person, defamation through pornography, assault caused by specific pornography, trafficking in pornography as sexually explicit sex-based subordination – are not protected expression,' she says.

This legal claim was condemned by the American Civil Liberties Union for promoting censorship and by a section of the women's movement (which MacKinnon describes as 'a tiny élite academic group'), for reinforcing stereotypes of dominated women. No court has yet accepted the ordinances and they were declared unconstitutional in 1985, although this legal result is, MacKinnon points out, not final.

'It is the effectiveness of this law in stopping the harm of pornography to women and children – without which the industry and the materials cannot exist – that gives rise to the virulent and vicious opposition to it. One strategy of this opposition is to focus on the individuals who have proposed this remedy, rather than on the social reality that has given rise to the need for it,' she says.

Her argument had more success in Canada where the Supreme Court reinterpreted its obscenity law – which defines obscenity as sexually explicit material that involves violence or degradation – as a sex equality provision. In a recent case, when Canada's obscenity laws were tested against the country's sexual equality provisions, the damage done to women and sexual equality was found more important than the risk to free speech.

In America she made her mark in legal history when she pioneered the concept of sexual harassment as a form of sex discrimination, which included the notion of a hostile environment in the workplace. This was embraced by the Supreme Court in 1986.

Such unconventional work – MacKinnon says it is 'clear that the substance of my views makes some people uncomfortable' – meant that she had difficulty in achieving tenure or even making a living. For years, after acquiring a first degree from Smith College and graduating from Yale Law School, where she also gained her Ph.D., she moved from one university law school to another until she was granted a tenured position by Michigan in 1990. MacKinnon was then in her forties, an advanced age for a law professor to be given tenure.

She did not help herself by eschewing the conventional route to a tenured job. Aspiring academics in law schools have to write a substantial 'tenure article', a piece of work which gets them taken seriously and leads to tenure in two or three years. After that, law professors can go off and do radical work, but MacKinnon did the radical work first.

There is no doubt that she is extraordinarily bright – as well, for some, as extraordinarily difficult. 'She has an extremely aggressive confrontational style,' says Stanley Katz, president of the American Council of Learned Societies. 'It's always in your face.'

In addition, she does not write or speak in a conventional scholarly mode. Her books, although footnoted, are written in a direct style which, at first reading, appears almost sensationalist compared with the theoretical convolutions of much academic writing. MacKinnon herself, objecting to descriptions of her style as 'personal or emotional', says 'It is an uncompromised, unapologetic woman's voice telling you about reality'. She adds that her analysis is 'precisely predicated on a massive amount of data. It is only because the truth of what is done to women is so pervasively covered up that it looks stunning when anyone simply describes it in public.'

A group of writers and academics called Feminists for Free Expression take issue with MacKinnon's ideas on pornography and censorship. One of their members is Nadine Strossen, a law professor and president of the American Civil Liberties Union. She was invited to speak at a conference of women judges a few years ago, but found her invitation withdrawn. Why? She believes it was because MacKinnon had also been invited to speak, and that the conference organisers did not want to risk offending her.

MacKinnon queries Strossen's claim, saying there is absolutely no evidence that the withdrawal of Strossen's invitation had anything to do with MacKinnon's own appearance. 'She (Strossen) has no god-given right to speak,' she says.

There is little doubt that MacKinnon is a bigger draw than Strossen. People – even judges – love to hear her. She is glamorous, beautifully dressed, extremely forthright and clever. Her rocky relationship with the media is unsurprising, given her views and visibility.

She dislikes prying questions from interviewers, particularly about her personal life. And she makes it quite clear she does not care for profiles – she says not because she has experienced a number of hostile articles but because 'it is trivialising to an analysis of women's status to personalise it to any one individual'. What matters are the issues, she says. Phrases which would 'further the demonization of me' are rejected, personal questions are off-limits.

When I asked her how she had become involved in the women's movement and in arguing cases brought by women in the courts, her reply reconfigured the question to answer it as follows. 'The women's movement began throughout the US in around 1969–70, pursuing the lived experience that women are second-class citizens in public life and civil society. The law, integral to a hierarchical social order and maintaining it forcibly, has resisted taking women's needs and injuries into account. The theory and practice of feminist jurisprudence, developed by the legal arm of the women's movement, has aimed to change this since its beginning.'

Married once, Catharine MacKinnon is no longer married. She has no children and beyond these bare facts does not wish to comment.

Today she is working on a legal casebook, to be called *Sex Equality*. This is the product of fifteen years of teaching and compiling edited materials on US law in a comparative, international and social context, according to MacKinnon. She is publishing a new collection, *Women's Lives, Men's Laws*, which is made up of previously unpublished or uncollected writings and speeches and legal briefs from 1980 to 1995. And she is also producing, with Andrea Dworkin, an edited version of the civil rights hearings against pornography, in which women and men speak in public about what pornography has done to them. It is being called *In Harm's Way: The Pornography Civil Rights Hearings*.

When she is not writing and giving speeches she is working on lawsuits, such as the one on behalf of the raped women of Bosnia-Hercegovina, which she recently won in the Court of Appeals. She, with the National Organisation for Women as local counsel, is suing

Radovan Karadzic, the head Bosnian Serb, for genocidal rape, war crimes and torture.

Based on victim accounts, MacKinnon argued, in an article in the American magazine *Ms*, that men in the former Yugoslavia had been saturated with pornography and that the availability of pornographic materials contributed to the wave of sexual atrocities unleashed in the war. She quoted survivors describing how the rapes of Bosnian Muslim and Croatian women by Serb soldiers were filmed and shown on Serbian television as war propaganda and ended by querying the effect on a survivor 'when the films of her rape are sold as pornography – emblem of democracy and liberation in post-Communist Eastern Europe and increasingly protected as speech worldwide.'

But this material, she says, plays no role in the lawsuit against Karadzic. In what she describes as 'an exceptionally ill-founded decision', a district judge dismissed the action for lack of subject-matter jurisdiction. Now that her appeal has been won, she is 'looking forward to going to trial against Karadzic, a genocidal war criminal, for the sex-and-ethnic-based rape of Bosnian Muslim and Croat women I represent', she says.

Like many of MacKinnon's battles it looks like a tough fight ahead. But it may be a mistake to underestimate the strength of her influence on the relationship between the sexes, not only in America – but, increasingly, as she herself argues, world-wide. 'I pioneered the whole field of feminist jurisprudence – seeing violence against women as an issue of sex equality, seeing women's rights as human rights,' she says. 'That is now a world-wide phenomenon' – and it is changing people's lives.

Publications include:

Sexual Harassment of Working Women: A Case of Sex Discrimination, 1979, Yale University Press.

Feminism Unmodified: Discourses on Life and Law, 1987, Harvard University Press.

Toward a Feminist Theory of the State, 1989, Harvard University Press.

Pornography and Civil Rights: A New Day for Women's Equality, 1988, with Andrea Dworkin, Organising Against Pornography.

Only Words, 1993, Harvard University Press.

(© Lucy Hodges)

Emily Martin, born 1944, is professor of anthropology at Princeton University. She is one of a small band of anthropologists who have turned their attention from foreign fieldwork to cultural research back home, in her case in the USA.

Photograph © Phyllis Berger

Why, all of a sudden, is 'the body' such a hot topic in academic circles? Emily Martin suspects that it's far more than a matter of intellectual fashion. Academic attention becomes focused on phenomena precisely when they are on the way out, the French anthropologist Claude Lévi-Strauss once claimed, and Martin agrees. We are seeing 'the end of one kind of body and the beginning of another kind of body,' she argues. 'We are undergoing fundamental changes in how our bodies are organised and experienced.'

Martin's latest book, *Flexible Bodies*, tracks 'immunity in American culture from the days of polio to the age of AIDS' and consolidates her reputation as one of America's most original social anthropologists. It is excellent, groundbreaking work, says Marilyn Strathern, professor of social anthropology at the University of Cambridge. It explores 'the way ideas breed, the way they spread through a culture like forest fires'. Focusing on cultural ideas about the immune system, Martin's most recent work establishes her as 'a pioneer in the anthropology of science', says Henrietta Moore, reader in social anthropology at the London School of Economics.

That's even more pioneering than it sounds, for what Martin means by science is not just the life and times of men in white coats. To understand what 'the immune system' means today, she interviewed immunologists and worked alongside them in their laboratories, accompanied clinicians on their ward rounds and worked as a 'buddy' to people dying of AIDS. She talked to 'ordinary' people about their immune systems, and asked them what they thought of scientific images

[156]

– electron micrograph pictures of killer T-cells and macrophages. She even put on mountaineering gear and jumped off 40-foot poles – as required by an Outward-Bound-type corporate training scheme – for in contemporary managerial philosophies she finds immune system metaphors. Everywhere, talk is of the need to be 'flexible'; our minds, our bodies, our immune systems must be adaptive, open to change, primed for competition in an unpredictable world.

'When I described my methodology – just the different sites that I was working in – to one of my friends who works in the social studies of science, she said, "What's the matter with you, don't you know how to stay put?" – meaning that I should go into the lab and stay there. There I would find out all I needed to know about science.' But Martin was not convinced. 'By not staying in the lab I wanted to broaden the definition of what science is, and to broaden the range of factors that might be thought to bear on what is done in scientific work.'

Even those sociologists of science who break down the walls between the laboratory and society focus exclusively on the movements of objects and concepts out of the laboratory and their impact on the rest of society, Martin argues. In such theorising, 'the only things that enter the laboratory come from other laboratories or other sectors of the scientific world. There is nothing cycling back into the laboratory from the street or from popular magazines or movies, certainly not from non-experts in any way, shape or form. In contrast, I am trying to show ways in which the flow of things out is accompanied by a flow of things back in.'

She began to try to chart this phenomenon ten years ago, setting aside her anthropological specialism in China to study her own culture. 'There was a lot of puzzlement about why someone should change from a foreign area to working on the US,' Martin says. 'I always wanted to study the US, I don't know why, it just always seemed to me fascinating.' Working in Taiwan and then China, Martin was persistently questioned about life in the United States. One of the things Chinese people asked over and over was why we put our aged parents in institutions, 'which was for them horrifying behaviour fit only for dogs. I realised I really couldn't give good answers. I didn't really know enough about what made my culture tick to explain.'

It was when Martin became pregnant with her first child that she hit on a way of doing fieldwork 'on something that I was actually experiencing in my own home culture'. The result was an innovative exploration of cultural ideas about menstruation, pregnancy and menopause published as *The Woman in the Body*. Meanwhile, other anthropologists in the US – notably Paul Rabinow and Rayna Rapp – had also switched from foreign fieldwork to cultural research in the US. 'All of a sudden there was company – people you could talk to about the particular problems of doing fieldwork here, in one's own culture.'

One of the worst problems, Martin says, is how to pick a problem. 'All the traditional questions don't really apply; at least, it's not clear how they apply. And the units you might choose to study – communities or occupational groups – just aren't enough to get at the sort of things that are going on.' Another problem is how to behave as an anthropologist on your home ground. 'Usually as an anthropological fieldworker you are supposed to be a co-participant/observer. In an agricultural society, it would have been considered perfectly acceptable to go and participate in the planting or harvesting of the crop while chatting with people or listening to their conversation. But there were no models for how to study illnesses that I don't have any direct experience of, or how to translate the experience of working as an AIDS volunteer into something that would be acceptable as anthropology – most medical anthropology doesn't involve any actual hands-on grappling with ill people.'

As she worked on *Flexible Bodies*, Martin puzzled over how to write about her experiences. 'The book kept crossing over into other genres. I didn't want it to be a memoir, I didn't want it to be about me, but somehow I wanted to have the things I had learned through doing that kind of work come out. It was a struggle.'

The result is a compelling read. *Flexible Bodies* documents, in a lively and personal way, the eerie links between the business philosophy of 'flexible accumulation' – now said to be the hallmark of capitalism in the 1990s – and the way Americans in the late twentieth century think about their bodies. Martin illustrates the ways in which contemporary American culture places a premium on agile responsiveness – on adroit, supple, nimble, flexible, innovative bodies poised to meet any conceivable challenge. Just as corporations seek to teach workers to be open to unexpected challenges and risk-taking, so responsible citizens train their bodies, tone their muscles, stretch their physiques; now they even seek to 'educate' and 'nourish' their immune systems through diet, exercise and avoidance of 'stress'. No wonder everyone from journalists and biomedical researchers to aerobics teachers and acupuncturists all talk about the 'immune system' these days.

But what exactly are these connections between political, social and economic change and our ideas about ourselves? 'My personal feeling is that what we need is to get more complex imagery around the question of causality, rather than looking for things that are essentially causal arrows. There are different kinds of images that might be more fruitful for working with what is happening today. For instance, there's the image of an archipelago. Deep down at the bottom of the sea you would have everything that is, and poking up through the sea you have islands – who knows how they come up or when they come up or why they come up? The analogy to my work would be that I hop around from island to island, from science lab to corporate training grounds to neighbourhoods, and I see things that are similar; yet the connection between one island and another is not obvious, it's discontinuous. Such an image allows you to think about things being part of the same whole setting but not mechanically linked. I think we need to explore other models of causality than ones which come straight out of Marxism or structuralism because the phenomena today are not mechanical in their nature.'

Martin's recent work has a darker side: it charts the emergence of a new vocabulary with which to justify social inequalities. Martin sees disturbing parallels between the cultural representations of people who fall by the way in the world of work – through unemployment, 'deskilling' or lack of training – and those who fall ill as a result of 'inferior' immune responses, leading to AIDS, cancer or a host of other diseases. She fears the rise of a new form of social Darwinism, in line with contemporary business practices that put a premium on 'total quality management'.

'This is what I am hoping to work more on now. I have a sense that the comfortable terms of analysis of social hierarchy that we're used to, based on class, race and gender, have been picked up and redeployed by corporate image makers in ways that have changed the whole setting in which we are attempting to understand social hierarchy.'

For example, she says, the stress on 'multiculturalism' or 'diversity' may mean many different things in many different contexts. 'But in the corporate realm in the US these concepts are being used in very particular ways to change the make-up of the workforce at the top, especially in managerial realms. The desirable management team is no longer all white and male, quite the reverse. For companies that are trying to maintain their place in intense global competition, the desirable management team is heterogeneous by ethnicity or race and gender and age. The implications of that are not clear, and some people would say, it's just windowdressing. But it could be that the nature of the desirable corporate organisation really is changing, connected to the fact that they are all multinational corporations now, operating in many different parts of the world. Their fate as a corporation depends on their ability to operate smoothly and effectively and knowledgeably in relation to culture and language – all these wonderful anthropological concepts are now part of the corporate dictionary, for very concrete material reasons. I want to understand more about how the whole landscape, in which social hierarchy based on race, class and gender exists, has been shifting.'

Martin perceives two recent developments that bear on these issues. 'One is the increasing reliance on the biological features of a person to determine their worth as epitomised by genetic descriptions of people. People get to be thought of as having "good" genes and "bad" genes, as if someone can be reduced to these fundamental biological particles that they are born with and can do nothing about. It is very deterministic, which is bothersome for obvious reasons.'

'But the other trend almost goes in the opposite direction, and that is this incredible emphasis in the US on training and education and the ability of a person to change and grow. There is continuous talk, in schools and universities and in government and corporations, about the importance of education and training. Similarly, the emphasis of New Age and other kinds of alternative health movements is also on how you can train yourself to become a "higher order" being. This all seems to me to be highly problematic, partly because the resources are not at all freely available. It is an extension of the old story that if you just try hard enough you will succeed, but now you must try hard in all these other layers of existence from the physical make-up of the body, the mind and the immune system, to whether or not you get sick. I want to know more about how people can be categorised by the kinds of training they're investing in. It might go along with or counteract this other more biological determinist trend. We really have to rethink the way we are understanding these processes of social differentiation, to have even a prayer of keeping up with what's going on.'

On a more positive note, Martin discerns intriguing corridors opening up between traditional and alternative health treatments in the US. 'The discourse of the immune system is readily useable by acupuncturists and homeopaths and massage therapists, enabling ordinary folks trying to get help to move from realm to realm – from Western scientific doctor to alternative therapists and have a kind of common understanding of what the goal of treatment is. This is very revolutionary and I don't know what the effect will be. It could be that what counts as knowledge about the body is loosening, and that it is loosening more in the medical profession. The whole terrain of illness treatment could change, allowing people to handle things that are plaguing them without as many strict institutional barriers and with more openness to the possibility of help in a wider range of contexts.'

Emily Martin is not only an original and dynamic anthropologist, her colleagues say, she is also an awfully nice person, and her sensitivity to other people undoubtedly has its roots in an unusual childhood. Born in Alabama, she grew up on the East Coast in Pennsylvania and spent most summers with her paternal grandparents, who were Mennonite farmers living in a traditional community.

Her maternal grandparents were equally intriguing. Her grandfather was the coach to Auburn, a famous American football team, while her grandmother worked as a photographer's assistant in Birmingham, Alabama, in the days when women didn't do that kind of thing. She got her own television show in the 1950s, and for the rest of her life was the hostess of a cooking show called 'The Magic Kitchen'.

Emily Martin's immediate family was less 'interesting' and more problematic. Her brother died of polio at the age of two when Emily was seven; three years later, her sister was born. Unusually in the US, Emily was sent off to boarding-school, which proved something of a relief. 'I think anthropology appealed to me because it allowed me to be half in, half out. You're there but you're not quite there, you always have an escape and you have a licence to observe – you're supposed to be observant and figure things out. In my family the dynamics were so complex and frightening and disturbing, I adopted the stance of being on the edge of a group and constantly trying to figure out what it was doing. I'm sure was what made me leap at anthropology when I first became aware there was such a thing.'

At the University of Michigan she studied Japanese music in its ethnomusicology unit, learning 'the theory behind what makes the music move, what makes it beautiful – you experience, noise becoming music. It was quite an amazing experience, and that was what I was looking for in anthropology.'

She set off for Cornell intent on studying Japan, but when she got there the Japan specialist was on leave, and she was lured away to study China instead. She did a great deal of fieldwork in Taiwan, and wrote scores of articles and three books on China before her 'switch' to American culture.

The mother of two daughters, aged 21 and 13, Martin is married to a biophysicist who teaches at Johns Hopkins. Her recent move to Princeton, after twenty years at Hopkins, gives her a change of scene and an opportunity 'to teach at an institution that puts a high priority on undergraduate teaching'. Princeton also produced some of the pioneers of modern personnel management; 'I had the idea it would be fun to look into the history of some of these management ideas.'

In the best possible way, Martin is irrepressible, blessed with an openness and enthusiasm all too rare in academia. Where did she get her guts and drive? 'If I had to say who influenced me most, it would be my grandmother and her TV show. I got this picture of this woman who was just fantastically competent doing these amazing things; I'm sure it was my grandmother who was the most important influence on me, and her name was Emily Martin.'

Publications include:

The Cult of the Dead in a Chinese Village, 1973, reprinted 1988, Stanford University Press.

Chinese Ritual and Politics, 1981, Cambridge University Press.

(Ed.) *The Anthropology of Taiwanese Society*, 1981, with Hill Gates, Stanford University Press.

The Woman in the Body: A Cultural Analysis of Reproduction, 1987, Beacon Press.

'The egg and the sperm: how science has constructed a romance based on stereotypical male-female roles', 1991, *Signs: Journal of Women in Culture and Society*, 16, 3, pp. 485–501.

Flexible Bodies: Tracking Immunity in American Culture from the Days of Polio to the age of AIDS, 1994, Beacon Press.

(© Gail Vines)

Mary Midgley, born 1919, is a moral philosopher who for twenty years was lecturer in philosophy at the University of Newcastle. Author of nine books, she has a particular interest in the nature/nurture debate and the relationship between religion and science.

There's a paragraph in Mary Midgley's latest book, *The Ethical Primate*, that seems to contain an important clue to her philosophical approach. 'If we consider the development of the human baby – something which celibate philosophers have often been unwilling to do,' it begins, towards the end of a discussion on freedom and the growth of consciousness.

How heartfelt is this parenthetic remark about child-free philosophers? As it happens, I am meeting Mrs Midgley only a few days after she has addressed a conference in Manchester on the nature of freedom. There, her subject was freedom and families: in her words, 'the way the great Enlightenment propaganda for freedom had actually left out the rest of the family. The voter had to be free, but nobody else'. From there she goes on – 'though I don't want to be beastly about the mighty dead' – to talk about the 'self-deception and moral cowardice' of Rousseau; Kant's struggles with poverty and reluctance to go in for the 'disturbance' of marriage; and the hostile Victorian reaction to John Stuart Mill's views on the suffrage of women. (Mill is, she notes, one of the few non-celibate philosophers of the past: other 'exceptions' are Aristotle, Hegel, and Berkeley.)

'It is a great deformity in this wonderful edifice of freedom which the Enlightenment built up . . . this unwillingness to look at one side of it,' she says. 'The way that learning has grown up still has that twist. It isn't really that I don't like men – I do – but there's a way of arguing that is so different. I can't help thinking, particularly in philosophy, that [women's] style of talking is different.'

Although she says she does not 'keep on about it normally', this view of the differences between men's and women's approaches to philosophy colours the recollections of her early life. Born in 1919, she went to Oxford in 1938, where she read Greats at Somerville. 'I started philosophy in 1940,' she says, 'and there was no undergraduate doing it then who did not very seriously want to do it. Nobody was there because they wanted to show off, or because they were good at winning arguments.' In other words, the 'clever young men' were all away at the war, and a generation of women that included Iris Murdoch (her exact contemporary), Elizabeth Anscombe, and Philippa Foot could flourish.

Graduating during the war, even with the first that she gained, meant there was no question that the young Mary Scrutton, as she then was, would stay on for a further degree. Instead there was work in the Civil Service and as a schoolteacher – although she ended the war in a quasi-academic role, as secretary to the classical scholar Gilbert Murray, translator and populariser of Greek tragedy, especially Euripides, and League of Nations activist. ('He was finishing his autobiography and was sorting out his letters . . . from people concerned with his plays, and politicians of all kinds.')

After this, she returned to Somerville and taught there while starting a doctoral thesis on Plotinus: 'If I'd known before I started what an enormous subject that was, I probably would have done something else,' she says now. But she did meet a fellow philosophy postgraduate, Geoffrey Midgley: 'He was of that very interesting generation [at Oxford in the late 40s] when all the war people came back. It was a very lively philosophical life, a great mixture of the oncoming logical positivists and the people who wouldn't have that at any price.' (Geoffrey himself recalls that 'I don't know that I cared for either side at the time.' Dubious about logical positivism, he also 'found the unctuous moralising of the moralists depressing'.)

Somerville was followed by a year and a term spent lecturing at Reading, after which – her doctoral thesis on Plotinus abandoned – she and Geoffrey, now married, headed north to Newcastle University. He taught there for nearly forty years, retiring in 1986, just as the philosophy department that he had chaired was heading towards extinction – a politically charged episode that still rankles with them. The Midgleys still live in the Newcastle area, though. They occupy the extended ground floor of a comfortable stone house in Jesmond and let out the first floor; in earlier years, with both younger and older generations in residence, the whole house was theirs. These days, Mary writes philosophy in a study that doubles as a dining room, while in another room Geoffrey may be found puzzling over computer programs.

Mary Midgley began her life in Newcastle by taking time away from academia to have children – the Midgleys have three sons – and this, too, she sees as an advantage. While at home, she reviewed books for such outlets as the *New Statesman* – novels, children's books, and 'what you might call feminism' – but otherwise, she says, 'I read what I wanted to read, and what I wanted to read suddenly was animal behaviour. I picked up Konrad Lorenz [the Austrian zoologist who identified the nearly irreversible learning process of "imprinting" in the young of certain creatures, and who argued that aggressive impulses are in some way innate] and was hooked. From that I went on to try to get the hang of evolution.' (Midgley's latest book is dedicated to Jane Goodall, whose pioneering studies of primate behaviour also made a deep impression on her.)

Of course, she adds, as a mother she could observe 'plenty of animal behaviour on the hearthrug' and develop her own views on the nature-nurture debate: 'The point about innate tendencies really struck me when I considered the way children do things without anybody having to put them in their heads. And when I had two and then three children, I was greatly struck by the differences between them, too.'

Such experience makes her think she was 'jolly lucky' not to have completed her doctoral thesis: 'A thesis has to be defended, so you get terribly obsessed with qualifying things and not saying more than you can defend. That would be all right if after the PhD there were a sort of conversion course.' (Later in our conversation she quotes C. S. Lewis on how 'the learned world' has been 'almost entirely cured of worrying about whether something is true or not' – again, it seems, a dig at conventional philosophical practice.)

At home with her sons, then, rather than 'running up against the regular crew of philosophy', as she puts it, she began to combine her reading in animal behaviour and evolution with the philosophy she had learned earlier. And when Newcastle offered her part-time work, at the point when her eldest was twelve, 'it began to come together.'

What came together was the group of ideas that formed her first book, *Beast and Man*. She had resumed writing serious philosophical articles in the early seventies, and one of them, 'The Concept of Beastliness' led to an invitation from Cornell to talk to an interdisciplinary programme there – and thence to a book commission from Cornell University Press. *Beast and Man* had 'moderate success', she says, 'because, I think, everybody was pig-sick of the sociobiology debate. There was this terribly polarised dispute, and anybody who said there's some truth on both sides was welcomed.'

It was a dispute largely between scientists and social scientists, the former committed to the notion that human behaviour may be influenced by genes, the latter, fearing eugenics and genetic determinism, resisting the notion in favour of environmental factors.

Written, in her words, 'in ordinary English because it is meant to be about ordinary life', *Beast and Man* was an argument directed at both opposing camps. On the one side, it argued against the sociobiology propagandists who explained human nature in the same terms as animal behaviour; on the other it refused to accept that arguments about human ethics have nothing to learn from the study of evolution and animal interaction: 'We are creatures of a definite species on this planet and this shapes our values'.

Since publishing that first book – the first substantial contribution to the sociobiology debate by a philosopher – only a year before her fiftieth birthday, Midgley has been comparatively prolific. She took early retirement from Newcastle in 1980, since when eight more books have appeared under her name.

Wisdom, Information and Wonder examines the phenomenon of academic specialism, whereby various 'tribes' – biologists, physicists, sociologists, etc. – operate blindly within their own conceptual frameworks. Philosophy, she argues, can play a role in bringing the tribes together.

The latest book is *The Ethical Primate*. 'After writing *Beast and Man*, I felt there was serious business left over on two fronts – wickedness and the nature of freedom,' she explains. One of the two fronts was covered in her generally well-received 1984 'philosophical essay', *Wickedness*. The other is dealt with in the new book, in which she continues her arguments against the reductionism of various philosophers and scientists while seeking to reconcile free will with the apparently deterministic ideas of evolution.

As in her earlier books, Darwin again looms large in *The Ethical Primate*. This time, it is his contention, in *The Descent of Man*, that conscience can be understood to have developed within the parameters of evolution 'without anything being somehow imported from elsewhere', in Midgley's words, that she finds most telling. It is, she concedes, 'terribly hard for people to take in. To say that conflict (of motives) should actually be a great advantage, that it's the condition of everything we value – I know it's been said before, and I may not be saying it newly enough, but I'm trying to. If one asks why is morality there, it seems to me it has to be because our motives are not naturally harmonised, but unlike the animals we are capable of looking back and forth and seeing that they have to be harmonised.'

Her target is the common assumption that morality is an optional extra, 'something added' – an assumption to which she objects: 'You couldn't have even the simplest, crudest and most beastly human life without some sort of structure of priorities.' And thus, as she puts it in *The Ethical Primate*, 'human freedom centres on being a creature able, in some degree, to act as a whole in dealing with its conflicting desires.'

Alongside this is the central Midgley theme, what she calls (again to quote *The Ethical Primate*) 'the mistakenness of trying to find a single "fundamental" form of explanation for very complex matters such as human activity.' In other words, sociobiology, neo-Darwinism or any other 'reductive enterprise' can never be the answer to everything.

Much of Midgley's work has patrolled that territory where science and philosophy meet uneasily. 'I've never, you'll note, had any proper science training,' she concedes. 'But it's been a great help to talk at conferences with the kind of person you meet there.' Former Newcastle colleagues such as biologist Ursula Philipp and paleontologist Alec Panchen have been helpful, too. And she continues to try to keep up with science; lately, as well as re-reading Scott ('working in the local Oxfam shop pricing books, I got a lovely big edition') and William James's *Varieties of Religious Experience*, she just finished the neurobiologist Gerald Edelman's book *Bright Air, Brilliant Fire* – 'Which I rather like. I don't say he's got it all right, but he's got much more idea of what he's writing about than most people who talk about consciousness.'

She is saddened, though, by most British scientists' lack of interest in philosophy. 'On the continent, scientists know that they are one province on a map. It's an awful shame that (British scientists) are educated in such a way that they don't know that. You can often tell if an apparently ordinary English or American scientist has had a European education, because right away they put things in context.'

Midgley's sceptical approach to some scientists' recent claims to 'theories of everything', given a good working over in her 1992 book *Science as Salvation*, may suggest that she has an axe to grind on behalf of a belief in God. Those hostile to what they see as religion's claims, such as the Oxford chemist Peter Atkins, have attacked her 'false interpreta-tion' of science's progress. But Midgley herself says she finds religion 'puzzling', and is 'unclear (what to make of it) . . . I like a lot of Christianity, but I can't do with the personal relation. I do not see a person out there.'

The Midgleys' eldest son David, meanwhile, is a Buddhist: 'He came to it after great difficulties and confusions, sorting himself out through it. I can't see anything wrong with that.' (He is thanked in the preface to *Wickedness* for his support while 'ploughing a neighbouring philosophical furrow'.) Beliefs have certainly changed through her family's generation: her father was a vicar, but his father, a High Court judge, was a militant atheist.

While in no way reaching the heights reached by another Oxford-phi-losophy-educated Mary, namely Baroness Warnock – 'I could not do the job that she did chairing the committee of inquiry into human fertil-isation and embryology' – Midgley has not shrunk from public duty. She chaired an RSPCA committee on animal experimentation, but admits that it was hard work 'trying to get the two wings, the moder-ates and the extremists, together'.

And after the Newcastle philosophy department was closed, she and her husband helped form the Applied Philosophy Trust, which has done research on business ethics; locally, they are at the centre of APIS (Applied Philosophy Ideas Section), a discussion group of 'people in Newcastle interested in general topics'.

Applied philosophy, though, is 'a funny sort of name,' she observes. 'It's as if there was some pure philosophy which one then went and applied. But all the great philosophy has come out of particular problems.'

'There's something a bit distorting in the syllabus about the way we tend to go for the biggest and most abstract works. In themselves they're pretty good, like the *Critique of Pure Reason*. But Kant also wrote a lot of political stuff. He didn't just write that on Thursdays for amusement – it's where his thought was coming from. The notion that it isn't really philosophy unless it's totally pure and abstract is wrong.'

Publications include:

Beast and Man: The Roots of Human Nature, 1978, Cornell University Press.
Animals and Why They Matter, 1983, Penguin.
Women's Choices; Philosophical Problems Facing Feminism, 1983, with Judith Hughes, Weidenfeld and Nicolson.

Wickedness; A Philosophical Essay, 1984, Routledge.
Evolution as a Religion; Strange Hopes and Stranger Fears, 1985, Methuen.
Wisdom, Information and Wonder; What is Knowledge For?, 1989, Routledge.
Can't We Make Moral Judgements?, 1991, Bristol Classical Press.
Science as Salvation; A Modern Myth and Its Meaning, 1992, Routledge.
The Ethical Primate; Humans, Freedom and Morality, 1994, Routledge.

(© John Davies)

Photograph © Jerry Bauer

Born in 1947, American philosopher **Martha Nussbaum**'s work has ranged from Hellenistic ethics through the classics of English literature to development economics. Consumed with the question of how we should live our lives, one of the low points in her own trajectory was failure to win tenure at Harvard in the early 1980s.

As a child Martha Nussbaum spent solitary hours reading to herself, reading to her dolls and acting out stories. Until the age of nine she lived in American upper-middle-class opulence in an estate owned by the Earl of Surrey and translated to suburban Philadelphia brick by brick.

'As a little child I had the complete run of all the forests and fields in this really quite romantic English-looking place, so I think my love of story-telling was very much increased by this,' she explains. 'I would drag my dolls around and find deserted corners of some little out-buildings where there were strange statues that had been stored for the winter and just hole up there and read books for hours.' Perfect training for an intellectual.

Today, with seven books and various prizes behind her, Nussbaum is still reading avidly. But her life is in flux. Having completed eleven years as a professor of philosophy, classics and comparative literature at the Ivy League Brown University in Rhode Island, on the East coast, she is moving West, – to take up an appointment as professor of law and ethics at the University of Chicago. It will be a big jump for her, away from the East where she was born, grew up and flourished to a new frontier, away from a cosy niche in classics and philosophy to a more bracing and public role in the fearsomely intellectual law department at the University of Chicago. She will find the change invigorating, and Chicago is likely to appreciate her.

Martha Nussbaum has acquired a formidable reputation as an American philosopher who is as at ease with literary criticism as with Hellenistic ethics, who has more recently ventured into the world of development economics with Harvard economist, Amartya Sen, and who is consumed with the practical, if high-minded, notion of how we should live our lives. Her work is immensely learned, as well as provocative and original. It says a lot about America that one so highly regarded should be so unknown outside academe. But then Nussbaum does not write in sound bites. Her books require knowledge and an attention span of several hours, if not months or years.

Like so many American academics she defies labels. Her first book to set people talking was *The Fragility of Goodness*, published to mixed reviews in 1986. People either loved it or hated it. 'It brought literature and philosophy together in a way that had not been done very often before and it really argued that you need to do this in order to see what philosophers are grappling with,' explains Nussbaum. 'You really need to set those problems in their cultural context by holding them up against the thought of the literary authors.'

A supremely scholarly work, the book looked at what the various Greek thinkers thought about making human life immune from the slings and arrows of fortune. It asked the general question: how much chance do these Greek thinkers believe we can humanly live with? Our lives were threatened in various ways beyond our control, said the Greeks. And some bits of our lives were more susceptible to reversals of fortune than others, for example, political participation, citizenship, love, and having children.

'All these are parts of a life that seem valuable and seem to be included in many people's perception of what it is to flourish, but they are obviously very vulnerable to being upset by events that lie beyond our control,' explains Nussbaum. 'What should we say about that? Should that give us a reason for not including those elements in our conception of flourishing? Some philosophers would say yes, that we should define a flourishing life in terms only of things such as intellectual contemplation that seem much more within our control, to do or not do whatever we want.'

But even when things seem to be within our power, there are often conflicts among them that are produced by luck, adds Nussbaum. For example, you love your family as well as your city, but you may find yourself unwittingly in the midst of civil war. You have to make the difficult decision whether to fight members of your family in order to do your duty to your city, or vice versa. 'If you value more than one thing, that can put you at the mercy of luck because luck can throw up circumstances where you can't fulfil your duties to all those things,' she says. The Greek tragedians appreciated that problem.

Nussbaum also looked at the question of uncontrolled forces within the personality, the various emotions and desires that seem to put us at the mercy of luck by making us true to ourselves and out of control. What did the various thinkers have to say about that? Was that a reason not to include those emotions and their satisfaction in the picture of a flourishing life? *The Fragility of Goodness* took a decade to write and perfect, and was followed in 1990 by *Love's Knowledge*, a more accessible tome, which argues that questions of style and substance are intimately bound up with one another. Large chunks of this book are spent analysing Henry James's *The Golden Bowl* and Charles Dickens's *David Copperfield* as Nussbaum shows us how wonderfully well novels tell us about human life and what is important in it – things that contemporary philosophical prose does inadequately.

In a recent book, *The Therapy of Desire*, Nussbaum examines emotion by looking at the Epicureans and Stoics, who argued that many harmful emotions are based on false beliefs that are socially taught, and that good philosophical argument can transform emotions, and, with them, private and public life. One of the themes running through her work is the notion that practical reasoning unaccompanied by emotion is not sufficient for wisdom.

Emotions are often more reliable than intellectual calculations, she says. That is why she became involved in development economics, led by Amartya Sen, whom she was living with at the time. One could not reduce how well a country was doing to the Gross National Product per capita, she thought. 'Of course that doesn't even tell you how well income is distributed, much less tell you anything about some important other indicators of life quality that are not so well correlated with

GNP per capita, such as life expectancy, infant mortality, political liberties and so.' Such a viewpoint chimed with Sen's work. Together they worked on a project which came together in a book entitled *The Quality of Life* and in a new book *Women, Culture and Development*, edited by Nussbaum and Jonathan Glover.

Today Martha Nussbaum has become interested in the law: 'Over the years I have got much more interested in the connections between philosophy and law,' she explains. 'This is not really a new development in the sense that what the people in law have been interested in is finding accounts of practical reason that are alternatives to the accounts put forward by utilitarian economics.'

'For that reason they have taken a great interest in Aristotle and his account of practical reasoning. I would find that law schools and lawyers would invite me to lecture, and I was very interested in being a part of that discussion and bringing some of my arguments against utilitarianism into that domain.'

As an avowedly politically committed person, of feminist and compassionate leanings, Nussbaum is contributing in this way to public debate in America. And she will do so even more in Chicago. 'It seems to me very appealing that I should have colleagues who are in the judiciary and teaching students who would right away go out and be clerks for judges involved in writing judicial opinions,' she says. Brown had no law school, so it didn't offer the same opportunities.

How did Nussbaum reach this point? How come her overriding quest has been the ethical and moral question: how shall I live? She first become interested in ethical questions, she says, growing up in upperclass Philadelphia. What struck her was the gap between that upperclass milieu and the big changes that were taking place in America in the 1960s – the civil rights movement and women's liberation. It was a contrast between the unreflective life she was being brought up to lead, which never asked what was really worth caring for, and the changes that were taking place around her. The territory on which she conducted her search was ancient Greece, because, she says, she found the Greeks really grappled with the basic question of how to live. And she discovered the Greeks in high school.

She attended Baldwin, a private school for girls, which played a big part in her intellectual formation, she thinks. It had a 'feminist, intensely intellectual atmosphere' and impressive teachers. Nussbaum remembers particularly her English teachers, who taught her how to read literary works and ask questions about them, but also how to write. 'They would be absolutely merciless,' she says. 'They would put examples of people's writing up on the board, and they would dissect them and re-do them.' Baldwin also gave her a great grounding in French literature. By her final year of high school she and her friends were writing and producing plays in French.

At that time Nussbaum had set her sights on becoming an actress. 'I found it very rewarding emotionally,' she explains. 'I thought I could express things in acting at that stage in my life that I couldn't express otherwise.' She acted the parts of heroines in Greek tragedies. And her passion for drama continued at Wellesley, the all-female liberal arts college outside Boston, Massachusetts, where she went as an undergraduate, her father having vetoed what he called the 'pink' colleges of Oberlin and Swarthmore, which were co-educational.

At Wellesley, already loving ancient Greek literature, she also began to learn ancient Greek. But Wellesley was probably not the right place for her, she thinks. It was too much a pale imitation of her high school. She was ready for something else, and might have been happier at one of the 'pink' places dismissed by her father. Half-way through her second year she received an offer of a job, acting Greek drama in repertory. So she threw in Wellesley – against the wishes of her lawyer father – and went off to act, having secured a place in drama school for the following autumn at New York University's new school of the arts. It didn't take long for reality, and wisdom, to hit. 'When I got into the world of the theatre I saw that it was a very bad atmosphere for being creatively expressive because there was no job security and no sense of a permanent repertory system,' she says.

Anyway, she decided she was better at thinking and writing about plays than acting in them, so she transferred back to the regular part of New York University, and finished her degree there studying classics. At NYU she made the decision to go to graduate school. And at NYU she met the man who was to become her husband, in a Greek prose composition class.

Until that time Martha Nussbaum's name had been Martha Craven, a good white Anglo-Saxon Protestant name to go with her striking, fair-haired WASP looks. (Her father was a Southerner from Georgia.) On marriage, she converted to Judaism, and still feels herself to be Jewish. That is one reason she never reverted to her WASP name, despite the ending of her marriage in 1987. Back in 1969, before they exchanged wedding vows, Martha Craven and Alan Nussbaum were the two classics majors at NYU doing advanced courses. After marriage they attended Harvard graduate school together, and today Alan Nussbaum is a professor of classics and linguistics at Cornell.

At Harvard, Martha's attention shifted pretty swiftly from classics to the ancient philosophy programme directed by G. E. L. Owen, a Welshman who ended his career as the Lawrence professor at Cambridge in England. 'I felt that what he was doing was tremendously exciting,' she explains. 'It was much more exciting than anything else I was seeing.' During this time she was studying for her examinations in Latin and Greek in the classics department. But her abilities were clear, and at the end of her third year she was awarded the junior fellowship in the Society of Fellows at Harvard – an attempt to create in the United States a cross between the Trinity prize fellowships and the All Souls prize fellowships.

It was a terrific break, because it carried kudos and money. Nussbaum was the first woman to be awarded the fellowship, which had been restricted to men until that year, 1972. She had already published two articles on Heraclitus, and had plans for a PhD thesis on Aristotle's *De Motu Animalium*, so now she could beaver away to her heart's content, without having to worry about where the money was to come from.

Before being awarded the fellowship she had come across the British philospher Bernard Williams, who conducted a seminar at Harvard on moral luck. 'It was very exhilarating for me because it made me recognize that what I was interested in – the issues about luck, moral conflict, emotion, and so on in the Greek tragedies – actually had a place in philosophy. And I wasn't sure of that before. Moral philosophy was certainly reviving very powerfully because John Rawls was just publishing *A Theory of Justice* . . . but it was a different kind of moral philosophy.'

As well as her work on Aristotle, Nussbaum began to write material which would eventually lay the ground for her book, *The Fragility of Goodness*. She showed much of her work to Bernard Williams. It was a frenetically busy and productive time because she also had a baby to look after, a daughter, Rachel, who was born as she took up her fellowship. But Martha Nussbaum remained unfazed. In fact it was a good time to have a baby, she says, because she had three years with no teaching responsibilities and a flexible schedule. In a burst of enlightenment Harvard also decided to attach a stipend for child-care to the fellowship.

Happily for the Nussbaums, and perhaps unsurprisingly given the gene pool, Rachel was a bookish child, who learnt to read early. She is her mother's pride and joy, having just graduated this summer from Brown with all kinds of honours, as well as a Fulbright award to study intellectual history in Germany for one year. After that she is destined for graduate school at Cornell, where she has a six-year fellowship in the history department.

Back in the autumn of 1975, when Rachel was still a toddler, Martha Nussbaum was offered, and accepted, a job as assistant professor at Harvard. There began eight years of teaching at that university. But she faltered at the ultimate hurdle. She failed to win tenure, because, she says, Harvard's classics and philosophy departments disagreed about whether to award it. Philosophy was in favour, classics against, by a very narrow margin. As Martha Nussbaum re-lives her own tangles with fate, one can almost hear the pain in her voice. Some colleagues urged her to bring a grievance against the university for sex discrimination, she says. But there were so many factors clouding the issue. 'Anyway I'm just a very non-litigious person by temperament, so I decided, whether wisely or not, I'm not sure, not to bring a grievance.' In any case, the offer from Brown was appealing because that university's classics department was more enthused by the role of philosophy inside classics.

It was while she was at Brown that her career began to take off. In 1990 she won the Brandeis Creative Arts Award in Non-Fiction. Three years later in Edinburgh she was invited to give the Gifford lectures, called 'Need and Recognition: A Theory of the Emotions'. These are being reproduced in a book to be called *Upheavals of Thought: A Theory of the Emotions*, which is a quote from Proust. Martha Nussbaum will spend time on the shores of Lake Michigan revising that for publication.

As if that wasn't enough, Nussbaum is also taking on a more political task, writing a book about some of the controversies in America on diversity in higher education. She has been drawing on the Stoic idea of world citizenship, the idea that one should not be a citizen of some local or narrow group but a citizen of the whole world. And she has a small book coming out, based on lectures she gave in 1991. Called *Poetic Justice: The Literary Imagination in Public Life*, it looks at literature and, in particular, Charles Dickens's *Hard Times* (a favourite of hers), to defend a non-utilitarian conception of the public imagination. That is an uphill task in America, but Martha Nussbaum is undaunted.

Publications include:

The Fragility of Goodness, 1986, Cambridge University Press.
Love's Knowledge, 1990, Oxford University Press.

The Therapy of Desire, 1994, University of California Press.
The Quality of Life, 1995, with Amartya Sen, new edn., Oxford University Press.
(Ed.) *Women, Culture and Development*, 1995, with Jonathan Glover, Oxford University Press.
Poetic Justice: The Literary Imagination in Public Life, 1995, Beacon Press.

(© Lucy Hodges)

Ann Oakley, born 1944, is a sociologist and novelist whose subjects include gender roles, the situation of women and medical sociology. She is professor of sociology and director of the Social Science Research Unit at the University of London's Institute of Education.

Photograph © Geoff Franklin

Dusting her husband's books at home one day, Ann Oakley's eye fell upon *Alienation and Freedom* by Robert Blauner. It argued that although female factory workers have the most 'alienated' jobs, they don't mind because their fulfilment comes from being wives and mothers. Suddenly, Ann Oakley, who married a fellow Oxford student at the age of 20, had two small children and hardly any paid work outside the home by the age of 25, was angry.

'I was furious. I thought – what on earth are women like me doing if it is not work ? Why is housework not regarded as work ? I became obsessed with the idea of doing research on housework – on why it is not treated as labour – as manual labour.'

She threw away the red and blue pills she was taking for depression and started an academic doctorate on the sociology of housework –

'though in 1969 it was hard to find a supervisor who would take such a subject seriously'.

This is an oft-told anecdote which, of course, pinpoints a more than personal moment. The late sixties/early seventies was the period during which the women's liberation movement and academic women's studies first got off the ground in Britain. The concurrence with the start of Oakley's own career as a sociologist was thus no freak accident; her reputation was established with pioneering (and politically uncomfortable) sociological studies of issues relating to women's lives and health: issues such as antenatal care, housework and the impact of motherhood.

Perhaps the one all-inclusive label, in a life which has encompassed complementary careers as novelist, academic, policy-aide and mother – is that of feminist. Oakley lived through many of the feminist battles of the era and her own work has made a not insignificant contribution to changes since then in society's treatment of women.

Her doctoral material formed the first chapters of a book, *Sex, Gender and Society*, commissioned by the magazine *New Society*. Two more books, *Housewife* and *The Sociology of Housework*, drawing on the same research, followed. In her study of forty London housewives Oakley demonstrated that it was not just middle-class women who were dissatisfied with housework; working-class women also showed signs of discontent. Every woman in the survey spent a minimum of 40 hours a week doing housework (the maximum was a staggering 105 hours – 15 hours a day). Dispelling the myth, current even in the early seventies, that men were taking an increasingly equal role in the home, Oakley argued that marriage and housewifery were, for women, impediments to sex equality in the world of work outside the home.

Charting the historical and cultural conditions which produced the role of housewife, she challenged the supposedly biological arguments which claim an innate home-making/nurturing urge in women and a bread-winning/aggressive urge in men. Drawing on anthropological research into, for instance, the division of labour and organisation of society among the Mbuti pygmies of the Congo forest, she showed that in many societies being a mother does not restrict opportunities for labour outside the home, nor is a mother left almost single-handedly responsible for child-rearing. In *Housewife* Oakley dismissed as 'myths' the twin notions that women are uniquely fitted to be housewives and rear children and demanded the abolition of the categories 'housewife', and 'family'.

As well as having an impact on the conceptualisation of women and gender within sociology, the housework project helped produce a re-think about the division of labour within the Oakleys' own household. It was the start, as she puts it in her autobiography, *Taking It Like a Woman*, of a long journey, from a very traditional set-up, where depressed and isolated wife did the bulk of the housework and child-rearing while husband (Robin, also an academic sociologist) went out to work, to the 'unrecognisable egalitarian affair' of 1982, in which both the Oakleys had paid full-time work (roughly equal incomes), and shared the child-care, cooking and shopping. At the time of this inter-view, in the early 1990s, Ann Oakley (who is now separated from Robin) was living in North London with 15-year-old Laura, the youngest of her three children.

The last paragraph is, arguably, irrelevant – it wouldn't be found in a discussion of a man's academic work – but for Ann Oakley the stuff of women's private, personal lives has always had a wider, political signif-icance. Her own experience of miscarriage led to a general book for fellow sufferers. Her autobiography is an attempt to use her own expe-riences to answer general questions like 'What makes someone into a feminist?', 'What is the nature of love between men and women?' and 'How can a feminist be part of a society organised in terms of sexual "difference" and "the family"?' Her novel *The Men's Room* – which was turned into a BBC drama series attracting record-breaking audiences – focused, in particular, on the second question. It uses the device of an adulterous affair between two sociologists – an affair which, inciden-tally, ends the female academic's marriage, though not that of her male professor – to explore the differences between male and female reac-tions to the same emotion, love.

From studying the unfairness of housework Oakley moved on to look at the passage to motherhood. The result of that research, funded by the then Social Science Research Council in the mid-seventies, was two books: *Becoming a Mother* and *Women Confined – Towards a Sociology of Childbirth*. The latter, which she describes as 'one of my most original pieces of work', is a study of sixty-six women, following them through pregnancy into early motherhood. Including 900 taped conversations between women and doctors in antenatal clinics, it tests the hypothesis that medical management influences how women feel about themselves after giving birth as well as affecting their later, social, experiences of motherhood.

Oakley was shocked by what she found – not only by the doctors' attitudes towards the women in their care, but also by the lack of any sound scientific basis for the medical interventions they recommended. 'I assumed that when the doctor said "You need a Caesarian section" – this was the right thing to do. That, by and large, was not the case. It is still the case that a high proportion of these procedures have not in fact been found to be effective, appropriate and safe.'

Ask whether these research findings have changed the way doctors treat mothers-to-be and Oakley's answer comes in two parts. The medical treatment of labour and delivery, she says, has changed more than have hospital procedures for antenatal care. Since 1974 the proportion of medically-induced births has fallen, partly because of social science research into how women felt about such intervention coupled with monitoring of health standards which revealed no advantage to such procedures. But in antenatal clinics, says Oakley, little has changed since the late seventies. 'Women are still being processed like cattle on an assembly line, tests are being done without being explained, causing stress-related problems. There is no space for young children, the waits are long.'

The highlighting of such findings led in the eighties to dissatisfied, middle-class women seeking alternatives to hospital care. 'Natural' childbirth was much touted; birthing pools became fashionable; women demanded the right to give birth at home, attended only by midwives.

One would expect Oakley to applaud such moves. But not without reservation. Her novel *Matilda's Mistake* explores the dilemmas. Exactly what Matilda's mistake is we are not quite sure. Is it to have fallen in love with Stephen, the charismatic but morally suspect director of an alternative birthing clinic, or is it to have let him off the hook in the consumer report she writes about his clinic's record and work? The author's point is that 'natural' birthing procedures are all well and good, but they too must be subjected to rigorous research and testing of the risks as well as the benefits. 'If one is demanding that what doctors normally do to women should be based on good evidence that it is the right thing to do, one must also make that demand of alternative medical practices.'

Oakley has never thought of herself as having a career and indeed the concept of career ('starting at the bottom and working your way up to the top'), as well as the notion of a division between work and home, are ideas which she has critically re-examined. She has spoken of her horror of the nine-to-five job and of her attempts to avoid being slotted into such routines. 'I have thought of myself as doing the things I wanted to. In terms of progressing through the academic world I have not done the things which would have got me a top job early on. I do not fit the conventional career path.' In her novels too heroines think little of discarding well-paid careers and promotion in search of liberation and personal fulfilment (almost always including having, and rearing, children). In *Scenes Originating in the Garden of Eden* Flora Penfold quits her post as head of an arts organisation for a financially uncertain future in her dream country cottage. Oakley's heroines are always aware of other options, other possibilities, other lives they struggle to lead outside the dictates of a modern, middle-class, patriarchal world.

In juggling the dual responsibilities of part-time work and child-care, Oakley took the route many of her generation chose – research projects, consultancy work and novel-writing, all of which could be conducted from home and dovetailed with looking after the children. (She is proud of having undertaken the bulk of the care of her infant children herself, without use of day-nurseries or nannies.) That pattern has for many female academics proved disastrous. In middle age they find themselves locked into part-time lectureships, with little hope of promotion to the levels reached by their male counterparts.

Although she has written movingly about the frustration of years spent on short-term research contracts, Ann Oakley avoided the typical traps that ensnare part-timers, gaining her own research unit at the University of London as well as a personal chair. But her elevation was preceded by a time of great uncertainty. She was deeply disappointed when, in 1990, as deputy director of the Thomas Coram Research Unit in the university's Institute of Education, she applied for the top job – only to see it fall into someone else's lap.

Having left Thomas Coram for her own completely new research unit (still within the Institute of Education), Oakley is pursuing an agenda which she describes as 'social and cultural analysis of policy and practice issues in education and health'. It is, she adds, 'an unusual venture these days,' striving to conduct research 'independent of the fashions of the policy climate.' Studies underway at the seventeen-strong unit (staffed largely by women) include projects on: the meanings of 'informed consent' in healthcare research and practice; methods of describing the ways families discuss (or don't) health education topics; the background to racist attacks at Thamesmead and children's beliefs about cancer.

She describes the impetus beind her research unit as an attempt to improve the relationship between such professional services as health and education and the well-being of their customers. Arguments about professional ownership of human experience are common in healthcare, where doctors' claims over management of childbirth, for example, have been widely questioned. But they are less common in education and social work, a comparable set of 'interventions' in people's lives, though, argues Oakley, no less applicable. 'We are in a period of history in which we are beginning to understand that there are problems with professionals who say "This bit of life belongs to me, this bit to you." People lead whole lives and it is damaging for different professionals to claim ownership of different bits of these lives.'

Oakley contends that appropriate research on the effects of education – essentially an activity devised by middle-class professionals and seen as 'good' largely by the same class – has not been done. 'The question is: are education services of different kinds effective in their stated aims, are they appropriate to the needs of different social groups (ethnic minorities, special needs, working-class children, for example) and are there, perhaps, ways in which different kinds of education do the opposite of benefit, that is, harm people?' Similar questions about appropriateness, effectiveness and safety are, she points out, commonly asked in the medical domain.

Part of the strength of Oakley's research relies on her ability to think laterally, and innovatively, across disciplines, challenging established methodologies and theories. In this she resembles her father, Richard Titmuss, who left school at fourteen and had no further formal education of any kind. Titmuss, who developed a career as an influential social historian and critic, gaining the chair of social administration at the London School of Economics and building up the discipline over twenty years – despite 'never sitting an examination or securing a formal credential' – is obviously an important influence.

The same willingness to challenge disciplinary boundaries and re-define methodology is evident in Oakley's book-length description of a research project which began in 1983 and in which 509 women participated. In *Social Support and Motherhood: The Natural History of a Research Project* Oakley hits out at sociology's reliance on quantitative rather than qualitative research. 'In aping the natural sciences sociology committed itself to a biologically determinist model of behaviour and has spent much of its short life' trying to escape from the problems this poses, she writes. By contrast, the 1983 project used both qualitative and quantitative methods to gauge whether social support in pregnancy – home visits and chats with midwives – could improve the health of women and their babies. (One aim was to try to alleviate maternal stress, a factor linked to babies of below average weight at birth, who are at risk of suffering from a range of physical and mental disorders in later life.)

'Friendship, support and non-professional forms of help are at least as relevant to the production of health as medical-risk factors and medical interventions,' writes Oakley, who goes on to point out that qualitative research also has potential in terms of creating a sociology more suited to women's needs and lives.

In the late seventies Oakley fell seriously ill with cancer of the tongue. She also gave birth to her third child, Laura. Characteristically, both events prompted a radical rethink of her priorities, and, again characteristically, she opted for more time with the family. Academic responsibilities and committee commitments were shelved. 'I did not expect to survive. Spending more time with a recent child was definitely more important than being on the ESRC social affairs committee.'

But survive she did, going on to take up a three-year fellowship at the Wellcome Trust studying antenatal care (resulting book *The Captured Womb*), which she coupled with a consultancy at the new National Perinatal Epidemological Unit at Oxford.

Then came the appointment as deputy director at the Thomas Coram Research Unit where she ran a number of programmes, including one on the effect on parents' health of having children. In 1990, five years later, came the blow of being turned down for the directorship.

A woman who has spent her life trying to redefine female stereotypes and assumptions, she is pessimistic about women's opportunities in the present. When, recently, she had a chance to examine 1990's women's views of their male partners' roles, she concluded that men are still unwilling to undertake the 'more public health' aspects of childcare and housework; cleaning, changing nappies, laundry. 'Their favourite activities are playing with the baby and helping with the shopping.'

Radical change is not, she thinks , on the immediate agenda. 'We are in one of those historical periods where that is not where the emphasis is, but we will come back to it: because the problems have not been solved and because I do not think women will be content to accept what is being said to them.'

Publications include:

Sex, Gender and Society, 1972, Maurice Temple Smith.
Housewife, 1974, Allen Lane.
The Sociology of Housework, 1974, Martin Robertson.
Becoming a Mother, 1979, Martin Robertson.
Women Confined: Towards a Sociology of Childbirth, 1980, Martin Robertson.
The Captured Womb: A History of the Medical Care of Pregnant Women, 1984, Blackwell.
Taking It Like a Woman, 1985, Fontana.
Social Support and Motherhood: The Natural History of a Research Project, 1992, Blackwell.
Essays on Women, Medicine and Health, 1993, Edinburgh University Press.

Fiction
The Men's Room, 1989, Fontana
Matilda's Mistake, 1991, Fontana
The Secret Lives of Eleanor Jenkinson, 1992, HarperCollins.
Scenes Originating In the Garden of Eden, 1993, HarperCollins.

(Sian Griffiths, © Times Higher Education Supplement)

Camille Paglia, born 1947, is professor of humanities at the University of the Arts, Philadelphia and, since the publication of her book *Sexual Personae*, the new *enfant terrible* of American letters.

Photograph © Luca Babini

Camille Paglia won't talk to journalists unless they agree to tape her every word. Shorthand won't do. You see why as soon as she opens her mouth. Words pour out in a mad, nervous rush, cascading over one another, as she explains, ridicules, tells her story, and repeats herself, on and on, interspersing frequently with 'OK?', rubbishing Derrida and Foucault, women's studies, academic Marxists like Terry Eagleton, Warton professor of English literature at Oxford, the Ivy League.

It's a terrific perfomance, witty, erudite, megalomaniac. Clearly Paglia believes it would be a tragedy for the interviewer to miss one peerless *bon mot*.

You can't get a word in edgeways. The only way to ask a question is to interrupt the stream of theatrical street talk, which is not easy for a bashful Brit. But it doesn't matter because she asks the questions for you. As in: 'If you were to ask how did I develop my powers of social analysis, it came from the fact that my earliest memory of my parents is of constantly discussing and dissecting the surrounding American culture, the alien culture, and what was wrong with it, in other words the emphasis on cheerleaders or the emphasis on dating . . . whatever it would be, and so some of my earliest memories are the sense of being an embattled minority.'

In case you have been asleep for the past few years, Camille Paglia is the new *enfant terrible* of American letters, a small, feisty Italian-American with a very loud mouth. Just as she is lauded by some as the most important lesbian intellectual in the US, she is dismissed by others as inconsistent and sloppy.

Paglia was completely unknown until 1990 when her first book, *Sexual Personae: Art and Decadence from Nefertiti to Emily Dickinson*, which was her PhD thesis, was published. Aimed at an academic audience, it had been turned down by seven major New York publishing houses, but the readers lapped it up. It is long, 673 pages, peppered with attacks on feminism and liberalism, and comprising a huge, synoptic view of Western history and culture, starting in ancient times and moving to the modern. It covers literature, art history, psychology and religion and is full of X-rated sexual material. Sadism, voyeurism, pornography, you name it, it's in the book. 'What is art?' she writes in the preface. 'How and why does an artist create? The amorality, aggression, sadism, voyeurism, and pornography in great art have been ignored or glossed over by most academic critics.'

Christianity, argues Paglia in the book, did not succeed in suppressing the pagan, 'which still flourishes in art, eroticism, astrology and pop culture.'

More controversially, Paglia goes on to draw the conclusion that civilisation has been created by men rather than by women. Paglia sums her ideas up thus in some of the most widely-quoted sentences in the book: 'When I cross the George Washington bridge or any of America's great bridges, I think men have done this . . . If civilization had been left in female hands, we would still be living in grass huts'. In the preface she states baldly: 'My stress on the truth in sexual stereotypes and on the biologic basis of sex differences is sure to cause controversy . . . I see the mother as an overwhelming force who condemns men to lifelong sexual anxiety from which they escape through rationalism and physical achievement.'

And it's written in Paglia's inimitable style, at the same time immensely learned, while being outrageously raw and rude – short, staccato sentences packed with ideas and running off at tangents. 'The Rolling Stones, the greatest rock band, are heirs of stormy Coleridge,' she writes. 'But rock has an Apollonian daylight style as well, a combination of sun and speed: the Beach Boys.' From the Beach Boys she arrives at Byron. The connection? Both displayed an effeminate heterosexuality. A better parallel for Byron is Elvis Presley. Both had white skin and dark oiled hair, she points out, and revolutionary sexual personae.

Paglia's explanation for the male domination of art, science and politics is based on an analogy between sexual physiology and aesthetics. Men are anatomically destined to be projectors, she says in *Sexual Personae*.

'Man is sexually compartmentalised. Genitally he is condemned to a perpetual pattern of linearity, focus, aim, directedness. He must learn to aim.'

Woman's eroticism is diffused throughout her body, she says. 'Man's genital concentration is a reduction but also an intensification. He is a victim of unruly ups and downs. Male sexuality is inherently manic-depressive . . . Men are in a constant state of sexual anxiety, living on the pins and needles of their hormones. In sex as in life they are driven beyond – beyond the self, beyond the body.'

Lust and aggression are fused in male hormones, she continues. Anyone who doubts this has never spent much time around horses. Thus profanation and violation are part of the perversity of sex.

'An aesthetics and erotics of profanation – evil for the sake of evil, the sharpening of the senses by cruelty and torture – have been documented in Sade, Baudelaire and Huysmans. Women may be less prone to such fantasies because they physically lack the equipment for sexual violence. They do not know the temptation of forcibly invading the sanctuary of another body.'

Our knowledge of these fantasies is expanded by pornography, which is why pornography should be tolerated, though its public display may be reasonably restricted, she writes. 'The imagination cannot and must not be policed.'

It was deeply unfashionable to be writing a great narrative which accepted what Paglia calls 'the canonical western tradition', however hip the style, at a time when the post-structuralists said it wasn't done any more. 'It turned out there was a tremendous thirst obviously, OK?' she says. 'The book found its audience in some mysterious way.' Letters began to pour in from all over the world, sixteen-page letters from artists, she says, and from people who would not normally read an academic tome, who said they couldn't put it down. They must have heard about the book by word of mouth, because they couldn't have learnt about it any other way.

Slowly the media began to catch on. 'Suddenly all at once, by some mysterious law of Jungian synchronicity [sic], suddenly, like, five different magazines or newspapers all approached me, virtually simultaneously, without any contact with each another, and asked me to, like, write a piece on Madonna, who was in the middle of a controversy, or a piece on the current date-rape controversy, or to talk about television and the attack on television by conservative educators in America, and so on.'

'I seemed to burst on the public in this way, OK? Political correctness was also in the news . . . and I attacked French theory. In women's studies, I was the first feminist to say women's studies is an atrocity which is destroying the education of the young.'

Paglia thinks she may have been the right person to come upon the scene at the right time. Until 1991 her life had been a struggle. No one understood what she was about, except Harold Bloom, who had taught her at Yale and is the eminent defender of a classical education.

Camille Paglia grew up in an Italian-American family in a small town in upstate New York close to the Great Lakes. Her parents were working-class, she says, but her father managed to acquire a university education via the GI Bill, and eventually became a professor at a small Jesuit college.

Luckily for Paglia, he had advanced ideas (for an Italian American) about women. She was encouraged to get an education, and learnt from him how to defend herself verbally – and physically. He taught her how to stand up for herself in conversation and to put up her fists like a boy, a skill that she has put to good use. She is famous for getting into fights. 'I have a long history of punching and kicking,' she told *Playboy* in an interview. 'I just kicked someone here a few weeks ago. Some guy who didn't know I was a faculty member, because I was wearing sneakers, tried to move me out of the way. I kept kicking him and got into a huge scene.'

She tells another story about an incident at a Madonna concert when she felt spattering at her feet. 'I turned around and saw this guy peeing behind my seat,' she explains. 'I just slugged him.'

Paglia read voraciously, did well at school and got her first degree at the local State University of New York at Binghamton in the mid-1960s. It was a flagship campus, full of poor New York Jews, whom she describes as very politically radical. It gave her an excellent education, rigorous, creative, and exciting, she says, particularly compared to Yale, where she attended graduate school.

'My direct encounter with authentic leftism has made me utterly contemptuous of what now pretends to be leftism, these professors of the Ivy League institutions whose whole idea of politics is reading Foucault in their armchairs.'

She was unusual in college in that she was interested in studying, and had a passionate desire to achieve as a scholar. She was also a sixties person, drinking in the revolutionary messages, putting development of her own learning before advancement.

Eventually the highmindedness paid off. But, until *Sexual Personae*, her career was 'a disaster', she says. At Yale, where she went in 1968 to study literature, she was the only graduate student doing her dissertation on a sexual topic. This was bizarre at the time. 'I was considered a freak,' says Paglia.

Thus she found it hard to get a job. Her personality didn't help either, she admits. 'I was a true sixties personality, surrounded by this, you know, very grey kind of environment where you had to adopt a very low-key manner.'

At Yale she was even more flamboyant than she is now. 'I am a shadow of my former self,' she explains. At seminars at Yale she would wear a big, pale-blue Tom Jones shirt, purple suede waistcoat, white eye-liner, and hippy stained-glass ornament round the neck. And she made no secret of her passion for astrology and popular culture.

She was saved by Bennington, the posh, private, liberal arts college in Vermont, which gave her work and where she was able to continue to do her own thing. 'I was completely out of control as a sixties person,' she says. 'I just had this completely arrogant sense, as did many of my generation, that the world was going to change immediately.'

'We did not conceal our sense of superiority towards the older faculty. Well, good heavens, I mean I had to learn some harsh lessons about life.'

Paglia spent eight years at Bennington, 1972 to 1980, and does not conceal the deep personal problems she had. Without going into details, she says she got into one scrape after another. Over time, she said, she began to understand the needs of institutions and that it was necessary sometimes to renounce egotistic expression for the good of the whole. But she may not have taken the lesson to heart enough. After becoming embroiled in a fist-fight at a college dance, when a female student thought Paglia had called her a lesbian (it wasn't true, says Paglia, she simply said the girl was attracted to another), she was fired.

This was a watershed in her life, a searing experience. It seemed another disaster at the time but it forced her to take stock. For the next few years she was deeply in debt and on the unemployment line. But she scraped by, teaching factory workers in night classes, and came out the other end full of provocative ideas about the cushiness of academe.

'When we hear all this nonsense about how we should be teaching the poor students about the peasants of Guatemala in Marxist rhetoric, I say, excuse me, the factory workers I have had contact with, black and white, they don't want to read about the peasants of Guatemala. They want Sophocles and Shakespeare. That's why they're taking the damn course, OK?'

'They want to learn about art. It's the height of condescension to teach ghetto sensibility to people who are trying to escape the ghetto.' That's why she can rail at Oxford University's Terry Eagleton, she says. What's he doing at Oxford when he's such a Marxist?

During her period in the wilderness she finished *Sexual Personae*, but still couldn't get a job. Finally the University of the Arts in Philadelphia picked her up. She is still there today teaching first-year art students about literature and art history. 'I am blessedly free of the toxins of post-structuralism here,' she says. 'I can go the whole year without hearing the names Derrida, Lacan or Foucault. It's wonderful, it's absolutely wonderful.' She also teaches a women's course, but that's OK because there's no ideology.

Paglia has deliberately kept her life the way it was before fame struck, she says, sharing her office with two other people and teaching the same schedule. The only change is that she moved out of a two-room garret apartment into a small house.

'I have tried to keep absolutely the same, OK?, because I see the terrible lesson of Germaine Greer, OK? and Susan Sontag, because the moment those brilliant women became famous they altered their lifestyle in certain ways that, I think, truncated their continued development as writers.

'Germaine Greer made the mistake of leaving the University of Warwick after seven years there as a Shakespearian scholar. I think that was disastrous for her. She should have stayed.'

For her, Greer has become like many other feminists, anti-sex and men. Paglia casts many feminists as whinging prudes who believe the world would be fine if only men could change their beastly ways. But men will always be savages, she says, so it's up to women to rebuff sexual harassment and to avoid any situation that could lead to date rape.

Thus in her second book, *Sex, Art and American Culture*, a collection of essays, she criticises Anita Hill for whining about Clarence Thomas ten years after she alleges he harassed her. 'If Anita Hill was thrown for a loop by sexual banter, that's her problem,' she writes. 'If by the age of 26, as a graduate of Yale Law School, she could find no convincing way to signal her displeasure and disinterest, that's her deficiency.'

Such talk incenses feminists. They see her as part of the anti-feminist backlash, a neo-conservative who misrepresents feminism's aims and stereotypes its supporters. As the author Naomi Wolf has written in the

American magazine *New Republic*, 'By decorating a stale set of values with the baubles of pop culture and postmodernism, she reassures social conservatives – traditionally the dweebs of the intellectual schoolyard – that to hang out in the rearguard of social change is not uncool after all.'

Paglia doesn't care, though she rejects the conservative label. 'What are they talking about?' she asks. 'I am a radical, sixties libertarian.' She delights in offending everybody, declaring that she is pro-porn, pro-homosexuality, pro-abortion, pro-legalisation of drugs. OK?

She maintains she is a feminist. In a conversation with feminist Suzanne Gordon in the magazine *Working Woman*, she declared: 'I totally support what I consider to be the feminist agenda – the full political and legal equality of women.'

'But the movement has drifted into an exclusive concern with white, upper middle-class problems, often involving fast-track, high-achievers' problems.'

Today Paglia is a media star and *Sexual Personae* is a best-seller. She has been featured in magazines all over America, as well as in Russia, France and Japan. One of the reasons for the attention is that she has strong – and interesting – views about all sorts of subjects, including education.

She advocates a core curriculum based mainly on the classics, and dislikes the frills like gay studies, women's studies, African-American studies, and so on. In fact, she would go further and end all departmental boundaries between subjects under the heading of humanities.

'My model of multiculturalism is one based on learning, OK,' she says. 'I want a world perspective. I want to totally smash the curriculum. I believe I am the only person who is calling for a core curriculum for the world, OK?'

Thus, students should learn about the great world religions, and about archaeology, palaeontology and geology, she believes. True multiculturalism is opening children to the distant past, to the origins of civilisation. From her own experience with poor black students in Philadelphia, that is what fascinates the young. And it has the great merit of being beyond political argument. No one objects to students being taught about what happened in ancient times.

Today she is writing the second volume of *Sexual Personae*. The first volume went from the cavemen to Emily Dickinson. The second will go from Dickinson to the Rolling Stones. She is staying as professor of humanities at the University of the Arts, she says. Not that anyone is trying to steal her away. 'I am happy to say that I am *persona non grata*.' There are blessings to being politically incorrect.

Publications include

Sexual Personae: Art and Decadence from Nefertiti to Emily Dickinson, 1990, Yale University Press.
Sex, Art and American Culture: Essays, 1992, Vintage.
Vamps and Tramps: New Essays, 1994, Vintage.

(© Lucy Hodges)

Griselda Pollock, born 1949, is professor of social and critical histories of art and director of the Centre for Cultural Studies, University of Leeds. Her book *Old Mistresses* is an exploration of the work and lives of neglected women artists.

Photograph © Financial Times, photograph by Ashley Ashwood

In the course of researching this profile I rang up an academic art historian. Griselda, she said rather curtly, does not need any more 'hate articles'.

It is for her withering attacks on the tradition of the 'great', invariably male, painters of Western art that Griselda Pollock, using a mix of psychoanalytic theory and historical investigation, has provoked most outrage.

This is Henri de Toulouse-Lautrec, acclaimed artist of those garishly energetic Parisian cabaret dancers, as seen through Professor Pollock's irreverent eyes: underlying Toulouse-Lautrec's 'stylistic signature' of a dancer's black-stockinged, cocked leg (concealing a glimpse of more private parts) is the insecure young boy's anxiety for his penis, she suggests. Lautrec's own legs were buckled by a genetic condition; the dwarf artist's images of female artistes have, for Pollock, a debasing, nightmarish quality.

In *The Black Gloves of Yvette Guilbert*, Lautrec, according to Pollock, reduces a contemporary Parisian singer, 'to the empty, limp but fantastic shapes of inanimate things which none the less trail down the steps like some hydra or multi-headed snake. Empty, they [the gloves] still gesture, they do not form a five-fingered hand, but a kind of webbing produces a grotesque, almost inhuman shape.'

Sitting in her Pudsey living-room, on the outskirts of Leeds, (a Greenham Common print hangs above the fireplace, photos of children jostle along a shelf), Pollock proffers critical descriptions of herself. Hilton Kramer, for instance, conservative American critic, who penned a savage critique of her lecture 'Can art history survive the impact of feminism?' 'He thinks I am the end of civilisation.' Others demonise her, she jokes, as 'the Wicked Witch of the North', dogmatic, driven, theoretical. She feels 'out on the margins', 'out on a limb', and not just because of the choice to stay in Leeds (where she became one of the first women in Britain to gain a professorship in art history), away from London's incestuous artistic circles.

It is for the book *Old Mistresses*, (co-author Rozsika Parker, 1981) that Griselda Pollock's fans – who regard her as a guru and not at all marginal – are most grateful. To counter the 'Old Masters' approach to art appreciation, Pollock and Parker embarked on a search for the neglected women artists of history. Dozens are featured, including Judith Leyster, many of whose works were wrongly attributed to Frans Hals; Artemisia Gentileschi, raped by her teacher and then tortured at the trial to ascertain the truth of her allegations; and Marischol Escobar, part of the 1950s Pop Art generation, whose legendary beauty commanded newspaper inches denied to her work.

Old Mistresses veers towards a reappraisal of the canon of artists whose work is *de rigueur* on undergraduate courses. Its research enables the insertion of forgotten women, yet its co-author is profoundly unhappy with questions such as 'Why are there no great women artists?'

Pollock is disinclined to play the canon game, even in rebuttal. She sees the task as different – the need to redefine the assumptions we bring to art. It's not enough to say that women weren't trained as artists or weren't permitted to paint male nudes (the central image in so much Biblical/classical painting) – that's why they weren't great. It's not even enough to say well, some of them were great – but neglected by male 'connoisseurs'.

Rather, what she wants to establish is 'a view from elsewhere', a critical practice that can examine what was going on in society both when the paintings were 'produced' and when they were interpreted. Why, for instance, have women's genitals in art been smoothed down and idealised? (Art critic John Ruskin apparently failed to consummate his marriage, shocked that his wife was not hairless like classical statues.) Why are Mary Cassatt's images of motherhood not granted the same importance by critics as are those of Picasso's 'cut up women' or Paul Gauguin's full-frontal female nudes?

'I am not interested in an expanded canon. It is always going to be exclusive, it is always going to leave someone out.' She describes worrying about 'who is better than whom' as 'Oedipal' – killing off one's predecessors to create a space for oneself. Infinitely preferable, she thinks, is French intellectual Luce Irigaray's notion of a 'cult of admiration'.

As an example of what she is trying to do Pollock offers an exhibition in 1916 at which Mary Cassatt and Hilaire Germain Edgar Degas, both Impressionists, were represented. With Cassatt's paintings of mothers and children critical appreciation is hampered by the fact that 'everyone thinks – "Oh God, motherhood"'. There is a weight of criticism within patriarchal societies which devalues female experiences such as motherhood and middle age. This makes it difficult for the viewer to respond positively to paintings, like Cassatt's, which depict such experiences. With Degas's paintings of bathers and young ballet dancers, on the other hand, the reverse is true. There is a weight of words saying 'this subject is interesting/original'. What, asks Pollock, do you have to do to the two walls of paintings to enable the formal brilliance of both to shine through on equal terms?

Mothers and the theme of motherhood become increasingly important in Pollock's later work. Her own mother, who she says, inhabited a world of bridge, golf, and art galleries, died thirty years ago, when Pollock was fourteen, a loss she describes still as 'the worst thing that happened to me'. She has been in analysis, partly to explore this 'trauma which shaped my life' and to prevent her children, Benjamin and Hester, now twelve and nine, growing up affected by their mother's unresolved grief and fear. Her son never asked about his grandmother.

Her daughter did, only to follow up with: 'How old was she? – Are you that old?'

Psychoanalytic theories are a later thread in Pollock's move away from long-standing critical traditions. As a postgraduate at the Courtauld Institute in the early 1970s, she found herself increasingly frustrated by a combination of a dilettante ethos and an approach focusing exclusively on 'scholarly formalist analysis, histories of style, monographic studies of artists'. Although grateful for the ability her art history training gave her to walk into any art gallery and say 'That is a Klee, that is a Klimt' – her own enthusiasms (her first degree was in history) propelled her to follow Marxist art historian Tim Clark to Leeds University, where he was pioneering precise historical study of the nature of the societies within which painters worked.

Feminism and art history came together when Pollock, again with Rosie Parker, wrote an introduction to the journals of Marie Bashkirtseff, a nineteenth-century artist who died before the age of thirty and used her journals to rail against the restrictions imposed on women artists.

Criticisms of the education offered by the Courtauld as 'narrow, élitist and limited intellectually' provoked a sharp exchange of letters in *The Independent*. She remembers too how Anthony Blunt, Courtauld director until 1974, asked whether she would give up her scholarship in favour of a man.

Pollock herself freely acknowledges that 'to anyone on the outside psychoanalysis is a ludicrous science'. Some of its unprovable assumptions about the childhood traumas and complexes which supposedly influence the adult's actions, behaviour and creations may, she admits, turn out, in the end, to have been no more than fantasies. None the less, as a means of exploring images, in the cinema or on the canvas, she has found it a tool as fruitful as her earlier forays into history.

Historically, too, she says, psychoanalysis has a sound track record. It emerged out of people, notably Freud, listening to the pain of women trapped in restrictive social roles. Today the process continues. French intellectual Julia Kristeva 'writes a book about women and dependency because she listens to suicidal women talking about themselves'. One of the reasons for pursuing psychoanalysis is that it enables women to imagine roles other than those ascribed by social norms.

Psychoanalysis says that we operate at the level of fantasy, of suppressed impulses not understood by the conscious mind. A lot of art, says Pollock, is produced from that space. In exploring Toulouse-

Lautrec she draws on the theory about the moment the small boy glimpses his mother's genitalia and recognises that his possession of a penis makes him different; a recognition that means he is no longer at one with the safe, all-encompassing female world of early childhood. The black cocked leg of the Moulin Rouge dancer can thus be interpreted as a fetish, a substitute for a penis, a denial of the anxiety-provoking recognition of the artist's difference and subsequent isolation.

Pollock moves on to a discussion of a Van Gogh drawing of peasant women bending over. She finds it offensive to see an elderly woman made to take up such a vulnerable position by a middle-class artist with economic clout, but she also receives from the painting powerful feelings of 'aggression and love'. It is this co-existence which hooks the viewer, says Pollock. Again the aggression is ascribed to the child's shock of expulsion from the maternal world of early childhood. For Van Gogh, as for so many others, the principal adult carer in early years was likely to have been a working-class nurse. But filial love is there too. These feelings, she says, have to be taken on board. Otherwise you are left with idealised interpretations along the lines of 'Van Gogh loved the peasants/was a great humanist'.

All kinds of signals come into play in such interpretations. How do the women in the paintings stand, or more commonly lie? At what are they looking? What kind of spaces are they given?

Vision and Difference, her 1988 book, is spattered with phrases like 'The artist is one major articulation of the contradictory nature of bourgeois ideals of masculinity'. Yet confront Pollock with the charge that, in places, she writes so obscurely that the excitement of the ideas is lost and she bridles. To me she says 'I never could write'. Her PhD supervisor told her to buy a thesaurus to increase her vocabulary, Rozsika Parker used to edit down her 'great long sentences'. Later she used the technique of imagining an intelligent reader and addressing her writing directly to that imaginary person – she subsequently won praise from editors for the clarity with which she expressed complicated theoretical ideas.

Now her writing is moving into terrain more familiar to the artist. With three books on the go, 'at a point at which I have lost faith with a certain kind of academic argument', she uses autobiographical stories (that feminist slogan the personal is political), as well as imaginative writing in language sometimes closer to 'poetry'.

Inevitably, perhaps, for one who has spent so long analysing art and in the company of artists, Pollock has 'wanted to do it too', undertaking video and photographic projects, though never painting. There is pleasure when audiences praise her lectures, illustrated with slides, as 'artwork'.

Enthusiastic advocacy of certain contemporary artists has been criticised by female colleagues, with some of whom there is an uneasy relationship. Pollock has championed the feminist artist Mary Kelly for instance, whose 'Post Partum Document' has been interpreted as an attempt to provoke new ways of seeing by ignoring traditional images of women and their children in favour of displaying fragments of their relationship – from dirty nappies to jottings on the child's early experiences.

But the attacks on Pollock are contradictory. On the one hand there is whinging about the way in which artists championed by Pollock sometimes gain a degree of fame from the association, while research on artists by less well-known academics makes less of an impact. On the other hand are complaints about restriction of praise to a select few. 'Why so much about Mary Kelly?' (One answer might be because Kelly, who is also influenced by psychoanalytic and feminist theory, is a fruitful subject for Pollock's style of art criticism.)

But Anthea Callen, a close friend and a senior lecturer at the University of Warwick, is unequivocal: 'She has managed to balance being a very committed feminist/feminist art historian with being very successful, which some people find difficult to take. She is probably a source of great envy. So much for sisterhood.'

The interview turns to toddler James Bulger, murdered in 1993 by two ten-year-olds. Pollock also teaches film theory and sees a connection between video and real-life violence. She welcomes the demand for more media education to enable children to respond critically to TV and film. 'I say to my students "People die because we do not understand what is happening."'

Confronted with an appeal for a more sophisticated analysis of our visual culture, the description of her own appearance on BBC2's programme 'Without Walls' (demolishing Van Gogh's reputation – she herself jokes that it is perhaps her work on this male artist, still uncompleted, which will finally bring her into the mainstream) is unintentionally ironic. TV critic Christopher Dunkley wrote, '(She) not only knows her stuff and speaks well but looks good too, a fact which should ensure her as much TV work as she cares to have'. When it comes to images of women, *plus ça change*.

Publications include:

Millet, 1977, Oresko Books.

Vincent Van Gogh, 1978, Phaidon Press.

Mary Cassatt, 1980, Jupiter Books.

Old Mistresses; Women, Art and Ideology, 1981, with Rozsika Parker, Routledge and Kegan Paul.

The Journals of Marie Bashkirtseff, 1985, with Rozsika Parker, Virago.

Vision and Difference: Femininity, Feminism and Histories of Art, 1988, Routledge.

Avant-Garde Gambits: Gender and the Colour of Art History, 1992, Thames & Hudson.

(Sian Griffiths, © Times Higher Education Supplement)

Mamphela Ramphele, born 1947, a former medical doctor and Black Consciousness activist in South Africa, is the first black vice chancellor of the University of Cape Town, a historically white university.

Photograph © Eric Miller

For decades non-racist white South Africans – rather few that they were – shouldered a heavy weight of guilt for the sins of apartheid. This was too bad, since in every other way apartheid benefited whites. What was surprising was to have the burden shared by black people who had succeeded in a hostile world. 'Like the survivors of the holocaust, one is sometimes overwhelmed by a sense of guilt,' explains Mamphela Ramphele, a former Black Consciousness activist and medical doctor who is now a social anthropologist and who became, at the end of 1995, the first black vice-chancellor of a historically white university.

Guilt about surviving when others have died. Guilt about achieving things when others, perhaps with better abilities, have failed. 'It is part of the culture of survival to make one feel guilty about success. In a sense the whole activist culture says the individual doesn't matter. What matters is the cause. Anything that focuses on individual achievement becomes a tension point.'

Still, it is hard to comprehend why guilt stalks a person who has endured poverty, bad schooling, prison and banishment, the hardships of township life, the violent death of several loved ones – including Black Consciousness leader Steve Biko, the father of her eldest son – and a deeply sexist society.

It is also difficult to understand why the wise, self-assured and witty woman sitting across the table in her sedate university office is there at all. From anti-establishment 'BC' to 'V-C' of the University of Cape Town, a liberal, historically white institution? The decision to accept the post was not an easy one, she admits, but by 1991 change in South Africa had advanced to the point where unless black people engaged with the institutions that wield power, they would have little impact on the transition process. 'My focus has been to help the university nego-tiate transformation, to look at what new policies should be adopted to enable the institution to play the critical role universities must play in higher education and development in South Africa. I believe there cannot be development without a capacity for serious reflection. Academia is not just about degrees and books. It is also about the ability to stand back and reflect on what one is doing, where society is going, and what the alternatives are. If South Africa does not have that capac-ity as a nation we are doomed to become a society of victims. We have to generate new ideas and knowledge. Africa has sunk to the bottom of the pit precisely because we have not asserted our right to be in the market-place of ideas. That cannot be done without nurturing and cre-ating centres of excellence.'

'We must stop thinking of intellectual life and academic excellence as a luxury or an élitist pursuit. It is a matter of life and death.' Death was the one, rather important aspect of the profession Ramphele first pursued, that she could never really handle. It was one of the reasons she decided to swop, in the mid-1980s and in the middle of an admit-tedly erratic career, to anthropology. She has subsequently written four acclaimed books on issues ranging from poverty to politics, the environment and life in migrant labour hostels. She has published nine chapters in books, and twenty-two journal articles, reviews and reports. She has also earned two more degrees, one a PhD, more than a dozen awards, and directorships of four major organisations, including Anglo American, the massive corporation which owns the bulk of shares quoted on the Johannesburg Stock Exchange. There are two more books forthcoming, one of them called *Stretching Across Boundaries: An Autobiographical Reflection*, which Ramphele wrote while on sabbatical last year. It is a chronological biography which dips in and out of different themes: 'How I was introduced to politics. Community life. Survival in the wilderness. The struggle to define who the hell I am.'

'It is really about how I have negotiated an independent lifestyle within the context of the society I live in, where people have very conflicting and different expectations of me. It is about my role as a woman, mother, academic, executive and political actor. South Africa has a very traditional, patriarchal society in which people have a definite view of what a women is supposed to be like.'

One of Ramphele's earliest memories is of her father, Pitsi Ramphele, complaining to her mother that the brains in the family had gone to a girl. Her father felt she would be unable to exploit her intellect. The Rampheles lived in a rural village at the foot of the Soutpansberg mountains, in far northern South Africa. Both of her parents were teachers, and they taught their children for most of their primary schooling. 'Life was uneventful and schooling was effortless, boring and unstimulating.' Her father's patriarchal view was perpetuated at the Bethesda Normal College in Pietersburg, a conservative – Dickensian, she recalls – Dutch Reformed Church school where the dominee responded to Ramphele's announcement that she wanted to be a doctor with a sad shake of his head and the comment: 'Girls become nurses'. The school did not offer maths, since the subject was thought to be beyond the capacity of black people. She met maths for the first time at Setotolwane High, where she completed her schooling in 1966. She also met a supportive white science teacher there – the first person to encourage her to become a doctor. Later, after studying pre-medicine at the University of the North and enrolling at the University of Natal's Medical School, he would send her 25 rand each time she got a distinction: 'It was my only pocket money at university'.

Ramphele did not enjoy her medical studies at all: she was squeamish, and couldn't bear the sight of blood or corpses. 'I was in the wrong profession. But it was the only one that could give me the independence I wanted, so I persevered.' She graduated in 1972.

King William's Town, 1974. A massive groundswell of opposition to South Africa's apartheid government was gaining momentum, and Ramphele was in the thick of it. While working as an intern at the Mount Coke Mission Hospital in the Eastern Cape, she became swept up in the Black Consciousness movement with Steve Biko, Barney Pityana and a core of medical students who were at the forefront of launching the radical South African Students' Organisation. They set up Black Community Programmes, worked in poor communities, and the following year started the Zanempilo Community Health Centre in King William's Town. Ramphele was the medical officer, and ran the centre. 'Those were crazy days. I felt I was actively participating in changing society. The excitement of being part of this wave of history was intoxicating. We worked hard and did excellent things for people with little resources – with none of the millions that came later.'

'It was a time of enormous creativity. We knew we were doing things that went beyond commitment. We helped lay the foundations for a society which had a vision of greater equity, and of people being treated with dignity. It taught us, firstly, that black people have creativity and, secondly, that they can do excellent things.'

But they were also hard days. Ramphele and her colleagues worked seven days a week, every week, and earned a pittance. The lifestyle was destructive: no rest, lots of smoking, drinking and parties. 'It was the culture of the 1960s and early 1970s. It was a time we can look back to with pride.' In 1976, after the Soweto Riots, the South African government panicked and launched a wave of preventative detention. Thousands of people were imprisoned, including Ramphele. 'The police plonked me in a cell, and that was that. The circumstances were very painful. A friend, Mapetla Mohapi, had been murdered in detention and I was asked to observe the post-mortem. I was outraged.' She used the four and a half months spent in detention to catch up on sleep, be on her own and gather her thoughts together. 'The power of the medical profession helped me in detention, and later when I was banished. There is a sudden reverence with which people treat you when they find you are a medical doctor. It didn't prevent me from being locked up, but it did make things more comfortable.'

Ramphele was released on 28 December 1976 – her 29th birthday. She went back to work at the health centre and also took over management of the Black Community Programmes. But not for long: on 27 April 1977, she was banished by government decree to Lenyenye, a desolate township near her childhood home in Northern Province. The decree spelled Ramphele's name wrong, and messed up other details – mistakes which gained her ten days of freedom before she was unceremoniously dumped in Lenyenye. In those few days she fell pregnant by Steve Biko. In August she heard that Biko had been detained and, shortly afterwards, she was admitted to hospital with a threatening miscarriage. 'I was a bad incubator.' This, together with Biko's detention and news the following month of his death, laid Ramphele in hospital for the remaining four months of her pregnancy. In January 1978 her first son was born. She named him Hlumelo, which means 'the shoot from the dead tree'.

Banishment was horrible. 'It was like surviving in the wilderness.' In 1978 she set up the Ithuseng Community Health Programme in Tzaneen, and for the next six years threw herself into community development. The programme was a remarkable success, helping to improve the lives of 50,000 poor people in Lenyenye. 'They were tough, tough times but I had a lot of support.' Community work made Ramphele very aware of the central role women play in South African society. Migrant labour policies tore many black families apart, with men leaving rural areas to seek work in urban centres and women being left to care for their families. Yet the role of women remains unrecognised. Women, she told the upmarket magazine *Leadership*, can do a lot to improve their situation – especially through organisation. But in a traditional society it is often risky for them to assert their rights. 'Women are still primarily responsible for socialising their children. This gives them real power to shape the attitudes of the next generation. If it's too difficult to raise the issue of gender discrimination with their husbands, there's nothing to stop them raising the issue with their children, making them sensitive to the practices and structures that discriminate against women.'

Ramphele had been briefly married as a student, and she married again in 1982. Both marriages lasted less than a year. 'I hadn't reckoned with the fragility of the male ego,' she told *Leadership*. 'I have since decided that I am unmarriageable. That realisation has given me a great deal of inner freedom. I accept the fact and get on with my life. For this generation of women it will be very difficult for strong women to find marriage partners. It's best for them not to waste too much of their time looking.'

By the early 1980s Ramphele had gone back to studying. In 1982 she gained a diploma in Tropical Health and Hygiene at the University of the Witwatersrand, and in 1983 – the year her second son, Malusi, was born – she graduated with a Bachelor of Commerce degree from the University of South Africa, a distance learning university. The following year, when her banishment ended, she returned to the Eastern Cape and later got divorced. In October 1984 she moved again, this time to the University of Cape Town to take up a research fellowship at the Southern African Labour and Development Research Unit. After a decade of relentless community work, she was tired and in need of intellectual stimulation. Francis Wilson, a leading economist, had lured Ramphele to Cape Town to work with him on the second Carnegie Enquiry Into Poverty in South Africa: the first had looked at poverty among whites. They worked on the project – which produced more than 300 papers and was the most comprehensive study ever conducted into poverty in the country – for the next two years.

In 1989 *Uprooting Poverty: The South African Challenge* was published and became a seminal work. The report challenged the then government to introduce policies which would enable people to move out of circumstances of helplessness and denial, and raised the issue of poverty high in the public consciousness. 'It concentrated minds and made it explicit to those with starry eyes how difficult it will also be for the new government to deal with poverty.' *Uprooting Poverty* was a gratifying study for Ramphele. It taught her that she could write well, and fast. She drew on her experience of the struggle and her strength as someone who had lived with poverty.

In 1986 she took up a senior research post in anthropology. 'I didn't set out to do a PhD, but discovered an affinity with the subject. That's how I ended up being an anthropologist.

'It quickly became clear that one cannot be an activist without using anthropological methods. Participative observation, used by anthropologists, is the same method used by activists. Living with people, seeing how they see the world and so on. So I was not foreign to anthropology, and it dealt with issues dear to my heart.'

Two years after *Uprooting Poverty*, Ramphele and old friends, including Barney Pityana, produced *Bounds of Possibility: The Legacy of Steve Biko and Black Consciousness*, a vibrant history of the black consciousness movement in the Eastern Cape. Meanwhile, Ramphele had begun working on a two-year study of migrant labourers living in appalling conditions in hostels in Langa, in Cape Town. She saw the project as a natural outflow of the poverty study. 'It was one of the most sustained painful projects I have done, and it generated deep anger in me. I was dealing with people who were being treated like animals. I saw destruction and degradation personified. I saw pain on people's faces. I saw abuse of children and of the environment: people who are destroyed do not care about hygiene. I played with metaphors around space. When people's private space is so circumscribed, they reduce their psycho space to survive. Society doesn't expect anything of such people, and these low expectations are self fulfilled.'

The project was a crucial learning experience for Ramphele. 'My idealistic activist's notions of empowering people were seriously dented. I realised that activists do not take sufficient cognisance of the lack of capacity of very poor people, who have not been exposed to any form of effective organisation. Organised and democratic cultures take a long time to develop. South Africa is going to suffer from its lack of capacity.' The migrant labour study earned Ramphele her anthropology PhD and resulted in her book *A Bed Called Home: Life in the Migrant Labour Hostels of Cape Town*. It also made her acutely aware of the cost of neglecting children.

In 1991 she began a new study of children and a book on the subject, *Produce from Untilled Fields: Adolescents in New Crossroads*, is in its final draft form. Half of South Africa's African population of 30 million is under the age of nineteen – a proportion which is projected to rise to 60 per cent by the turn of the century. 'It became quite clear to me that we have a huge time-bomb ticking away and we are not getting to grips with it. I don't understand how we have come to where we are. We blame young people for ill-discipline, entitlement and lack of a culture of learning. But we need to ask how we produced such children: they didn't grow on trees. The chickens of negligent social policies are coming home to roost with a vengeance. Migrancy, impoverishment, neglect and anti-education policies have produced a family dynamic which is not capable of creating young people who are critical, participative members of a democratic society. People have no time for caring so they practice an authoritarian system in their homes. We find tyranny in schools, homes and in the streets.'

In January 1995, Ramphele became director of the Institute for Democracy in South Africa's Public Information Centre, a project which tackles issues of public policy. 'We will make sure that politicians are kept accountable for what they claim to have been elected for. It is crucial in a new democracy that people feel their opinions matter, that they understand politics and the fact that the government cannot do everything for them. South Africa's Reconstruction and Development Programme is not about what the government can do for people, but about the whole country getting its act together.'

'I have a vision of a more equitable society. That vision makes me feel very good about being a South African, about participating in the reconstruction of society – and about saying things that others may feel uncomfortable about me saying.' Ramphele's life has been dominated by the pursuit of excellence. She has never been prepared to accept anything less, and at times it has made her unpopular. 'I will never compromise on excellence. From cooking to lecturing, we have got to strive towards excelling at what we are doing. I'm very comfortable about that, and have enormous joy talking about it to young people.' It is perhaps this passion which has kept her out of politics, despite requests for her to join South Africa's new government.

Mamphela Ramphele has a birds-eye view of the country. She has worked with the very rich and the very poor, male and female, young and old. The role she is playing outside government, in a country whose fragile new democracy depends on a vibrant civil society, is even more valuable. Delivering her first graduation speech, Ramphele said she had begun to come to terms with her guilt as a survivor. She steered those still troubled by their élitist positions as intellectuals to the words of sociologist Peter Berger in his book *Pyramids of Sacrifice*: 'Myth fosters total commitment, and people who are so committed tend to be blind to inconvenient facts, and indifferent to the human costs of their mythologically legitimated programmes. For this reason demythologisation is both theoretically and politically important in the area of development. There is no alternative to having intellectual and political élites, but it makes sense to prefer theorists who have doubts, and policy-makers with scruples.'

Publications include:

Uprooting Poverty – The South African Challenge – Report of the Second Carnegie Enquiry into Poverty 1989, co-authored with Professor F. Wilson, 1989, David Philip Publishers and W. W. Norton.

Bounds of Possibility: The Legacy of Steve Biko and Black Consciousness. An Overview, 1991, co-edited with B. Pityana et al.

(Ed.) *Restoring the Land: Environment and Change in Post-Apartheid South Africa*, 1992, Panos.

A Bed Called Home: Life in the Migrant Labour Hostels of Cape Town, 1993, David Philip Publishers.

(© Karen MacGregor)

Jessica Rawson, born 1943, is warden of Merton College, Oxford. She is a renowned oriental scholar who has revolutionised thinking about ancient Chinese jades and bronzes.

Photograph © Rob Judges

It is hard to believe that Jessica Rawson has not always walked across the cobbled quadrangle to Merton's timbered library. As she reaches the hallowed oak door, her step quickens and her voice drops to a reverential whisper.

'These are the oldest bookshelves in England,' she says, with a 'room-of-my-own' enthusiasm, pointing to some modest-sized stacks which nevertheless represented a revolution in library technology when old Mertonian Sir Thomas Bodley introduced them from Italy in the sixteenth century. Amid the ancient tomes, and with the halo of cerebralism which the headship of an Oxford college confers, she looks every bit the scholar of Chinese art and archaeology who, according to Gordon Johnson, her former teacher and now head of Wolfson College, Cambridge, 'has turned the preserve of the connoisseur into an academic venture of profound originality and discovery'. But until last year, Rawson was a curator at the British Museum and it was by no means obvious that the scholar in her would finally prevail, that the academic would triumph over the administrator.

Rawson was always academically precocious. At the age of ten, she was mesmerised by the magic of Chinese characters, coming across them after reading about the Rosetta stone and Egyptian hieroglyphs. Seven years later, she toyed with the idea of reading Oriental Studies at Cambridge. But her school, St Paul's, put her off: what was suitable for Ian Fleming's suavely outlandish James Bond was evidently not suitable for the strait-laced bluestocking girls at one of England's premier public schools.

Rawson fetched up at New Hall, and graduated in 1965 with an unremarkable career in history. She half planned to do research, securing a place at the School of Oriental and African Studies. But when her father died, she decided 'it was better to get a job and have a steady income', and so she headed off to the Civil Service to become an assistant principal in the Ministry of Health. She thrived in the milieu of the paper-pushing bureaucrats. As she acknowledges, 'I had a considerable inclination towards administration.'

A solid, even spectacular career in the Civil Service beckoned. By her own testimony, she was something of a 'hot prospect'. Yet after two years, the lure of the East tempted her away to the British Museum, where she accepted the post of assistant keeper in the department of oriental antiquities. It was a now-or-never moment, and Rawson was lucky. 'I should not have got in,' she admits, 'because I did not have a degree in Chinese.' But she explains, 'It was the 1960s, and those rare people who did have Chinese degrees were going off to the new universities to found chairs.'

For the budding researcher, the new job was a step in the right direction, rather than a leap into heaven. 'It was a very intricate jigsaw-puzzle type of a job and although there were opportunities for research there were wide-ranging administrative duties – the cataloguing, housekeeping and displaying of rare objects.' As with the Civil Service, she thrived in her new-found administrative role, even taking a degree in Chinese at SOAS between curatorial shifts. She might have continued on this path, especially after developing a passion for purchasing ancient bronze carvings, which would lead her to the cluttered market stalls of antique dealers along Portobello Road.

But in 1978 she started work on the famous Arthur M. Sackler collection in the United States, joining a team of academics from Harvard. 'It raised my aspirations,' she now says, adding that 'from the late 1970s onwards research became the primary element of my life.' Certainly, her reputation as a indefatigable researcher rose steadily, and according to one insider, 'rumour has it that she goes to bed with huge catalogues of Chinese archaeology'.

Rawson does nothing to dispel this image of single-minded scholarship. 'I have had very little time for family life because I have worked absolutely continuously, day and night, all holidays and all weekends.' Her daughter had to get used to seeing her working on the latest catalogue, lecture or article: 'When she was young, my husband and I would take it in turns to go to the park and push her on the swings. We would not all go together.'

But what Rawson has lost in domestic bliss she has gained in professional recognition. Her election to the British Academy in 1990, and later her award of a doctorate of letters from Cambridge, testifies to her contribution to the understanding of the Western Zhou, a people who ruled China between 1050 BC and 750 BC, by reference to their manufacture of beautiful, ritualistic objects of jade and bronze. This marks her out as unique in Britain. As Craig Clunas, lecturer in the history of art at Sussex University observes: 'There is no one in this country with whom Jessica can have an intelligent conversation about her specialism.'

The British Museum is blessed by magnificent collections of bronzes and jades, mostly brought back by travellers and missionaries in the last century. But in recent years, this has become something of a mixed blessing, because new archaeological finds, especially in the 1970s, have turned the world of Chinese scholarship upside down, serving to transform the avant-garde into the old hat almost overnight. Rawson has not been unaffected. Her first academic work, *Chinese Jade Throughout the Ages*, was published in 1975. The following year, the tomb of the Shang queen, Fu Hao, was discovered, dating back to 1200 BC and containing 700 jades. It changed the orthodoxy dramatically. According to Dr Clunas, her comments on the early period are 'now purely of historiographical interest'.

Rawson has now revised her thinking in a new book, *Chinese Jade from the Neolithic to the Qing*, which describes a technologically and intellectually sophisticated neolithic culture which 'was not dreamed of before'. In other fields, the fact that she has revised her views might be interpreted as intellectual vacillation, but not in Chinese art and archaeology. The mere fact that she revised her views on the basis of reading the cascade of archaeological catalogues that are coming out of China every month is a source of wonder.

She has become one of the great interpreters of the new material outside China, renowned especially for the idea that there was a 'ritual revolution'. Based chiefly on a hoard of 103 bronzes found in the mid-1970s, the theory endeavours to explain why ritualistic wine-vessels were in vogue in 950 BC but were out of fashion and replaced by food vessels by 880 BC, just 70 years later. As she told the British Academy, 'this must have effected major changes in ceremonies and even in beliefs'.

Rawson is also recognised as having led what Clunas calls the 'intellectual break-out' of Chinese scholars into other disciplines. 'She is even interested in chaos theory,' he says, evidently awed. Gordon Johnson endorses this view of a broad intellect, observing that she has 'demonstrated relationships between Assyrian and Gandhara palmette design, between Iranian and Tang silverware, betweeen lotus patterns in the Mongol empire and in Turkey and between bird designs in the Yuan dynasty and in far western Staffordshire'.

But Rawson's claim to a more lasting achievement is based on her work on the importance of objects. A museum is a treasure trove of objects, and the BC period necessarily has few extant written sources. So it might seem like special pleading for a museum curator spotlighting the ancient Chinese world to privilege objects. But Rawson's point is that objects and texts often tell very different stories – they are not equivalent, they are not an either-or. 'If you don't have both, you have lost half the information,' she contends. 'People often assume that if you have got the text that is enough. But I disagree. If you wanted me to understand what your life was like, just to write a potted biography would not be sufficient because it would not tell the whole story, it wouldn't convey the colour and the nuance.' As proof she leaps to her feet, picks out a burly catalogue from her office book-shelf and points to a larger than life size bronze human figure found in a once isolated province which rivalled the main Bronze Age capitals but was not recorded in the textual evidence.

For Rawson objects tell alternative stories, they challenge the canonical consensus. More than this, they are a metaphor for and a mobiliser of cultural thought. Confucius said jade represented the paradigms of human virtue and immortality, much as gold does in the West. Rawson adds that this established a dialectic between physical reality and cognitive structure, since an individual would treat somebody with jade quite differently and probably more deferentially than somebody without jade. But isn't it something of a paradox that a gifted linguist like Rawson should be so transported by objects, by the realm beyond language? She does not think so: 'I think that once you have learnt Chinese, you realise that languages are not all equivalent, they are only arbitrary constructs. It becomes clear that you need more than one access to a people's mind.'

If Rawson became ever more dedicated to research in the 1980s, she never let her museum work slip. Exhibitions, she realised, are a good vehicle for research. In 1984–85, in an exhibition called 'Chinese

Ornaments: the Lotus and the Dragon', she presented her work on the origin, migration and transformation of some key ornaments through the cultures of Eurasia. Two years later she got the top job in the department and set to work on what most regard as her finest curatorial achievement, the Joseph E. Hotung gallery.

Finding £2 million of sponsorship from Hotung, a millionaire Hong Kong businessman, Rawson completely refurbished a gallery that was first built in 1914. Like her exhibitions, this permanent gallery contains the fruits of her latest research, and the presentation crosses cultural boundaries – with the beautiful jades and bronzes of the East set in the golden surroundings of the West. According to Robert Knox, who succeeeded Rawson to the post of keeper: 'She transformed what was an old and worn and grey and lifeless gallery attracting 50 people each day, into a gold-leaf-covered treasure chamber attracting several hundred people every day.'

As if for emphasis, Dr Knox adds: 'And that's a big thing'. Certainly it set her up well in the competition for the ultimate museum job: director of the British Museum. Sir David Wilson retired in 1992 and Rawson put her name into the hat. At the time the *Financial Times* said she was 'the joker in the pack'. Rawson says she applied, but not 'terrifically whole-heartedly' and she was 'not surprised by the decision' to appoint Robert Anderson. A close colleague confirms that she applied, 'in part because she thought that if she did not apply she would be accepting the British Museum view that oriental material is in some sense marginal to the Greek and Roman material'.

Soon afterwards, anyway, she left for Oxford. 'That was lucky for Chinese scholarship,' says one observer, and Rawson acknowledges that as the British Museum's director she would have had 'little time for scholarship'. Research now takes precedence, although she has not left the British Museum behind completely, since she is preparing a new Chinese exhibition for September 1996 which is expected to rival the famous Tutankhamun exhibition of the 1970s. But if she ever doubts the wisdom of her move, she can look back on the day soon after she arrived at Merton when she discovered a long-forgotten Chinese bronze incense burner in a dusty library cupboard. For a sinologist, that was heartening enough. But the ritual vessel turned out to have been a gift to the college from Sir Aurel Stein, a turn- of-the-century explorer who gave to the British Museum one of the most precious collections of ancient oriental artefacts. For a former keeper of the British Museum's oriental antiquities, that was indeed a good omen.

Publications include:

Chinese Jade Throughout the Ages, 1975, catalogue of exhibition at the Victoria and Albert museum.
Chinese Ornament: The Lotus and the Dragon, 1984, British Museum Publications.
Chinese Bronzes: Art and Ritual, 1987, British Museum Publications.
Chinese Jade from the Neolithic to the Qing, 1995, British Museum Press.

(Simon Targett, © Times Higher Education Supplement)

Condoleezza Rice, born 1954, is provost and professor of political science, Stanford University, California. She was American President George Bush's special assistant for Soviet affairs.

In the early nineties *Time* magazine pinpointed a small group of rising stars in American life. One was Condoleezza Rice, the first black and the first woman to occupy the number-two job at Stanford University in California. She was someone to watch, said *Time*.

The provost's job at Stanford is widely regarded as a stepping-stone to the presidency of a major American university. But another striking aspect of the appointment was that Rice is a paid-up member of the Republican party, having been the then President George Bush's special assistant for Soviet affairs in the early nineties, helping to shape US policy when the sun was setting on the Soviet empire.

Stanford, for all its élitist reputation, is a pretty laid-back, roller-blading, Californian kind of place. Some academics were worried that her selection, coming as it did hard on the heels of conservative Gerhard Caspar's appointment to the presidency of Stanford, signalled a shift to the right. What it seems to have brought is relative tranquillity after a period in which Stanford's reputation was tarnished by scandal. The former president, Donald Kennedy, had been claiming a yacht and flowers in his mansion, among other things, as expenses incurred in the course of federal government research. Congress began to investigate, Kennedy was grilled and Stanford was left licking its wounds.

Rice is part of the new broom sweeping through the administrative corridors. Not everybody likes her. She has set about cutting services and firing staff to meet a $43 million budget shortfall. Her most controversial act, which led to a hunger strike by Mexican-American students, was to sack a Mexican-American administrator. But Condoleezza Rice remains unfazed by such conflict. While she admits that campus politics in America are 'quite something', she says: 'I think I tend to just assume that that's part of the job and not to find it actually all that disconcerting. I don't like going through a spring like we went through (in 1993), but I don't find it overwhelming in any sense.' With a little laugh, she adds: 'I didn't sleep badly.' Which shows how cool she is in the midst of turmoil.

But you have to remember that Rice has worked in the White House, in one of the most pressurised jobs in the world. Not too many higher education jobs can be as high-pressure as the one she occupied from March 1990 to March 1991, when Poland was being liberated, the Soviet Union breaking up and Germany coming together again. She was the only Soviet adviser at the National Security Council. Her job was to advise George Bush, write his briefing papers, take notes of his meetings with Russian politicians like Gorbachev and Yeltsin, and jet about the world with him.

Later she was one of three people preparing the actual documents for the foreign secretaries to consider at the time of German unification. Between March and September of 1990 she travelled to Germany twelve times. It was a heady and chaotic time. Rice describes it as a 'spectacular' experience. The White House staff was very small. 'You feel that you're always living at the edge of making some very big mistake,' she says, with another endearing laugh. 'You get called at two o'clock in the morning to make a snap judgment about what should or should not be done, what should or should not go to the President. That kind of pressure. I don't think I'll ever have a harder job.'

The other contrast between a Stanford administrator's life and her job at the White House – and one which helps her with perspective – is the stakes involved. 'I can remember going down to talk to Baltic Americans a couple of days after the Soviets stormed the television tower in Lithuania,' she says. 'And you have people looking at you and saying, you know, the blood of seventeen Lithuanians is on the hands of this administration. And that's tough. Standing up in front of a group of students is not tough.'

Condoleezza Rice is a pragmatist, not an ideologue. Her views are considered, middle of the road, pro-affirmative action, thoughtful on political correctness, the kind of views any Democrat-voting university administrator might articulate. Although chosen to give a speech at the Republican National Convention in 1992, the convention which was hijacked by the Republican Right, her speech, which was on foreign policy, was quite unlike the usual political rant. Washington insiders noticed the carefully worked-out positions, the logical argument, the intellectual as opposed to emotional content.

One has to remember that she is first and foremost an academic. She would never have got the provost job otherwise. A scholar of Soviet affairs (she was made a full professor a month before her appointment to provost), Rice has written two books on the Soviet Union. A third, on German unification, was published in 1995.

Born in segregated Birmingham, Alabama, she was brought up to believe in herself. Her father, a Presbyterian minister who later became associate vice-chancellor at the University of Denver, and her mother, a high-school teacher, were incredibly ambitious for her. 'They had me absolutely convinced that I might not be able to have a hamburger at Woolworth's in Birmingham, but I could be president of the United States, if I wanted to be, and probably ought to be, from their point of view,' she explains (more laughter).

As an only child, Rice had their undivided attention, which was to stand her in good stead. She has a robust attitude towards the subject of racism. It is not something she dwells on. She tells a story about a counsellor at her Denver high school who underestimated her because of her colour. (The counsellor thought Rice was not college material.) 'I use that as an example of how sometimes people will underestimate others – and that I think is the most pernicious form of racism,' she says.

No one seems to have underestimated Condoleezza Rice after that. She became an undergraduate at the University of Denver at the tender age of fifteen, thinking she would major in music because she had been playing the piano since she was three. She had learnt to read music before she learnt to read words. But at college she ran into some hard realities. Although pretty good at the piano, she was not exceptionally talented. 'I started to run into true prodigies and I thought I'm going to end up teaching thirteen-year-olds to murder Beethoven. And that really isn't what I want to do with my life because I didn't like teaching piano at all.' So, she cut her losses, and switched to international politics, which was taught by a Soviet specialist, 'a wonderful man', according to Rice, who had been the Czech ambassador to Yugoslavia and had fled Czechoslovakia at the time of the *coup d'état* in 1948. This man was Dr Josef Korbel, father of Madeleine Albright, President Clinton's ambassador to the United Nations. 'He just brought it all alive for me,' she explains. 'I had always sort of had an interest in things Russian. I liked Russian music and Russian culture and read Russian literature. But it was that class that really stimulated my interest in maybe doing this as a profession.'

Condoleezza Rice speaks Russian. Her doctoral thesis was on the Soviet Union and the Czechoslovak army and it became her first book. It is a study of civil-military relations in states that are not completely independent – client states. She looked at how Soviet influence affected the Czech military. That may be ancient history now, but the problems remain. 'What I'm really interested in now, for instance, is how you deal with the military in democratising countries, because militaries are a threat to democratic rule in so many countries,' she says.

Rice cites Africa and Latin America, in particular, with their repeated *coups*. People always ask why militaries intervene. But Rice thinks the real question is why they don't intervene more often, and what are the forces that make civilian control of the military stable. Her research has concentrated on the structures and values that support civilian control of the military, and includes the early American period when the Founding Fathers were grappling with the question. The Soviet Union never had to think about it, but today's Russians do.

Is she hopeful about Russia's future? She gives a rehearsed answer. 'Well, Russia's a little bit like a critically ill patient,' she says. 'You have to get up every day and take the pulse and hope that nothing catastrophic happened the night before, but every day that it lives it's got a chance.

'And I think that they're getting up every day and they're trying to just go through the process of building democracy and it's a mixed picture. I think there are some very good signs. I think the development of a free press is an excellent sign. And it really is a free press now in ways that it hasn't been ever.' She favours the 'shock' therapy for economic reforms and points out how very hard it has been for Russians to make some reforms, because encrusted attitudes have got in the way. Their attitude towards private property, for example, has prevented them making the progress in agriculture which they should have done.

Rice didn't become a Republican until 1980, and the reason was Jimmy Carter's foreign policy. By then, she was studying Soviet politics. 'I thought the Soviet Union was on the march in the seventies,' she says. 'And I thought there was little resistance to that, and that President Carter didn't fundamentally understand the nature of the Soviet Union.' In retrospect Rice believes even more strongly that she was right. 'I think that was a horrible, as President Reagan put it, a "sad" episode in human history,' she says. 'And I think that everything that's coming out now about how the Soviet Union conducted its affairs in foreign policy, what it did to its own people, only confirms that.'

The way in which Stalin built vast, military cities like Tomsk and Chita, way out in the Soviet hinterland, shows what a monster was created, Rice says. She visited these cities on the Trans-Siberian Express in 1988, three years after Gorbachev came to power. 'You would go through these cities and you would hear "Attention, Attention", and it was because you were going through a military city. If it was daytime they would put up curtains so you couldn't see anything. They created this monster really. What are people in places that only make rocket motors for inter-continental ballistic missiles supposed to do? What are they supposed to do?'

Rice's second book, *The Gorbachev Era*, which she edited with Alexander Dallin and which is based on a conference, looked at the problems Gorbachev faced when he came to power. Her third book, completed after four years, is a detailed study of the negotiations and diplomacy in 1990 that surrounded German reunification. Entitled *Germany Unified and Europe Transformed: A Study in Statecraft*, it is co-authored with Philip Zelikow, a professor at Harvard's Kennedy school of government. The pair had access to all the American documents under a rule that permits former officials to use their own documents. They were required to undergo a clearance process with the US government, but will nevertheless be revealing far more than would be possible in Britain under the thirty-year rule.

They had a letter from Bush to Gorbachev, and through a great stroke of luck some key documents from the Russian side which were made available to them by a 'wonderful young woman working for

Gorbachev'. Also they had very detailed diaries from the German side, and some from the Soviet side, and they conducted interviews in Britain and France.

Condoleezza Rice has seized all the chances that have come her way. She became involved in government through asking Brent Scowcroft (later National Security Adviser under President Bush) a tough question when he came to dinner at Stanford in 1984. She was then twenty-nine. He had come to talk about special commissions being set up to look at US nuclear offensive and defensive strategies. The opinionated Rice said she didn't think such commissions were a good idea because they usurped the authority of Congress. Didn't he agree? Soon she and Scowcroft were friends. 'When President Bush asked him to come to Washington, he called and said "I'd really like you to come with me. I need a Soviet specialist."' she explains. 'And he said "This guy Gorbachev, he's doing really interesting things, and this could really turn out to be an interesting period." And I thought hard about it and thought, well, he's probably right.' Her experience was so extraordinary that she's not sure she wants to go back into government again. Could it be that good a second time?

She wonders, but doesn't rule it out. Rice had been back at Stanford for two years when she was asked to be provost. She had doubts about whether she could give up the excitement of international travel and research at this moment. The doubts are still there in her tone of voice. 'But I love this university and I thought I had a chance to do something good for it, so I put those concerns aside,' she says.

Being provost is a huge management load. Effectively, she is the chief operating officer, dealing with finances and the running of the institution. One is left wondering whether she finds it sufficiently intellectually demanding. For Rice loves to talk about ideas. Asked about political correctness, for example, she launches into an articulate and thoughtful exposition of the subject. 'I think it's one of those phrases that oversimplifies what is a very complicated problem,' she says. That is not the kind of response one would hear from most Republicans. 'The complicated problem is that this is an increasingly diversifying society, and people are coming into much closer contact with each other than they ever did.' When Rice was growing up in segregated Birmingham, she and her friends didn't have to think about how they talked to other people because they were all black. They didn't have friends of other races. But today, particularly on university campuses, the races are mixing as never before. There's a cacophony of different views and experiences, and people's feelings are easily hurt. In that context it is perfectly proper for people to take account of one another's feelings, she says.

However, it's another matter to say, you can't make that argument, because it might offend me. 'I find that a problem for a university, because bumping up against people who disagree with you is fundamental to the creation of new knowledge. And so universities can't go silent. You can't have a place where it's not permitted to make a certain kind of argument.' But you can have a place which forbids epithets to be thrown at people, she says. 'I think those two have gotten confused.'

Debate about what should be taught at American colleges and universities, another hot potato, is 'somewhat vacuous and superficial', she thinks. Of course, it's desirable to have a true historical record of blacks in the US and of the cultures of all who contributed towards the US But people also need to understand that Western values dominated the founding of America, and they need to know about these ideas. Although she is against quotas, Rice is in favour of affirmative action, i.e. voluntary action to broaden the pool of people you look at to find people who are first-rate. 'Sometimes you have to look places you wouldn't normally look, like the University of Denver,' she says archly.

Rice has been asked time and again whether she is an affirmative action appointment, somebody who would not have got where she has without helping hands. 'I understand it's a double-edged sword,' she says. 'I can't tell you how many times I've been asked by people "Do you think race and gender contributed to your success?" How the heck do I know. I can't repackage myself as a white male and see whether I would have gotten this far.'

Publications include:

Uncertain Allegiance: The Soviet Union and the Czechoslovak Army, 1984, Princeton University Press.

(Ed.) *The Gorbachev Era*, 1986, with Alexander Dallin, Stanford University Press.

Germany Unified and Europe Transformed: A Study in Statecraft, 1995, with Philip Zelikow, Harvard University Press.

(© Lucy Hodges)

Susan Richards, born 1948, is professor of public management at Birmingham University. A former civil servant, she was an advocate of the new public service managerialism introduced by Conservative governments since 1979, who then went on to establish her own successful management consultancy.

Photograph © Sharron Wallace

There can be few organisations anywhere within the public sector which have not in recent years had a brush with management consultants. Sometimes these rationalisers have appeared like angels of death in suits, whose reports, high-quality laser-printing *de rigueur*, and presentations (what is a presentation without an OHP and a whiteboard?) eventually pronounce a sentence of 'downsizing', and if not that then a rigorous course of 'culture change'. Universities, funding councils, Whitehall departments, non-departmental public bodies, local authorities, health trusts: they have all met these dark visitors. Only those institutions which need change the most, the House of Commons, say, or the minister's private office, are spared the consultancy.

Behind the consultants there has of course lain financial reality, the desire to secure more for less, wrest savings all round, in reponse to a perceived mood-switch on the part of a more individualist and tax-averse electorate. In an individualist age much of the action has been inside collectivities, organisations. But for all their apparent influence consultants have been oddly invisible within the wider culture. They have not spawned soap operas. Little girls and boys don't usually tell their primary school teachers that what they want to grow up to be is a management consultant. They have, like the accountancy firms which shelter many of them, been famously grey.

That is not much of an introduction to Sue Richards, who is a consultant, a very successful consultant moreover, who recently moved to a high-profile position as professor of public management at the burgeoning School of Public Policy at Birmingham University. A grey woman? Well no, yet someone whose style is very much that of the organisation's psychotherapist, who seems to know what the employees and the executives obviously do not, cannot know about the pathologies of their . . . council, health trust, broadcasting corporation.

For consultancy is a form of talk therapy, and therefore its best practitioners are masters of timbre, nuance, tone and volume. One of the first things you notice about Richards is her voice, pitched low and in its softness able to stitch disparate positions together, to move people apparently on opposite tracks back on the main line, to get discussion going. A female skill, I wondered, this 'listening without competing' as she calls it?

Sue Richards is more than a listener. Career civil servant, entrepreneur and, in such books as *Improving Public Management,* a theorist, at least the kind of conceptualiser able to give a name and a shape to a new empirical phenomenon. It is, in considerable measure, thanks to her that the course of organisational changes in the public sector has a name, the 'new public management'. This embraces the doctrine of devolving managerial discretion down the line, 'empowering' lower-level staff to take more responsibility, writing all-encompassing 'mission statements', attending rigorously to costs, hiving off non-essential functions to contracted-out agencies, splitting the activity of contracting and strategy setting from that of delivering services or policy execution . . . It is manifest, in Whitehall, in the creation of the Next Step agencies, in the National Health Service, in the quasi-markets in which fund-holding general practitioners purchase medical services from hospitals, in local authorities, in competitive tendering for white as well as blue-collar services, and so on.

Never a Thatcherite, coming indeed from a left-of-centre background, Sue Richards was an early advocate and a prophet of the new managerialism. Now, while still an enthusiast for the reform of decision-taking, culture and practice in public-sector organisations, she is also its critic. As she settles into Birmingham she is thinking hard how any of these changes – Thatcherite in much of their inspiration – will survive the transition to a new, possibly Labour government. And what now of the argument that management change may have gone too far in substituting a can-do, business-oriented culture in public bodies where the public interest may demand caution, procedure and an innate sense of responsibility? The report, so long in arriving, of Sir Richard Scott into British arms sales to Iraq has come to symbolise the danger of a deficient moral and constitutional sense among public officials, elected and appointed. How much needs to be recuperated of an older, even Victorian notion of public service that orients itself not just towards the 'top of the office' – the minister's suite or the vice-chancellor's office – but to a wider conception of the public and its interest in good government?

'I think the Scott inquiry does show that there has been a decline in professional standards in the civil service, but I do not believe that this has been caused by managerialism. I see no reason why you should not have effective management for high public purpose. But public values have to be asserted and defended and that has not happened.'

'I don't align myself with the view that markets are better but I do think the health reforms have moved the NHS forward in all sorts of positive ways. In the civil service, management did improve, in cost and quality; it also even became more humanistic as notions of organisational culture, and winning the support of staff to achieve a vision and purpose took hold.'

But now Richards is about to embark on an Economic and Social Research Council-sponsored study of the effects of 'market testing' in central government – the programme by which public bodies are required to identify blocks of their work that could be performed by external contractors. Market testing, she feels, has produced some short-term cost savings, 'but may have damaged long-term capacity'. The name of the game for her, now, is to seek to provide the intellectual framework for thinking about the new public management as political and financial circumstances change.

For this theorist of change, her own trajectory has been – socially speaking – upwards, carried by the logics of education and employment out of working-class Bradford. The changing etiquette of culture and employment makes class identification ever more fraught, but how else, other than working class, do you describe a father who ran a cobbling business till he went blind then worked in a department store's petrol station, and a mother who made and decorated wedding cakes, in between raising a family of six children?

'There are two ways of handling the ladder of mobility. One is to detach yourself, leave it all behind. For me, strong family roots keep me going back there. My life is now very different, as part of the affluent middle class in the South East. I was lucky in having a warm supportive family who cared a lot for me, did not always understand where I was going, but none the less believed that anything I did was right as far as they were concerned. I see a very different world through the eyes of my mother and the rest of my family. That replenishes my anger if I am inclined to be too forgiving.'

What she did, after studying politics at Liverpool University and doing graduate work, first at Essex then at Birmingham Universities, was teach at Newcastle upon Tyne Polytechnic, where began her intellectual engagement with organisational life. Then to London, with a partner who is now a local authority museums officer, to teach middle-level civil servants about the political context of their work. This was at the Civil Service College, Whitehall's in-house training school. It is an odd, incomplete institution, part of whose job is to defend the faith that there is such a thing as a unified, professional civil service, rather than a group of departmental baronies loosely watched by a weak central authority in the Cabinet Office and Treasury.

It also did some research. Sue Richards fell among a group of people, a temporary phenomenon at the college, 'genuine academics' she calls them, who were trying to make sense of and explain what was happening empirically to public administration as Mrs Thatcher consolidated her power in the early and mid-1980s. Among them were Les Metcalfe, now at the European Institute of Public Administration, Robert Walker, now at Loughborough University, and Helen Wallace, now at the University of Sussex. The head of the unit was David Lewis, a career civil servant, and they were doing what the college was supposed to be doing but never quite was; giving back to practitioners a theoretically-informed account of their work, reflecting on practice in a theoretically-driven way.

'The culture of that little group was important in encouraging me to take myself seriously as an academic commentator on the Thatcher reforms then under way. I have a capacity to observe in the world of practice, to hear and to see partial truths. As a teenager I moved every day between my home culture and the culture of my direct-grant grammar school. This taught me early about cultural difference. There is, perhaps, a gender aspect to all this; intuition is not a magical property. If you stand outside the dominant culture you have to learn how to read it.'

The mid-eighties were an exciting time. *Improving Public Management*, written with Les Metcalfe, seemed to many to capture and explain the phenomenon for the first time, to make what was happening apace in health, local government and Whitehall acquire more coherence – more coherence, she now acknowledges, than perhaps it actually possessed. Critical research on public management within Whitehall was countercultural, easily killed at the flick of a mandarin's memo.

In seminars, in presentations and in papers Sue Richards became an advocate for the new managerialism and the criticism it contained of the mandarin class. 'Not a Thatcherite critique ... but something in my background chimed with the impatience, expressed among others by Sir John Hoskins, the Prime Minister's policy adviser, with the civil service's skill at the civilised management of decline. I felt a sense of outrage at the collapse of the manufacturing economies of cities like Bradford. I felt the smooth world of the mandarinate was part of the problem. What we badly needed was to modernise our government institutions so that we would be better equipped to solve social and economic problems.'

And she became, good Thatcherite transition this, an entrepreneur. After a spell at the London Business School she went into business. With Laurie McMahon and Greg Parston from the King's Fund College, she founded a management consultancy, the Office for Public Management, risking the family home, working all the hours eighties doers did. But OPM was intended to be different: it sought to achieve organisational reform for the sake of social purpose – to go into Labour councils, for example, with sympathy for their aims, seeking to help them realize their core values and objectives better.

But the aim was also to continue reflecting upon management practice. We had two aims, she recollects. One was to take the chaos out of the practitioners' world – the director of housing, the health chair, the agency executive – by reforming and reconceptualising their reality so that they could see cause and effect at play in their world and so handle it. 'We wanted to help them to understand and manage ... better.'

It did not feel very risky, she says. 'We were confident of our skills and in a service industry the primary assets are the people. Apart from having an office base and a few computers huge capital investment is not required.' OPM grew. It now employs fifty people, a third support staff, the rest professional consultants. So is she rich?

'We did not intend to take a profit. All the surplus has gone into developing the Office, and to funding some action research work.' It is a theme she comes back to, how hard it is to keep the process of reflection and concept development alive in the driven, competitive world of consultancy. OPM, she concedes, has done less thinking than she had hoped. And that fact goes some way to explain her move to

Birmingham. Because, she believes, in a university devoted to learning and enlightenment there will be strong support for the development of public management ideas which can influence practice.

What made her aspire to succeed in the world? 'I was turning thirty, no longer a pretty young thing, and realising that I could sink into the invisibility of middle age as a woman unless I worked out what my particular contribution to the world would be. When I had my daughter, there was the additional spur of wanting to set her an example, to encourage her achievement.'

Has the world welcomed her, as a woman? 'I suppose being a woman in the predominantly male world of commentary on public service has given me an added visibility, to my benefit.'

'Chief executives and directors of public service organisations are mostly male. Competitiveness seems to be built into the male of the species. Being different, complementary rather than competitive, allows access to issues which may be closed off to men – you are able to hold up that mirror even though it may contain distressing flaws, when you are not the gender competitor.'

'In our sort of consultancy understanding clients' culture and way of thinking is essential in enabling you to bring issues to the surface and manage them. The most powerful people in the organisation bear most responsibility for the state of their cultures and facing them with the often negative consequences of their own behaviour requires both delicacy and courage.'

Publications include:

Improving Public Management, 1987, with Les Metcalfe, Sage.
'Managing people in the new Civil Service', 1989, *Public Money and Management*, Autumn.
'Managing change in the Civil Service', 1993, with Jeff Rodrigues, *Public Money and Management*, Spring.
'Devolving public management, centralising public policy', 1994, *Oxford Review of Economic Policy*, 10, 3.
'Strategic management in a "re-invented government"', 1995 with Paul Jervis, *Strategic Management Society*, October.

(© David Walker)

Jacqueline Rose, born 1949, is professor of English at Queen Mary and Westfield College, University of London. Her work marries psychoanalytic theory with literary analysis – an approach which resulted in controversy when Rose applied it to the writings of the dead poet Sylvia Plath.

Photograph by Neil Turner © Insight

'We are talking about the Poet Laureate versus Virago Feminist Press.' Jacqueline Rose, professor of English at Queen Mary and Westfield College, pauses as she recalls the words of her Queen's Counsel. They were uttered on the eve of publication of Rose's controversial study of the works of the American poet Sylvia Plath, who committed suicide in 1963, shortly after her separation from husband Ted Hughes, the current Poet Laureate.

For a time it looked as though there might be legal disagreement between Hughes and Rose and her publishers, Virago. The headlines, as Rose's QC suggested, would have taken a predictable line. But the disagreement never got that far, although Rose still describes the period leading up to the publication of *The Haunting of Sylvia Plath* as 'one of the most extraordinary and difficult experiences I have ever had'.

Other authors might have bowed out under the weight of opposition: not only that of Hughes, now Poet Laureate, who inherited Plath's literary estate, but also that of Hughes's sister Olwyn, who, until recently, controlled the rights to her sister-in-law's work. Other studies of Plath before Rose's had encountered opposition from the Hugheses, including *Bitter Fame*, the biography by Anne Stevenson.

But, as Rose points out in the introduction to *The Haunting of Sylvia Plath*, 'This is not a biography'. Her book, she said, was not about Plath's life but her work. 'The publication of this book . . . represents an assertion of the diversity of literary interpretation and of the right of every reader of Sylvia Plath to form her/his own view of the meanings . . . of her work.'

Nonetheless, the Hugheses protested. The book was called 'evil' by Olwyn. Ted Hughes found Rose's reading of the Plath poem, 'The Rabbit Catcher', with its suggestion of bisexuality, particularly inflammatory. (Rose's reading of the poem was explicit, suggesting, for instance, a reference to oral sex in the Plath line 'the wind gagging my mouth with my own blown hair'.) In a letter to the *Times Literary Supplement* in 1992 Hughes described the 're-invention' of Plath's 'sexual identity' as 'humiliating' and damaging to Plath's (by then adult) children. In a letter to Rose herself Hughes suggested that in some countries such speculation, as he saw it, on a mother's sexual identity would be 'grounds for homicide'. Rose responded again drawing a distinction between life and work. In a letter to the *TLS* she elaborates: 'to read sexual ambiguity into a poem is to say nothing about Plath's lived experience as a woman – poetry being, among other things, a place where the unlived can be explored.'

But what Rose recalls of the dispute is not just a sense of strain but also of positive struggle, of co-operative feminist effort overcoming obstacles. True, she had to make 100 changes to her manuscript after taking legal advice, but she welcomed these, prefacing most of them with a phrase which made clear that one of the Hugheses had been the source of the new material. Nor did she change her basic reading of Plath's work. 'I thought I might have lost the book because the legal risks were so high. But to see how a feminist publishing house will rally round, with a real commitment coming from its own anti-establishment politics and history was tremendously encouraging. The press valued the book, thought the objections invalid and was determined to see it through.'

The binary opposition set up between establishment figures and feminist outsiders (she reels off a list of lone voices – including Marietta Higgs and Wendy Savage – all defended by the late Brian Raymond, Virago's 'brilliant' lawyer), is one angle on Rose's work. But it is not the whole story. For although her commitment to feminism is unequivocal, her complex and difficult vision, marrying as it does politics and psychoanalysis, has often brought her into conflict with feminists who want no truck with theories which have the potential to undermine their fight for rapid social change.

Such feminists are suspicious of what they see as the male story of psychoanalysis, with its impossible-to-prove explanations of how individuals develop, and they are especially suspicious of the theories of the founding father of the discipline, Sigmund Freud. The Oedipal crisis, for instance, when the male child is supposed to desire his mother but fear the wrath of his father (genitally directed, hence the boy fears castration, while the daughter believes her mutilation has already ocurred).

Rose herself says that although Freud could be 'a terrible chauvinist' who sometimes said 'preposterous' things about women, his theories on infantile sexuality and the unconscious, and his recognition that sexual identity is less fixed than society assumes, are 'very liberating' for a feminist. One of Freud's most radical insights, says Rose, is that the unconscious is bisexual. 'Freud treats the transition from being a bisexual, insatiable infant to recognising oneself as a stable, heterosexual, self-controlled person with a wonderfully creative form of scepticism', says Rose. 'For a feminism that thinks the dominant forms of sexuality and identity the culture offers are not desirable, Freud's insights are valuable because they give a way of thinking about that discomfort.'

As a student at Oxford University campaigning, at one key moment, for childcare facilities on the Cowley estate, Rose was a feminist before she became interested in psychoanalysis. She dates her feminism to 1969, when in one 'extraordinary week' both Germaine Greer and the Black Panthers visited the university. 'It was a turning-point – but I also felt that feminism did not have enough space for the inner life of the mind. When feminism did start to say the personal was political it was not saying it in terms of memory or desire or fantasy – it was saying it in terms of the political importance of private lives.'

So it seemed that in those early campaigns, vital as they were, there was no space to explore the pain of abortion, for instance, or the possibility that women's fantasy life might be enhanced by pornography, or the nature of children's sexual desire (the last because of the imperatives of an unambiguous stand against child abuse – can a child both be abused and have a desire for the father?). What Rose is seeking are connections between the black/white world of feminists like Andrea Dworkin and Catharine MacKinnon, with their concrete demands for social and legal change, and a much more complex 'interrogation of problems of self-identification and sexuality in the unconscious'.

Hence her fascination with Plath who, she has said, simultaneously protests against social institutions such as medicine, psychiatry and marriage while acknowledging women's 'sometimes self-defeatingly pleasurable engagement in the very structures against which they protest'.

In fact her book on Plath is characteristic of Rose's middle path –

steering a course between the generation of male critics, like Leavisite David Holbrook, who used psychoanalysis to pathologise Plath (he said she displayed schizoid characteristics and was unsuitable for school study) and the second generation of feminist scholars who, in order to politicise her, seemed to Rose to avoid what was most troubling about her inner psychic life.

It was in Paris, as a research student at the Sorbonne, that Rose first read Freud as part of her research for a thesis on children's literature (later completed under Frank Kermode in London and published as a psychoanalytic and cultural study of Peter Pan). 'I became clear that I wanted a feminism that could be agitational, that would take demands for political equality but would also talk about psychic life, sexuality and so on.' In fact *Sexuality in the Field of Vision*, the title of her collection of essays in the fields of psychoanalytic, literary and film criticism, can be read as a pun, not only talking about the representation of sexuality in the cinema, but also placing sexuality centre stage, where for psychoanalysis it belongs.

But the early 1970s were a bad time to try to be a feminist interested in Freud. For to be a Freudian was the cardinal feminist sin, a position that changed only with the publication in 1974 of Juliet Mitchell's book *Psychoanalysis and Feminism,* which gave Rose the sense for the first time that maybe 'two seemingly incompatible things could come together'.

In 1982, a decade after returning from France, while lecturing at Sussex University, she published, together with Mitchell, a translation of French psychoanalyst Jacques Lacan's theories, which were themselves based on a reworking of Freudian concepts; a rewriting of Freudianism in linguistic terms. Nearly fifteen years on, Feminine Sexuality; *Jacques Lacan and the école freudienne* is still required reading for students determined to get to grips with feminist literary theory. Isobel Armstrong, professor of English at Birkbeck College, London describes it (and its introduction by Rose) as 'absolutely the most important book of the early eighties, not only for feminism but for the subject of English studies'.

What it does, according to Armstrong, is put forward the notion that masculine and feminine roles are not fixed, but 'constructed' via 'the symbolic order', – the agreed set of categories and classifications which has to be accepted by everyone if we are not to go mad. The symbolic order, says Armstrong, is more than language or the legal system, although it encompasses linguistic and legal rules. 'The upside of the symbolic order is that you remain sane because you can communicate,' says Armstrong. 'The downside is that you are involved in oppression. In our society the symbolic order and patriarchy are the same thing. The symbolic order is enforced by "the Law of the Father". The Law demands repression. Psychoanalysis is interested in the repressed area of the unconscious.'

And in the places where the symbolic order slips, revealing the shifting ground beneath our assumptions of sexual identity. Plath is fascinating, Rose has said, 'because she regularly unsettles (such) certainties, troubling the forms of cohesion on which 'civilised' culture . . . often oppressively relies.'

After the Rose/Mitchell book feminism became much more complicated. The assumptions that feminine roles are biological or that they can be changed by nurture were revealed as too simplistic. Instead the task became to understand how sexual difference had been organised. 'We had to begin to think about the subject in a much more complicated way,' says Armstrong. But what remains ambiguous is whether Rose's position permits the possibility of a non-patriarchal symbolic order; whether in the political arena feminists have some grounds for optimism.

In recent years Rose has pushed further afield, into psychoanalytic explorations of other aspects of politics and history. 'What Rose believes,' says Armstrong, 'is that psychoanalysis is already political – because it refuses to accept a subjectivity which is coherent and uniform and in control of its world. The unconscious is always disrupting that.' From there it is a short step to investigation of phenomena, like violence, which break through controlling social structures.

'Violence', says Rose, 'has always been an issue in feminism, but its account of violence has always been one-sided – male violence against women. I feel that, while recognition of male violence is crucial, the question of violence is more complicated.' She raises the question of violence in women's fantasy life, of the glorification of state violence (the Gulf War, the Falklands, capital punishment debates) and in her most recent work, in South Africa and the Middle East. She asks difficult questions about where individual violence comes from – is it the expression of repressed instincts by civilisation? And what is the relationship between individual and state sanctioned violence?

During the Gulf War, says Rose, George Bush's public approval ratings went up to 90 per cent, the Falklands War was central to Margaret Thatcher winning the 1983 election. If states can draw on violence in these collective ways, is it something to do with people's unconscious relationship to violence? In an article, 'Why War?', published in a collection of her essays with the same title, she cites phrases which tellingly link images of sexual identity and aggression: Bush promising 'Saddam is going to get his arse kicked', a phrase he previously used for vice-presidential nominee Geraldine Ferraro. Or the *Sunday Sport* headline 'Saddam in Gay Lover Storm' or Saddam Hussein himself announcing that the 'ultimate evil of the West is demonstrated by the presence of American women in the desert', women in shorts, women baring their bodies, women at war. 'Why War?' concludes by asking whether the ultimate problem for the idea of a psychoanalytic cure is the problem of war.

Stuart Hall, professor of sociology at the Open University has shared the platform with Rose at the Institute of Contemporary Arts and admires the work she has done on the interrelationship between politics and fantasy. In his discussion of the 1987 general election Conservative victory, which saw Margaret Thatcher elected for a third term, Hall himself acknowledged that politics is partly a matter of fantasy, of the way people imagine themselves or imagine where they would like to be.

'What I like most about her writing is that it is very subtle and complex in its understanding of the relationship. It knows that the psychic and politics are connected but does not seek to reduce one to the terms of the other', says Hall.

Rose's essay on Thatcher and Ruth Ellis, the last woman to be publicly hanged in Britain, for instance, raises questions about women and power, women and violence and the roles of victim and executioner. Following her second election victory Thatcher permitted a vote on capital punishment. In discussions on the subject Ellis's image kept recurring. Advancing far beyond the simple pragmatic statement of whether Thatcher was for or against women, Rose raised deep and unsettling questions of how Thatcher's femininity was implicated in her political position in contradictory ways. 'That is exactly what foxed people, we expected the identifications associated with Thatcher to work in a traditional class way – but they so clearly did not. They cut across class boundaries,' says Hall. 'That can be explained in part by the nature of the psychic mechanisms going on, which enabled those kinds of investments to take place.'

Other cultures are now beginning to feature more strongly in Rose's work. An article entitled 'On the "universality" of madness', about the black South African writer Bessie Head, who wrote a semi-fictional account of a breakdown she suffered while in exile in Botswana, counters the criticism that psychoanalysis is only relevant to Western cultures. She is also republishing, with South African historian Saul Dubow, *Black Hamlet* by Wulf Sachs – the first psychoanalytic text to be published in South Africa in 1937. Jewishness and its place in British culture is under consideration in her article about Dorothy Richardson's *Pilgrimage,* which turns, crucially, on a Jewish man. (Rose's own maternal grandparents were first-generation Polish Jewish immigrants, who owned a shop near where she now teaches on the Whitechapel Road in London's East End.) Most recently, in her 1994 Clarendon lectures, 'States of Fantasy', she pursues these issues into a discussion of fantasy and politics in relation to South Africa, and Israel/Palestine, and their links to the British literary and cultural imagination.

Rose admits that her own interest in psychoanalysis does not originate from a solely academic curiosity. In her twenties she started an eight-year course of analysis (with a female Freudian psychoanalyst), to explore 'my complex childhood – which left a legacy'. Rose is reticent about her private life. She and her sister Gillian, professor of social and political thought at Warwick University, once turned down an interview with the *Tatler.* They felt that the personal focus might draw attention away from their work. 'There is a tendency to fetishise academic siblings,' she comments. In 1995, Gillian, who was diagnosed as having ovarian cancer and has since died, published *Love's Work,* a philosophical autobiographical narrative of mesmerising power, which gives some details of the family's history.

Jacqueline Rose has recently adopted a baby daughter, Mia, from China but never felt that 'motherhood and feminism or intellectual/academic work are or should be (within the limits of the possible) incompatible'. Her partner is child psychotherapist and writer Adam Phillips.

Since her first job was taken to pay her analyst's fees, it is fitting that she should have been able to carve a living from exploring her 'passions' – feminism, literature, film and psychoanalysis. Ironically, in leaving England for France as a research student she unintentionally turned herself into an 'oddly employable' commodity in the UK, where writers on cinema, and later, academics in universities, were starting to get interested in the writings of the French theorists.

The fact that her first writing was for the film world and theoretical magazines – *Screen, New Left Review, m/f* – was a reflection of the tardiness of university English departments in shedding the Matthew

Arnold tradition of literary criticism and coming to grips with the importance of French thinkers like Lacan and Julia Kristeva. Now, however, as psychoanalysis is pushed out of psychology departments it is finding a home in English literature faculties.

The interview draws to a close with Rose stressing how fortunate she feels to have been appointed to the chair at QMW, which must be unique among the male-dominated academic establishment for now having not just one female and feminist professor but two (Rose joined Lisa Jardine).

Some academics, remarks Rose, finally, have no time for psychoanalysis. 'They think the unconscious is too much of a problem. But I think that if you do not think about the unconscious, it thinks about you.'

Publications include:

(Ed.) *Feminine Sexuality: Jacques Lacan and the école freudienne*, 1982, with Juliet Mitchell, translated by Jacqueline Rose, Macmillan.

The Case of Peter Pan: or the Impossibility of Children's Fiction, 1984, Macmillan.

Sexuality in the Field of Vision, 1986, Verso.

The Haunting of Sylvia Plath, 1991, Virago.

Why War? Psychoanalysis, Politics, and the Return to Melanie Klein, 1993, Blackwell.

States of Fantasy: The 1994 Clarendon Lectures in English Literature, 1996, Oxford University Press.

(Sian Griffiths, © Times Higher Education Supplement)

Alice Stewart, born 1906, is senior research fellow at Birmingham University. She showed that the practice of X-raying pregnant women was causing childhood leukaemia. Now, in her ninetieth year, she is still working on the dangers of low-level radiation to human health; work which has made her a heroine of the anti-nuclear movement.

Photograph © News Team

In the mid-1950s, the pioneering epidemiologist Alice Stewart showed that the practice of X-raying pregnant women was causing leukaemia and other forms of cancer in children. It was the first evidence that low-level radiation could harm human health. Yet in the climate of techno-optimism that dominated the 1950s, many of Stewart's peers did not believe her data and did their best to refute them. Her popularity did not improve when she began uncovering new evidence that low-level radiation was damaging the health of workers in a American nuclear reprocessing plant that produced plutonium for nuclear weapons. Today, she remains a controversial figure, with friends and foes scattered throughout the world.

Stewart is still at the bench and still publishing papers to confound her critics. 'I was unpopular at first because undoubtedly X-rays were a favourite toy of the medical profession,' says Stewart. 'And of course I became unpopular when I focused on nuclear weapon manufacturers. But you can't blame yourself for that.' A heroine of the anti-nuclear movement today, she is keen to stress her impartiality. 'If the data had gone the other way I would have been just as strong.'

Stewart 'retired' from Oxford some twenty years ago, where she was reader of social medicine. But she immediately set up a new base at Birmingham University, where she still works with statistician George Kneale. Every weekday she walks to her office in the medical school, and gets on with the analyses. Where did she get the courage to buck the system, and to carry on despite the hostility her work has long inspired?

'People often ask me that,' she muses, 'and I think it's slightly to do with being a woman'. When Stewart – already the youngest woman ever to be made a Fellow of the Royal College of Physicians – became head of a pioneering department of social medicine soon after the war, the Oxford medical faculty had already decided there was 'no future' in public health epidemiology. But Stewart refused to go. Starved of funds, status and influence, she dug her heels in. 'I became head of this department that was deprived of everything. If I'd been a man, I would never have stood it – I would have gone. The prospects were too bad, the pay was too low. But being a woman I didn't have all that number of choices, and I have always found it rather difficult to spend money.'

'I also think it was a very good influence being a member of a big sibship because there is nothing so hard in life again,' she recalls. 'I was the second girl, the third child, with a boy and a girl above me, with one girl just a bit younger than me and then four boys. It was quite an awkward position to be in. So you learn how to handle it, and you don't really expect too much of life. To this day, it never phases me if nine people turn up for lunch and I've only enough for one. And you learn not to mind about battles – what would be the point of minding in a big family? You had better get on and get what you can. Needless to say my daydreams were all about how lovely it would be to be an only child.'

Daughter of two doctors, Stewart was actively encouraged to seek a medical career. But she found her fellow Cambridge medical students 'absolutely shocking'. 'There were four women and 300 men in my class. As I came into the lecture theatre and took my first step the men started to slowly stamp their feet in unison. I had to walk down the steps, to run the gauntlet, to sit on the front row with the other girls, along with one other person – I would never make friends with any medical student; I was having nothing to do with these "scum", I said to myself.'

It set the pattern for Stewart's later life. Her husband and her many friends were to come mostly from the arts or politics, rather than medicine. While not a political activist herself, she sees herself as 'instinctively a feminist and instinctively a socialist'.

Studying medicine at the Royal Free hospital in London, she discovered she had a flair for working out what was wrong with patients. She likens her diagnostic skills to her prowess at the game Scrabble. 'I don't reckon I'm a very clever person, and I don't think I have a particularly good vocabulary. But I have any amount of ingenuity about where the next word might go.'

She applied for hospital posts, but now married to a schoolteacher, and with two children, she found it difficult to land good jobs. The outbreak of the Second World War was her salvation. 'Suddenly I was *persona grata*, as I couldn't be called up. I was being offered jobs that normally would only have gone the way of men.'

Arriving at the Nuffield Department of Clinical Medicine in Oxford, she had her first taste of research. She tackled a problem that worried both the Medical Research Council and the War Office: how to safeguard the health of factory workers whose job it was to fill shells with the toxic and explosive chemical TNT. It was to be her first foray into the still embryonic field of 'social medicine'. Characteristically, she adopted a novel approach to the problem. 'I felt I didn't know enough about the thing, and the only way to do it would be to go and fill the shells myself, and then I might have some understanding of what it was about.' She had biochemical tests done on herself before and after. Then she began to recruit student volunteers to work in the factories during the long vacation under agreed conditions. 'They could do their war work this way and be paid for it, in return for the occasional blood test.' The work was a great success, revealing ways in which work practices would be altered to limit workers' exposure. After this triumph, she was popular with the Medical Research Council, which commissioned her to do three or four similar sorts of investigations during the war.

Stewart says her 'semi-ingenuity in thinking up things' won her a fellowship to the Royal College of Physicians at a tender age. 'I was the first woman under forty and there were only nine elderly women in front of me.' At the end of the war Professor John Ryle, who had what is today called a holistic view of medicine, decided that 'public health' lacked a proper university basis. He put his name to the first department of social medicine in Oxford. 'Before the war medicine was more or less a grocery business; you sold your drugs to those who could afford them. But the advent of war showed that doctors have a responsibility to the whole nation and need to find the answers to questions that are relevant to public health.'

Ryle asked Stewart to join him, but soon after, he died, 'unfortunately just as the medical faculty of Oxford was regretting founding the department'. The decision to close the unit was rescinded, only for fear of offending a living patron, Lord Nuffield. 'I was put back in charge but in very very mean conditions,' says Stewart. She began to look for something new and important to study, and settled on leukaemia, when her statistician colleague David Hewitt noted that there was something peculiar going on in children. He showed that there was an early peak of mortality from leukaemia between the ages of two and four. 'I said, let's go to the mothers of the children who died of leukaemia and other sorts of cancer and get their story. I suspected that the leukaemia peak was caused by something that was happening prenatally, and that the mothers might have collective memories of that which the doctors hadn't noticed.' But when Stewart took this project to the MRC, she was turned down 'on the grounds that leukaemia was too rare and you couldn't organise the survey and one thing or another'.

With £2000 scraped together from a charitable trust by a supportive colleague, she set out to do the project anyway. Stewart convinced the medical officers of each local authority to interview the mothers and set up a control group of children of the same age and area. 'We could see in the first thirty-seven completed forms there was one obvious difference: the mothers of children with all forms of malignant disease had been X-rayed before giving birth twice as often as matched controls. That set the jackpot going and roughly has kept me in the business of low-level radiation ever since.' Stewart's preliminary report came out in 1956, as she turned fifty, and caused a considerable stir. 'But lots of people chipped in saying we must be wrong, including the people on the MRC committee which had turned us down. So we said, we'd better go on.'

Stewart and her colleagues begin to survey all the children born in a given year and to continue to keep track of their health, year after year, for ten years and more. 'We went more or less to ground during this time,' says Stewart. 'Oxford University was still being very mean to us, but one of the great comforts of that was that it wasn't giving me any teaching or administrative work to do. So I was able to devote myself the whole time to this story. For years and years ours was the only evidence of low doses of radiation having a cancer effect.'

Throughout this period, American funding bodies provided the bulk of the modest 'glue money' that kept the childhood survey going. Stewart happened onto this source of funds almost by chance. In the 1950s a visiting American epidemiologist arrived late at her office, saying he had thought Keble College, across the road, was her establishment. 'I laughed and said we don't go that big here, I'm lucky enough to have one room.' He suggested applying to the US for funds, and sent her the documents. At last, after the forms languished in her in-tray for some weeks, she asked for £5000. She got it. 'I think I was part of the Marshall Plan aid,' she jokes, and year after year the grant was renewed.

Throughout her Oxford years, Stewart's private life had not been easy either. As her marriage broke up, leaving her with two children to rear on her own, Stewart acknowledges that 'there were times when things were a bit difficult. 'Yet,' she says, 'it was marvellous to have a mother who was herself a pioneer. The family I married into was the same, so I had a whole generation of feminism behind me, recognising the nature of the difficulties and helping in the way that was needed, never criticising you when things went wrong.' She also had to cope with the tragic death of her son, who left behind a wife and two small children whom Stewart helped to support.

Controversially, Stewart was never awarded a professorship, but she was made a professorial fellow of Lady Margaret Hall. 'I do remember thinking I had rather been taken off the streets when that happened. It made all the difference to my time in Oxford. My medical colleagues were being unhelpful to say the least, but the college filled the gap completely, again allowing me to make friends with people outside of medicine. It turned out to be a very good thing.'

International renown and the chance to travel came to Stewart after the childhood cancer report. She became 'rather well known' and began to establish links with American epidemiologists working on radiation exposure in workers at the Hanford nuclear plant in Washington state and on the A-bomb survivors. After the Three Mile Island accident in the US in 1979, she and George Kneale won a £1.2 million grant from the Three Mile Island Public Health Fund, which has been funding their work since the mid-1980s. Her determination not to let Kneale down – her collaborator for more than twenty years – has been 'another thing that kept me going'.

Against the mainstream, Stewart and Kneale argue that A-bomb survivors are not a reliable source of risk estimates for cancer. 'Time and again you read that A-bomb data are the gold standard, and anything that differs from that is wrong.' As a result, few researchers in the field are yet prepared to believe Stewart's and Kneale's analysis of the Hanford workers' data, which reveals an increased cancer risk even at low levels of exposure. She and Kneale argue that their critics are pooling different data illegitimately and neglecting the effect of age on health risks. The critics by and large ignore her. 'I don't think they're wicked, I think they've blinded themselves, they've got tunnel vision.' Her secret weapon, apart from her longevity, she says, is her 'latent conceit: I know that I am going to be right. I have known this for some time. It may not happen in my lifetime – in fact, it probably won't – but it will be found that we were on the right track. You'd be surprised how comforting that is.'

She sees conventional ambition as a snare and delusion. 'I like to think I stand for something, and that is, don't be afraid not to get to the top, it's a most uncomfortable position. I've always had enough money to do my work, never big grants, but always enough' – and not too much to turn her into an administrator instead. She says that 'one of the best things is not being a success; in fact, not being a success has almost been a necessity'. Her favourite quotation comes from Webster's *Duchess of Malfi*: 'Glories, like glow-worms, afar off shine bright, But looked to near, have neither heat nor light'. She chuckles: 'Don't you think that's lovely? I laugh about it, and say to myself, yes, those glow-worms, I don't really mind about them.'

Publications include:

'Malignant diseases in childhood and diagnostic irradiation in utero', 1956, with J. Webb, D. Giles and D. Hewitt, *The Lancet*, i, p. 447.

'Aetiology of childhood malignancies, congenitally determined leukamias', 1961, *British Journal of Medicine*, i, pp. 452–60.

'Epidemiology of childhood cancers', 1967, in R. W. Raven and F. J. C. Rose (eds.), *The Prevention of Cancer*, Butterworths, pp. 352–8.

'Radiation dose effects in relation to obstetric x-rays and childhood cancers', 1970, with G. W. Kneale, *The Lancet* i, pp. 1185–8.

'Low-dose radiation cancers in man', 1971, in G. Klien and S. Weinhouse (eds.), *Advances in Cancer Research*, Academic Press, pp. 359–90.

'Radiation exposures of Hanford workers dying from cancer and other causes', 1977, with T. F. Mancuso and G. W. Kneale, *Health Physics*, 33, pp. 369–84.

'Delayed effects of A-bomb radiation: a review of recent mortality rates and risk estimates for five-year survivors', 1982, *Journal of Epidemiology and Community Health*, 36, 2, pp. 80–6.

(© Gail Vines)

Marilyn Strathern, born 1941, is William Wyse professor of social anthropology at the University of Cambridge. Her work questions the concepts and categories Western anthropology has used to understand other societies and cultures.

Photograph © Chris Thomond

'Taking things for granted' is Marilyn Strathern's catch-phrase. During our Saturday interview, in her family home, teenage sons Alan and Huw banished from the kitchen while we lunched, she used the phrase no fewer than seven times. 'Taking things for granted' has been, she joked, 'the cause of my downfall'.

It is a mark of just how radical she has become that the phrase serves as an ironic commentary, not only on her work, where she has over-turned the categories and distinctions 'taken for granted' by Western anthropologists as tools to understand the non-Western cultures and societies they study, but also on her personal life.

Having begun her post-graduation life 'taking for granted' that the one institutional career in the family would be that of her anthropologist husband, Andrew, Strathern's promotion to the William Wyse chair of social anthropology at Cambridge in 1993 was achieved as a single mother who had brought up, almost single-handedly, three children for long periods of their lives. The slow, traumatic disintegration of a partnership which began in the early sixties when the pair were Cambridge students finally ended in the dissolution of their marriage in 1986.(The couple published one book together, *Self-Decoration in Mount Hagen*, about the meanings attached to the self-decoration of the people of the Papua New Guinea highlands.)

Strathern's award of the Cambridge chair was the culmination of a long process of challenging assumptions, her own included. But the seeds of her success were sown years earlier, in an untypical, English middle-class childhood. She grew up with a set of, for the times, unusual

[237]

views. Her mother, even in the fifties, an era when most British house-wives stayed at home, combined rearing her family with a career as a teacher of literature and history – to prisoners in Maidstone jail, to seamen, at adult education classes. Teaching classes on women's contribution to the arts, she imparted to her daughter 'the unself-conscious notion' that 'women were a reasonable area of study'.

So when Strathern, a newly-wedded Cambridge graduate, embarked with her husband for Papua New Guinea, an island group in the Pacific ocean, off the north-eastern tip of Australia, in the early 1960s, it seemed perfectly natural to choose as her research topic the role of women 'in between' clans, focusing in particular on the part they played in quarrels and disputes. It was spawned 'not of a strong feminist agenda at all, much more a taken-for-granted interest'. She was surprised therefore when a distinct lack of critical acclaim greeted the result, her first book, *Women in Between: Female Roles in a Male World*, published in 1972. It just missed the crest of the Women's Liberation Movement and hence was dismissed as 'dull', precisely because, says Strathern, of its perceived focus on women.

At the time Papua New Guinea was not a common destination for young anthropologists; Africa was more usual. It is characteristic of the way Strathern thinks that my question: 'Why did you choose Papua New Guinea?' is met with a long, and gentle, explanation of why the question is 'not interesting'.

'When migrants from Mount Hagen (in the Highlands of Papua New Guinea) go to the capital, Port Moresby, anthropologists are always desperate to know why. I undertook a study of migrants to Port Moresby – but I got very fed up with the reasons they gave. "Well, I wanted to see what it was like." "Well I jumped on the back of a lorry . . ." It took me a long time to work out I was asking the wrong question. It was not an interesting question.'

Similarly with my query about why the Stratherns chose Papua New Guinea as a research destination. All the Cambridge postgraduates could easily have chosen other destinations in which to carry out field-work. Obviously there were circumstantial reasons for choosing Papua New Guinea. 'But once you have been where you have been – you are changed irrevocably. For us Papua New Guinea became significant *after* the event, not before.'

Parts of Mt Hagen were still being opened up even as late as the early 1950s. The Stratherns chose a research area which had been settled by missionaries and of which a few written accounts already existed.

On the upstairs landing of her home Strathern opens a large chest and takes out strings of New Guinea shells. 'Men, in particular,' she says, 'organised their political life around the distribution of wealth. Pigs were the principal stock, but shells were also wealth objects. Money entered the system only later.'

Holding cowrie and mother-of-pearl shells sewn into headbands and belts she explains how Europeans airlifted thousands of shells into the PNG Highlands creating inflation within the shell economy. 'People gained prestige by giving away vast quantities of wealth to others. Political life is based on transfers of wealth between "big" men.'

Giving away symbols of wealth demonstrated two things: firstly, the status of the giver; secondly, the act served as a challenge – would the recipient be 'big' enough one day to return the pigs/shells? In her first book Strathern took an interest in the role of women in exchanges of wealth, political transactions between groups of Highlanders. Women who, via marriage, moved from one group to another were regarded as important 'roads' between the clans along which riches might flow. They were seen, says Strathern, as having 'loyalties to distribute'; they could ally themselves with the kin of their husband, or stay loyal to their parents family. A married woman could be described as 'in-between', i.e., acting as an intermediary across two sets of in-laws. But she could also be a source of bitter argument, over for instance, the amount of bride-wealth paid to the bride's parents by the husband's family, or in claims for compensation as a result of domestic violence. 'When there were quarrels between clans it was often possible to trace that back to a problem with women at some point – perhaps dissatisfaction with their husbands or a desire for divorce.'

Women in Between was a straightforward empirical piece of anthropological research, examining more than fifty cases in which women were directly involved with compensation claims, and arguing that women's 'intermediary status' gave them a hitherto unremarked 'autonomy of action', particularly in marital disputes. The book was followed by another manuscript, commissioned but never published. Its rubric was to present descriptions of gender relations (by both men and women, from a variety of cultures) and ask 'what might be distinct to anthropological specifications'.

By this time Strathern had a young daughter, Barbara, and was living in Papua New Guinea with her husband, who had been appointed to a chair at the university there. Strathern says that had that second manuscript been published and picked up by the early feminist movement the course of her career might have been very different.

As it was her Melanesian research left her with a foil to measure other cultures, a basis for her later, relativist thinking. *In Gender of the Gift*, which has been described as a rewriting of *Women in Between*, she re-analyses the great corpus of Melanesian ethnography with a critical eye.

According to Simon Harrison, professor of anthropology at the University of Ulster, Melanesia left Strathern with a strong sense that gender roles are culturally created, and vary enormously from culture to culture. 'What a man or woman is is only defined in terms of the particular culture one is looking at,' says Harrison. Such a viewpoint runs counter to 'essentialist' theories, which suggest that female/male behaviour is biologically determined – an innate 'essence', perhaps even genetically imprinted. 'Strathern would say that womanhood/malehood can only be understood in terms of different cultures because different cultures construct radically different kinds of power-relationships between men and women.'

Even more importantly, says Harrison, 'she developed the idea that the human person is also only a cultural construct'. 'The basic theme of her work is that there is an enormous difference between the way the person has been imagined in Western culture since the eighteenth century and the way the person is constituted in Melanesian culture.'

In the West, says Harrison, we think of the person as an individual – 'someone who cannot be broken down into anything smaller, someone who exists prior to any social relationships he or she might be involved in. Western philosophy begins with a collection of fundamentally anti-social, appetital individuals and then asks – how do these individuals enter into social relationships with each other?'

In Melanesia, on the other hand, Strathern argues that the situation is reversed. In Melanesia social relationships exist prior to individuals. The Melanesian person is constructed out of social relationships, born into a network of already existing connections and responsibilities which serve to define identity. In Melanesia the person is regarded as fundamentally sociable from the start. By extension the Melanesian gift economy is an exchange of commodities which exists to express relations between people. This contrasts strongly with capitalism, the Western economic expression of individualism, where exchanges of goods and services take place merely to create profit or gain.

Thus Strathern showed that our Western analytical concept of persons as individuals in society was useless when it came to rendering correctly the framework of Melanesian peoples. As Christian Toren of Brunel University says, after reading Strathern 'one has to find concepts which better capture the phenomena of Melanesian life, such as Melanesian sociality and gift exchanges between partible persons'.

Harrison also believes that 'between the lines', in her analysis of Melanesian culture, Strathern is, very subtly, criticising Western individualism. 'There is a tradition in anthropology of using other cultures as a hammer to bash Western culture with. She is doing that, but subtly. She says, between the lines, that at some sort of level Melanesian society has got it right. The individual is, in her view, inherently a social being. We in the West do not say that.'

Although all anthropologists 'are reflexive' – going into the field to carry out research which affects their understanding of their own society's categories – Strathern's critiques are far more radical: an unpicking of the very foundations on which the social science of anthropology is based. A colleague at Manchester University, where Strathern was head of the anthropology department, says: 'She makes the concepts through which anthropologists work part of what needs to be the subject of anthropological scrutiny. The taken-for-granted assumptions about the world are very much the subject of her analysis.' Harrison adds 'In some respects she is at the extreme end of cultural relativism. She takes a very very radical approach to the understanding of the person. To a certain extent she tackles a perennial problem of anthropology – to what extent can our own Western concepts apply to the understanding of other cultures?'

Concepts such as 'Nature' and 'Culture', for instance, scepticism with which Strathern traces back to her attendance at a conference on age and gender. 'People were talking about children being "natural" beings who had to be socialised into being fully "cultural" beings. I came away and thought: "I don't think there is any way one can translate nature/culture into real life. It just does not fit."' In *Nature, Culture and Gender*, a collection of essays edited by Strathern and Carol MacCormack, contributors amplify the point that 'the dichotomy between nature and culture and its association with a contrast between the sexes' was dreamt up by thinkers from Western societies.

Strathern's cultural relativism has laid her open to the charge of being 'difficult'. Her critics are those who dislike the move away from conventional positivist methodologies as well as the blurring of the boundaries between anthropology and other disciplines. They see her conceptual questioning as threatening, dismiss as pointless the way she subjects theories and analytical distinctions to informed interrogation.

Strathern, for all her success, is very alive to her critics' concerns. 'I think,' she says, 'I irritate people.' More seriously, she believes that cultural changes in Britain in the past decade are actually contributing to a backlash against the kind of thinking she favours. The stress now, she says, is on teaching as the imparting of neatly packaged answers to limited questions.

'What is in the wings, of course, is a new materialism. A sort of back-to-commonsense movement. What distinguishes the back-to commonsense people is the notion that you can have fairly direct access to knowledge – you do not need models, or if you do, they can be fairly simple ones. We do not need to interpret what is going on. You can see what is there. The back-to-commonsense people would regard the care one takes over how one interprets things as obfuscating. I am regarded as obfuscating, I am regarded as playing with concepts for the sake of it. They say all this superstructure of theorising and arcane concepts is unnecessary,' she says.

For Strathern, however, interpretation is at the heart of today's complex, self-aware societies. She has devised a 'beautifully simple formula' for describing social change – one of anthropology's traditional blind spots. The crucial ingredient, she says, is awareness of what has hitherto been unquestioningly accepted. 'People become aware of their own cultural system. In becoming aware of their own values they try to implement them. When you try to implement what before you took for granted – you change the terrain.'

Her own work around new reproductive technologies illustrates the point. The research of scientists and doctors has made explicit the elements which make up a birth, the nature of the blood-ties; who donates the egg, who the sperm, who carries the developing foetus, who fertilises the egg in the petri dish . . . The family ties involved in a birth and previously taken for granted are suddenly spelt out. 'People keep saying "There is nothing new about the new reproductive technologies – we are simply doing what has always been done". But we are being explicit – and that itself is changing things. Things can never go back to an implicit state again.'

In such a context, the importance of deconstruction, interpretation, explanation seems vital. But Strathern can be critical of her own practice. In a 1986 essay entitled 'The Study of Gender Relations' she writes of 'tackling analytical categories of all kinds', '(the nature/culture dichotomy: "woman" as a self-evident category; concepts of person-hood . . .)'. She adds, 'In a way it was too easy, once one was aware of the disjunction between categories of analysis and the representational system of those under study, almost any analytical endeavour could be criticised.' In the interview she describes it as 'like shooting a football at goal after the whistle has gone' and points out that her initial interest in cultural matters partly stemmed from being tied to Britain by the need to bring up her children, which prevented her for a long time from being able to carry out fieldwork abroad. (Rising early, before the children were awake, gave her precious time to write.)

A recent book, *After Nature*, hints at a deep melancholy for the way things were, for the past's secure systems of knowledge which could not be challenged or subjected to the kind of scrutiny she herself excels at. One review, in the *Guardian* newspaper, described it 'as a really first class nightmare', 'a splendidly lugubrious study', in which Strathern argues that the concepts of society and nature have collapsed. Instead we live with an individualism based on consumerism.

Caught in the midst of this phenomenon, says Strathern, 'I as a consumer feel nauseated. I just feel ill. There is no sense in making any choice, each entity is merely a combination. It is the same with academic life. Challenging assumptions was exhilarating but when that is all you are doing, there is a sense of glut. Of course, I am a principal culprit in producing this sense of glut.'

What she rescues from her sense of 'consumerism in politics, in academia, in morality' is that all are part of a contemporary mosaic and all are related to each other. 'All you can hold on to is the fact that there is an explanation for it – as long as you can think that – it is OK. As an anthropologist I hold onto the fact that one can be interested in this relationship.'

Publications include:

Women in Between: Female Roles in a Male World, 1972, Seminar (Academic) Press.

(Ed.) *Nature, Culture and Gender*, 1980, with C. MacCormack, Cambridge University Press.

Kinship at the Core: An anthropology of Elmdon, A Village in North-west Essex in the Nineteen Sixties, 1981, Cambridge University Press.

(Ed.) *Dealing with Inequality: Analysing Gender Relations in Melanesia and Beyond*, 1987, Cambridge University Press.

The Gender of the Gift. Problems with Women and Problems with Society in Melanesia, 1988, University of California Press.

After Nature: English Kinship in the Late Twentieth Century, 1992, Cambridge University Press.

Reproducing the Future: Essays on Anthropology, Kinship and the New Reproductive Technologies, 1992, Manchester University Press.

(Sian Griffiths, © Times Higher Education Supplement)

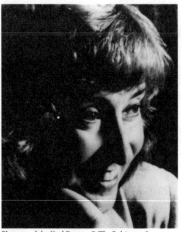

Photograph by Karl Ferron, © The Baltimore Sun

Deborah Tannen, born 1945, is university professor and professor of linguistics at Georgetown University, Washington DC. Her research, on how differences in male and female styles of speech can lead to misunderstanding, has brought her celebrity in America.

Sellotaped to the door of Deborah Tannen's office at Georgetown University is a photocopy of a cartoon from the *New Yorker* magazine. Portrayed is a couple exchanging wedding vows, and standing between them is Professor Tannen. The priest intones: 'And do you, Deborah Tannen, think they know what they're talking about'.

Mildly funny. For Tannen the point is not the humour but that the cartoon appeared in the *New Yorker*, that venerable American cultural icon now edited by Tina Brown. 'That they would assume that their readers would all recognize my name,' says Tannen. 'That was what was so amazing to me.'

Today Deborah Tannen is a household name, a sociolinguist of international renown, whose book *You Just Don't Understand* was an unexpected success and catapulted her into the *New York Times* bestseller list for almost four years. Also a bestseller in the United Kingdom and six other countries, it struck an immediate chord with the public for its explanations of how men and women talk differently, and end up misunderstanding one another.

Her latest book, *Talking from 9 to 5*, picks up where *You Just Don't Understand* left off and analyses, as she puts it in the subheading, how men and women's conversational styles affect who gets heard, who gets credit and what gets done at work. In this book, Tannen shows how girls teach one another not to appear bossy, to avoid standing out, and to find ways of saving the other person's face. Girls have conversational rituals, she explains, which mean the speaker takes what she calls 'a one-down position', and relies on the other person to bring her back up. Women, for example, often say 'I'm sorry' when they don't mean it literally. What they are doing is showing sympathy. To men, who are taught not to say 'sorry' all the time, who are more likely to boast and try to avoid 'one-down positions', it looks as though women are taking the blame. Similarly women's ritual self-deprecation can be seen as lack of confidence or even competence, and men's ritual self-protection can be misinterpreted as arrogance. All of which may explain partly why women hit a 'glass ceiling' and fail to climb to the top of the managerial greasy pole. Women in positions of authority are in a double-bind, she says. If they talk in ways expected of women, they may not be respected. But if they talk in ways expected of men, they may not be liked.

Tannen's books for popular audiences are a great read. She is writing about things that fascinate, and does so well. Her prose may feel a bit padded at times but it is rich in anecdotes, replete with stories about people, quotations and literary references. It comes as no surprise to discover she majored in English.

One of her best illustrations of the differences between men and women is the way women are happy to ask for directions when *en route* to an unfamiliar place, but men won't. Sometimes this can be downright dangerous. 'A Hollywood talk-show producer told me that she had been flying with her father in his private airplane when he was running out of gas and uncertain about the precise location of the local landing strip he was heading for,' she writes in *Talking from 9 to 5*. 'Beginning to panic, the woman said, "Daddy! Why don't you radio the control tower and ask them where to land?" He answered, "I don't want them to think I'm lost." Thankfully, the story had a happy ending.' The moral of such stories, according to Tannen, is flexibility. 'Sticking to habit in the face of all challenges is not so smart if it ends up getting you killed. If we all understood our own styles and knew their limits and their alternatives, we'd be better off – especially at work, where the results of what we do have repercussions for co-workers and the company, as well as for our own futures.'

She is careful not to say that one style is superior to the other. Although she generalises about the behaviour of men and women, she does not do so crudely. There are always exceptions to the conversational styles, she reminds us, and there are always cultural differences. What one must remember about Tannen is that she is first and foremost an academic. She may write fluently, but there are no easy solutions, no self-help manual for those who want to change their conversational styles. Tannen's work is based on research, years of listening to people talk into her tape-recorder, or, in the case of the new book, three years of observing and interviewing people at work. Her only advice is that people should become better aware of their own and others' conversational styles and how the two interact. Self-knowledge might help us to improve, but it's up to us to find the way.

Tannen shows no sign of letting up. She has the grand title of 'university professor', a special designation for extraordinary members of faculty, of which there are only three at Georgetown, awarded because of her success. She also has a secretary to herself, but she is still driving herself to write – at the moment plays about her family which are being performed in the Washington area. A tall, blonde figure, without make-up, she exudes a wry, no-nonsense friendliness, and bursts into cackles of laughter as she tells her life story. Her roots are New York Jewish. Both parents came to America as children, her father from Poland and her mother from Russia.

Listening to her talk, one sees striking parallels between her life and those of some other American women academics. Like Camille Paglia, flamboyant author of *Sexual Personae*, she derived great intellectual sustenance from her father, who was intellectual but not college-educated. He acquired a law degree at night-school but couldn't get work in the Depression, so took jobs as a prison guard and a cutter in the New York rag trade while becoming active in left-wing politics. Like Paglia, Tannen attended what was then Harpur College, and is now the State University of New York at Binghamton, on a scholarship. Both women came from working-class families, and were able to live the American dream through education – specifically at a low-cost, high-quality state college. Both women are childless, giving them the time to pursue their interests obsessively. Arguably, they were not circumscribed by having conventional career expectations made of them, as men might have had. They were able to follow their interests, and write about subjects, gender and conversation (Tannen) and sex and culture (Paglia), which could have landed men in hot water.

Tannen thinks it important that she was one of three daughters. Girls with brothers often have to watch while the boys of the family do things the girls are not allowed to do, she says. Not so the Tannen girls. She attended an all-girls high school in New York run by Hunter College. It was an élite public school with a competitive entrance exam and it was for intellectually gifted girls. 'I think that had a strong effect on me as well,' she says. At Binghamton during the 1960s she overlapped with Camille Paglia and had the distinction of rejecting one of Paglia's poems submitted to the literary magazine of which she (Tannen) was editor. Maybe Tannen did Paglia a favour. Because of that early rejection, Paglia claims, she never wrote any more poetry and devoted herself to a larger topic – the whole of Western culture. Tannen agrees with Paglia that Binghamton was an exceptional place, with good teachers, and students with a hunger for knowledge. In short, a superior place to the Ivy League universities. 'The time we were at Harpur was an amazing time,' says Tannen. 'It was the sixties, so it was political ferment. Also, schools like Harvard and Yale are very full of themselves. Harpur wasn't. We were all working-class kids who went there because we were smart. It was at that time the only small liberal arts college in the state system, and I think most of us were in the same position.

'We had gotten a Regent's scholarship, our parents didn't have enough money to send us to a big-name school, but they had just enough money that if we could have our tuition paid, they could manage.'

After her degree, Tannen followed the route taken by many other bold, young Americans of the time. She worked feverishly for a few months, saving money, and headed for Europe. In fact her goal was to go round the world and never come back. This was 1966. Graduate school did not beckon. 'I had no career goals at all,' she explains, chuckling at the memory. 'I just wanted an interesting life, so I wanted to leave the country and do something extreme and interesting.' In fact, Tannen never got further than Greece. She met a Greek man on the beach, fell for him, taught English and after two years returned with him to America. He was her first husband, who serves as material for the opening paragraph of *You Just Don't Understand*. As she explained in that book: 'Many years ago I was married to a man who shouted at me,

"I do not give you the right to raise your voice to me, because you are a woman and I am a man". This was frustrating, because I knew it was unfair. But I also knew just what was going on. I ascribed his unfairness to his having grown up in a country where few people thought women and men might have equal rights.'

Tannen and the first husband went to graduate school in the United States. She worked and supported them, and did most of his academic work for him too, she says, laughing. But she also did her own work and got her own Master's. With that qualification she was able to get work teaching English, and ended up at Leman College, part of the City University of New York system. In the early 1970s her first husband wanted to go back to Greece. For Tannen it was a chance to escape the marriage.

At that point she discovered linguistics. The summer of 1973 was spent luxuriating in her new-found freedom and the thrill of intellectual discovery at the University of Michigan, where she took courses in language and context, roughly what we call sociolinguistics. 'I got very excited by it, and decided I would apply for a PhD in linguistics,' she says. She was accepted at several universities but chose the University of California at Berkeley. Tannen was twenty-nine at the time. She threw in a safe job at CUNY, against the wishes of her father, and, like so many of her compatriots before her, headed West. That was the beginning of her career as a linguist. She spent four-and-a-half years at Berkeley, with a year off in the middle to write a book on Greek writer Lilika Nakos, and earned a Master's and a PhD in linguistics. Much of the time she supported herself by teaching.

Her dissertation was notorious in the annals of linguistics. It was about a Thanksgiving dinner conversation that she tape-recorded. 'I wanted to do a dissertation on conversational style,' she explains. 'That was my big interest and it still is.' At the dinner party were two Californians and a British woman, and three New Yorkers. After listening to the tape for a while she realized that the first three had quite distinct styles from the New Yorkers. They paused more and they did not 'talk along' with one another in the same way as the New Yorkers did. 'There was a whole range of features the New Yorkers used which had a positive effect when used among ourselves, in group talk, but a negative effect, seeming to be overbearing or dominating with the Californians,' she says.

Tannen was fortunate in landing a job at Georgetown before her dissertation was done. She was sought after because she had published articles as a graduate student and had a book contract in the bag. Almost immediately at Georgetown she was directing ten dissertations a year, teaching three courses a term, writing articles and attending meetings and conferences. She was working constantly, but loving it. 'I was so excited to be doing something I loved, and I was so excited to be living an intellectual life again. Those years when I was married and teaching composition were like a wasteland. They were like desert years.'

Tannen also had an extraordinary sense of fear that the world could blow up. That might have to do with having been a child in New York City when there were air-raid shelter drills, she says. Elementary school teachers would yell 'take cover' and the children would have to scurry under their seats. They wore dog tags carrying their names in case there was an atomic bomb and their bodies needed to be recognised. 'I remembered thinking I've got to hurry up and do this dissertation because what would happen if there was an atomic war, my father had a heart attack or something happened to get in my way?' Having a facility for writing meant her work was a joy. 'To churn stuff out was pure pleasure,' she explains. 'It was hedonistic.'

Tannen began to write for popular magazines, she got herself an agent and embarked on a book for a popular audience about conversational style. But her experience with the publishing firm, Dutton, was a nightmare, a lesson to any aspiring writer in how to be resilient. Four editors came and went as she was told to rewrite proposals, write the book, scrap everything she had written, do it a certain way, scrap that. Until, finally, she switched publishers. One of the things that kept her going was her sense of mission, she says. 'Linguistics had so much to offer society at large and everybody was thinking only of psychology, and subconscious feelings,' she explains. 'And I really felt I had a message to get out to people that sometimes what you think is psychology or intentions is really conversational style differences.' Her new editor at William Morrow thought the six chapters that editors 3 and 4 had found unacceptable were fine. She had to write a few more, and the book was published. Called *That's Not What I Meant: How Conversational Style Makes or Breaks Your Relations with Others*, it sold reasonably well and was a Book of the Month Club choice.

Writing the book about men and women, *You Just Don't Understand*, was not as arduous, but there were problems nevertheless. Her editor told her to write it in a more intellectual way than *That's Not What I Meant*, but when the publishers saw the manuscript they said it was too stodgy. Tannen was given six weeks in which to jazz it up. She rose at 5.30 a.m. each morning and worked until 9 or 10 a.m., after which she crammed in the rest of her hectic life. It was another sign, if one was needed, of her supreme competence. The book came out in May 1990, and as the months passed, it became clear it was a stunning success. In June, Tannen was invited on to the hugely popular TV show hosted by Phil Donahue. By August it had sold out of its first 30,000 print run, and had hit the bestseller list. The publishers couldn't believe it. Eventually they caught up with demand. Media interest intensified. Tannen took off the whole of the autumn term to meet publicity demands. The following spring, the pressure had not abated. About once a week a TV camera would follow her to her classes. For a whole year it took over her life. After the paperback edition came out, she began to say no to publicity. 'Now I have it under control,' she says. 'That first year it just about drove me nuts. But I don't do everything now.'

You Just Don't Understand completely changed Tannen's life. 'I had no idea what I was doing when I wrote that book,' she says. Given the choice, she would do it again. 'But it's a very mixed blessing, and I would say, all in all, I was happier before. I am not as happy as I was. Yet it's also very thrilling and fulfilling, as well as being a little over-whelming a lot of the time.'

Today Tannen is happily married for the second time – to an English professor at Fordham University in New York – and has no financial worries. She has just bought a large house in the Virginia suburbs of Washington for more than $1 million. But any best-selling academic is bound to receive criticism, and in Tannen's case, it is coming from feminists who accuse her of being an 'essentialist' (the theory that differences between men and women are biological, which Tannen says she doesn't hold), and from others for being recognised by Bill Clinton, who began to quote her after hearing her speak at a Renaissance weekend, a retreat for the chattering classes.

She is also the subject of criticism from her own colleagues in sociolinguistics. Any famous academic is bound to attract intense envy from less successful academics. Just as J. K. Galbraith was hated by fellow economists at Harvard, so Deborah Tannen is scorned by fellow linguists. She popularises, they say. She is not a theoretician. They point out how much her technical work differs from her popular books, and how much she generalises in the latter. Although she says it is important not to generalise, she goes ahead and generalises. That grates on the professional reader. She also over-simplifies, painting things in black and white when they are really shades of grey. Thus she says that men and women talk differently, but doesn't spend much time looking at exceptions to the stereotypes. She doesn't study variables such as the relative power and status of men and women, which might explain the phenomenon, or the fact that women might not want to talk like men.

Asked about this, she says her books are not about issues of power and status. If she had set out to write about these subjects, she would have done so. Some of the criticisms are justified. But it is fair to say that Tannen would never have become a best-selling writer able to communicate with a popular audience if she had written an academic tome full of qualification and nuance. In short, it is easy for academics to pick apart the work of someone like Tannen who has compromised to get where she has.

Is the criticism hard to take? 'I do get quite upset when I'm criticised for things I didn't say and when I'm criticised by people that I think should see me as an ally,' she says. One also gets the feeling she would rather not go down in history as 'the gender lady'. It is easy to forget that she had written reams of learned material on the relation between written and spoken language, frames theory and other esoteric subjects before venturing into the minefield of gender. But this is something she can cope with.

Publications include:

Conversational Style: Analyzing Talk Among Friends, 1984, Ablex.

That's Not What I Meant! How Conversational Style Makes or Breaks Your Relations With Others, 1986, William Morrow.

Talking Voices: Repetition, Dialogue and Imagery in Conversational Discourse, 1989, Cambridge University Press.

You Just Don't Understand: Women and Men in Conversation, 1990, Morrow.

(Ed.) *Framing in Discourse*, 1993, Oxford University Press.

(Ed.) Gender and Conversational Interaction. 1993, Oxford University Press.

Gender and Discourse, 1994, Oxford University Press.

Talking From 9 to 5: How Women's and Men's Conversational Styles Affect Who Gets Heard, Who Gets Credit, and What Gets Done at Work, 1994, New York Morrow.

(© Lucy Hodges)

Julie Theriot, born 1967, is a fellow at the Whitehead Institute for Biomedical Research in the US. Not yet thirty, she is a high-flying biologist, with a lab of her own and a research project which could lead to drugs preventing thousands of deaths.

In her lab in Cambridge, Massachusetts, Julie Theriot is busy growing nasty strains of bacteria. She nurtures *listeria* and *salmonella*, as well as a bacteria called *shigella flexneri* which results in an awesome statistic – 150 million cases of dysentery in the world and 500,000 deaths. Separately she tends live cells in an incubator.

What she does is to mix the bacteria with the cells and watch what happens under a powerful video-microscope. Don't worry, no animals are involved. There are no blood and guts at the Whitehead Institute for Biomedical Research. This is politically correct science. Ms Theriot's live cells came from an animal ten years ago and have been immortalised in cultures.

Still under thirty, Julie Theriot has achieved what many budding academics spend years working towards – a lab of her own. She has a staff of three, a technician and two postdoctoral students, and her own budget. All of which come from her appointment as fellow at the Whitehead Institute, one of the top biomedical research institutions in the world, set up 'to support innovative ideas by the finest young minds in science'.

The Whitehead fellowships are incredibly prestigious. Typically, only one a year is offered. Julie Theriot received $175,000 for equipment in the first year, plus her salary and that of a technician. A grant from the National Institutes of Health pays for some of the salary bill and operating costs.

Theriot is expected to go far. She is already winning awards for her research – including the 1994 Women in Cell Biology Award – and has appeared in a BBC television programme, *The Seven Wonders of the World*, to explain which natural phenomena have particularly interested her. One of her favourites is the bower bird, which lives in Indonesia and builds beautiful structures as a mating ritual. The birds gather twigs, brightly coloured flowers and shells, and arrange them into bowers, to entice females. A female bird picks the prettiest structure and mates with its creator.

'I think it's really cool,' says Theriot. 'Because the structure itself has no function at all. It's not a nest. It's not where they mate, it's not where they raise their young or anything. They build it for its aesthetic appeal.' This may seem a far cry from examining cells in the lab. But Theriot is interested in the interconnectedness of life. One of the things that fascinates her about her research on cells is the way that bacteria can communicate with animals and human beings. 'I think of all of life as being interdependent and interconnected,' she explains.

Since setting out on her research career, she has been studying cell motility, in other words, the way cells crawl around inside the body. Nobody knows how the process works – 100 years after anyone first began to look at the phenomenon.

Today she's trying to work out how bacteria 'talk' to the host cell in living things. Having discovered the protein on the surface of the bacteria which communicates with the host cell, she's trying to identify the corresponding protein on the host cell.

She is concentrating on the moment of communication between the bacteria and the host cell to see how it is the bacteria tells the actin (the protein) in the host cell to rearrange and form new structures and gets it to move around. It amazes her that bacteria have been able to evolve ways of speaking so specifically to the proteins in our cells that they can tell them what to do.

She is looking at how the bacteria infect the cells – the stages of the process – and the messages that are sent before a host cell capitulates and becomes an infected cell. In the case of *shigella flexneri* and *listeria*, the food-borne parasite that causes meningitis and stillbirths in human beings, the bacteria co-opt proteins on the surface of infected host cells to form 'comet tails'. The tails give the bacterium speed so that it can leap from an infected cell to an uninfected one, thereby spreading infection and reducing the bacterium's exposure to the human immune system.

The two species of bacteria – *shigella* and *listeria* – are entirely unrelated, yet they use the same strategy. That suggests to Theriot that the tail strategy developed independently more than twice in bacterial evolution.

Salmonella bacteria have a different method for invading cells. They persuade the host cell to undergo dramatic rearrangement before they even enter it. You can see what happens on one of Theriot's videos. When a *salmonella* bacterium approaches a human intestinal cell, the bit of the cell closest to the bacterium becomes disturbed. The whole structure of the cell changes. It develops huge waves (called 'splashes') that reach out and envelop the bacterium, drawing it into the body of the cell. The disease is now beginning to take over.

Julie Theriot wants to know how it is that the *salmonella* bacteria perform this trick. The point is that once science has found the answer, medicine can step in and prevent disease from taking over the body by fooling the bacterium that it's inside a piece of smelly Brie, for example, rather than in your gut, or by persuading the host cells to ignore the signals being beamed at them. All of which is comfortingly relevant.

Theriot is doing research which could help people, and which might lead to drugs that prevent hundreds of thousands of deaths. It's trendy too. Infectious diseases which were thought to have been killed off in the developed world have resurfaced. New, multi-drug-resistant strains of tuberculosis and pneumonia are popping up again in American cities, and the possibility of dying from such an infection has become a reality.

Julie Theriot's research has come at the right time. But what's important to the pure scientists is that her research is innovative. In the past, when scientists were looking at ways to fight disease, they would take bacteria growing on a petri plate and try to find chemicals to kill them. That is how penicillin and streptomycin were discovered. But that was somewhat simple-minded, says Theriot, because the presence of bacteria in the human body is not what causes disease. What causes disease is the body's response. 'Instead of trying to kill the bacteria, we can also try to mess up the way that they communicate with the host,' she explains. 'The human immune system is really very well adapted to clearing out bacteria and so basically all that you need to do is to slow down the process of infection, slow down the process of disease causation.'

Dr Gerald Fink, director of the Whitehead Institute, describes Theriot as 'a hybrid'. 'Some of the very best people end up being not in a field, but coming from outer space into what is an established area,' says Fink. And they sometimes end up changing the terrain quite dramatically. 'What she has done is to try to think like two different people. She has to think like a bacterium and like a higher cell, and combine them in some way.' There are not many people who can do that.

Julie Theriot has not always wanted to be a scientist. Perhaps because her father is a scientist – he is a high-energy physicist who works at the Fermi National Accelerator Laboratory (Fermilab) in Illinois, where scientists have just discovered the elusive top quark – she did anything but science until her second year in high school. Her interest in science was finally sparked by a biology teacher whom she remembers for his teaching of evolution. This, she says, was a 'ballsy' thing to be teaching in Wheaton, which is a home to Christian fundamentalism, and at Wheaton College, where evangelist preacher Billy Graham was educated.

But even after she woke up to science, she still spent most of her time in high school on her great loves, the theatre and the debate and forensics teams. (Forensics involved declaiming a speech which someone else had written.) Her intention during most of her high-school years was to be an architect and, with that in mind, she took a number of technical drawing classes. But by the time she left school she decided she wanted to be a physicist like her dad. 'I'd been working at the Fermilab during the summers for the last two years of high school, building equipment for experiments and it just seemed like it was so much fun,' she explains. 'The attitude everybody had there was just very exciting. The idea of trying to find things no one had ever been able to find before.'

All the time she was at school – and she went to a good high school – she did outstandingly well, ending up as a National Merit Scholar (awarded to those who do the best on the Scholastic Achievement Test, an examination which provides entry to college) and a United States Presidential Scholar. The presidential scholarships are awarded to the top male and female high school graduate in each state, and Theriot got the female award for Illinois. It came with much-needed money for college (like the National Merit scholarship), together with the chance to shake the hand of the President in Washington DC. Theriot passed up on the handshake because that year Ronald Reagan was in the White House and she wasn't that thrilled to shake his hand. In addition there was a national debating tournament she was taking part in (she had won the state tournament) that same week, which was more important to her.

Any of the top universities in America would have been delighted to have recruited such a high achiever, but Theriot opted for Massachusetts Institute of Technology because it had the best undergraduate physics department. As an undergraduate she says she spent most of her time in theatre groups. When it came to choosing a major, she decided on the double major of physics and biology. Her father talked her out of emulating him and going into high-energy physics. 'It's extremely competitive and there's a very small number of jobs actually available and there's very few places were you can actually do the work,' she says. 'Right now there's maybe four or five working accelerators in the world, and in order to do an experiment you have to get together with several hundred other people and it's a very long-term, large commitment. It's very difficult to do a very creative experiment that's sort of crazy just because it seems like it might be interesting. It has to be something you're fairly sure is going to work.'

She adds that there are a lot of over-sized egos in the glamorous field of high-energy physics. Theriot's ego is kept firmly in check. She is not the sort to brag about doing well or working hard – though she is no shrinking violet either.

Theriot may be modest, according to her boss Gerald Fink, but she is intellectually extremely aggressive, as he discovered when he engaged her on the subject of whether monkeys could be taught to do things like humans. He found her very well-read on the subject, he comments modestly. She is also well able to hold her own in a big meeting. She goes straight to the heart of an issue, and because she is so tiny, the effect is enhanced, says Fink.

As an undergraduate at MIT Julie Theriot enjoyed the physics classes more than the biology, because she found physics more intellectually satisfying. But she preferred conducting research in biology. By her final year she had developed an interest in cell biology, which is why she chose the University of California at San Francisco for her doctorate, an institution with a reputation for excellence in that field. She spent five years on her doctorate, working most of the time under a British-educated professor, Timothy Mitchison, and looking at how cells crawl around the body.

'When you start off you're just a fertilised egg and you are basically uniform throughout,' she explains. 'And in order to go from being a fertilised egg to being a human you have to first divide up a lot, and individual cells differentiate and change their states. But then one extremely important part of development, besides cell differentiation, is that they move around relative to each other.'

'So, for example, almost all the nerve cells in your body are derived from a little strip of embryonic tissue and at a certain stage of development they all start crawling out to where they're eventually going to go.'

Theriot explains that even as an adult you have cells in your body that crawl around, for example, white blood cells. Whenever you have a bacterium or any sort of foreign agent in your body, signals are sent to mobilise the white blood cells. These cells roll along through your blood vessels, inching their way towards the foreign body and engulfing it.

When Theriot was observing the crawling antics of cells, she was experimenting on goldfish skin. For some obscure reason, the cells of goldfish skin crawl very quickly so they are wonderful cells for looking at crawling. 'I had this big tank of goldfish on my desk,' she explains. 'One of the things I liked best about it was I was able to take primary tissue, the tissue directly from the animal, so there was no concern about it behaving unusually because it had been growing in the lab for so long.'

The beauty of it for Theriot was that she didn't have to kill the fish. 'I loved my goldfish. I had the same goldfish with me all the way through graduate school. Every so often I would grab one of them, pluck off a scale and put it back. It would huff around for a little while. But they don't have very big brains and they got over it pretty fast.'

In case you were wondering, fish cells work like human cells. And there is a one-word answer to why crawling cells are important – cancer. When a person develops a tumour, it is not the tumour that kills them, but the fact that the cells in the tumour suddenly become motile and start crawling, spreading the cancer all over the body. The crawling in metastatic cancer cells is very much like the crawling of fish skin cells, says Theriot. So, if scientists can figure out how it is they crawl and what the requirements are for crawling, they might be able to come up with some drugs that inhibit the activity, and thereby slow down the spread of the tumour. But for Theriot the real reason for studying cell crawling is that it's a fascinating unsolved problem. All cells crawl at some point in their development and all animals have cells that crawl. 'And if you ever see it, it's utterly fascinating how it happens,' she says. Her dissertation was on the crawling of cells.

Towards the end of her PhD she began to look at bacterial parasites and the way they move. She decided this was what she wanted to keep on doing. The Whitehead fellowship has enabled her to do that. Instead of moving on to a different topic, as is required of most postdoctoral fellows, she has been able to stick with her chosen subject – and get her own lab to boot.

The Whitehead Institute is gambling that it has been a wise invest-ment. It is notoriously difficult to predict which scientists are going to be successful. But Dr Fink believes Julie Theriot has what it takes to go a long way. As well as knowing the right questions to ask in experiments, she writes well, is a good collaborator and an excellent speaker. And she can see the wider implications of what she is doing.

Publications include:

'Actin microfilament dynamics in locomoting cell's, 1991, with T. J. Mitchison, *Nature*, 352, pp. 126–31.

'Bacterial pathogens caught in the actin', 1992, *Current Biology*, 2, pp. 649–51.

'Principles of locomotion for simple-shaped cells', 1993, with J. Lee, A.Ishihara, and K. Jacobson, *Nature*, 362, pp. 167–71.

'Regulation of the actin cytoskeleton in living cells', 1994, *Seminars in Cell Biology*, 5, pp. 193–9.

'The cell biology of infection by intracellular bacterial pathogens', 1995, *Annual Reviews of Cell and Developmental Biology*, 11, pp. 213–39.

'*Shigella flexneri* surface protein ICSa is sufficient to direct actin-based motil-ity', 1995, with M. B. Goldberg, *Proceedings of the National Academy of Sciences USA*, 92, pp. 6572–6.

(© Lucy Hodges)

Marina Warner, born in 1946, is best known for her work on fairy-tales and legends. She is author of a number of books which explore the relationship of mythic images of women to the reality of women's lives. Although she works largely outside the academy she holds visting professorships at Queen Mary and Westfield College, London and the University of Ulster.

Photograph by Neil Turner

'What is a woman from Vogue doing taking on the Church?' – that's what the critics were saying. You can imagine there was a lot of dismissive stuff about me.' Marina Warner is talking about the book that helped to make her name: *Alone of All Her Sex: The Myth and Cult of the Virgin Mary*, a breathtakingly ambitious deconstruction of a sacred icon from a woman in her twenties working outside academic institutions. Cutting across disciplines, she rummaged deep into historical and art historical sources; she analysed paintings, sculpture, religious and literary texts in her exploration of Mariolatry, showing how this social model of femininity had served to entrap Western women.

The book, published in 1976, became a landmark in the cultural history of the representation of women and induced excitement and praise as well as derision. On the one hand she was lauded for her elegant and compelling style, her scrupulous research and ability to mobilise material to provide new and refreshing insights into the images of virgin and whore as used through the ages. On the other she was attacked as a lightweight, a writer who, without qualms, blithely skated across the surface of areas that older scholars might enter with greater caution.

In her 'Afterthoughts', which accompanied a reprint of the book in 1990, Warner goes some way to acknowledging the criticisms. She writes: 'The hubris of youth astonishes me: now I feel that a single strand of something like the cult of the Virgin takes years to unravel, and the work can only be incomplete, whereas then, like Jack in the fairy-tale, I looked at the giant beanstalk and thought nothing of leaping up it.'

Around the time of publication she had been features editor on *Vogue* magazine and a contributor to broadcasting. *The Daily Telegraph* had appreciated her work, making her Young Writer of the Year in 1971 after a one-year stint working for its magazine. As a young undergraduate at Oxford she had edited the student magazine *Isis* and at the tender age of 14 had won the W.H. Smith Children's Poetry Prize. However, evidence of an institutional academic track-record there was none and this left her exposed to envious snipers and scholars who claimed authority over the territory she had ventured into with such verve.

The hurt she so evidently feels from such assaults, however, has never dampened her enthusiasm. The advancement of age and maturity has not curbed her daring. Marina Warner has been jumping up giant beanstalks ever since. More landmarks were to follow. *Joan of Arc: The Image of Female Heroism*, which maps the appropriation of the Joan myth in its many forms by different cultures and dynasties; *Monuments and Maidens: The Allegory of the Female Form*, an examination of female figures who have acted as allegories of Truth, Virtue, Justice, Liberty; the Reith lectures in the form of *Managing Monsters: Six Myths of Our Time*, showing how traditional and ancient myths, a syntax of stories, becomes the repertory through which we recognise the contemporary world.

Latterly we have *From the Beast to the Blonde: On Fairy Tales and their Tellers*: legends about Sibyls, the Queen of Sheba, Saint Anne, the sirens, Bluebeard, Cinderella, Mother Goose; searching for signs, in a fulsome and ribald fashion, of their rootedness in the social, legal and economic history of marriage and the family. Meanwhile she has also published four novels – one of which, *The Lost Father*, was shortlisted for the Booker Prize – two collections of short stories and a number of children's books, primarily written for her son Conrad when a young child but 'curiously lucrative'. Add to that any number of introductions to catalogues of artists' work, such as Helen Chadwick and Richard Wentworth, film scripts, opera librettos and numerous book and exhibition reviews, and you have a prolific body of work.

Marina Warner's abiding obsession has been with myth, its contribution to cultural and social practice and the fluidity of meaning of visual imagery and text. In particular she has concentrated on the various meanings that 'woman' has carried symbolically and the way this interacts with the reality of women's lives. She says: 'That is probably my central interest, so within the myths there is a strong emphasis on what they mean for women as individuals.'

This obsession began from a young age. A fluent reader at six, she developed a passion for Greek and Roman myths and for the figure of the wild woman 'who has access to something powerful. I think that has stayed with me always'. She graduated to tales of the Norse gods, tales of the Irish fables and legends and fairy tales of all kinds. In addition she adored the 'basement world of female secrets', which she entered by spending time in the domestic round with her Italian mother and young Italian maids. Here, speaking 'kitchen Italian', she was submerged in a world of 'Catholic superstition, boyfriends and the preparation of food'; here too she was introduced to the cult of the saints: 'I would be taken into the bedrooms and shown statues of the saints: "Now here is Sainta Rosa and this is what she can do for you". I must say it has had a tremendous influence on me.'

She grew up in Cairo where her English father was a bookseller, moving on to Belgium and then to England. Her family was comfortably middle-class (her godfather is Lord Longford). Her father's world was the loftier world of books, Englishness and male figures of authority. The spies Donald McLean and Kim Philby and the writer Lawrence Durrell were visitors. Her father, a Protestant, thought Catholicism 'a good religion for a girl'. Although Warner painfully departed from her faith on entering Oxford, a factor which largely drove her to write *Alone of All Her Sex*, she now describes herself as a Catholic agnostic and warmly acknowledges the sources of her cultural formation. Her second marriage, to John Dewe Mathews, the painter and a practising Catholic, helped to heal old wounds further.

A former pupil at St Mary's, Ascot, a private, convent school, she remains grateful for the two meditative practices that were taught there: examination of conscience and meditation on Holy pictures. 'These have remained completely part of my practice,' she said. 'That's exactly how I conduct my mental business all the time. We were given all these Mysteries and we were also taught to conjure them in our minds.' The world of female secrets has endured as an enticement, providing more exciting possibilities than the world of Englishness, of authority and of men. And she has remained a conjurer, mobilising her vast repertoire of stories to make connections between myth and cultural symbols and social reality which have hitherto been overlooked.

'You can tell by the way I try and anchor myth in social context that I think there are meanings that have reference. Often what's happened is that those references have been lost which has impoverished the meaning.'

The predicament of her quest lies in the fact that she employs an uneasy mix of psychoanalysis and historical investigation. She said: 'I think that it is a rather difficult way of treating myth in the sense that it requires a lot of investigation and a lot of Jungian ideas. The Jungian analysis is a much easier thing to do really, to trace the sequence of images or stories unanchored to context or social realities, but I have tried to relate them to function, which of course is relating them to some kind of experience of reality.' In that respect she is forced to speak with a voice of authority at a time when scepticism and incredulity are rife. She describes herself as an old-fashioned liberal humanist, one who resists the carnivalistic tendencies and wry despair of postmodernism.

By exposing the layers of meaning myth brings to culture and society she is attempting to provide us with tools for improving the reality of that society. For example in the first of her Reith lectures she roots the present-day attack on single mothers in an old story which has taken on new vigour. She writes: 'women in general are out of control, and feminism in particular is to blame. It has become a bogey, a whipping boy, routinely produced to explain all social ills.' Fear that the natural bond of motherhood excludes men and eludes their control, she argues, has coursed through ancient myths.

'The she-monster's hardly a new phenomenon. Greek myth alone offers a host – of Ceres, Harpies, sirens, Moirae. Associated with fate and death in various ways, they move swiftly, sometimes on wings; birds of prey are their closest kin – the Greeks didn't know about dinosaurs.' But Steven Spielberg does.

Ever alert to the way old myth adopts contemporary disguise she illuminates popular icons with her critic's gaze, revealing the ancient predator in a refreshing and exciting way. Female organisms in the film *Jurassic Park* prove uncontrollably fertile, 'resistant to the constraints of the men of power'. The velociraptors, the truly evil presence in the movie, are 'Voracious, cunning girls . . . Is the terror they inspire anything to do with their femaleness?' Her question is loaded.

Finally, in this first lecture, she exposes what she sees as the weakness of postmodernism: 'Ironies, subversion, inversion, pastiche, masquerade, appropriation – all the postmodern strategies of the last two decades are buckling under the weight of culpability the myth has entrenched.' Postmodernism's form of despair, which takes a rather 'bumptious delight in the richness of possibilities', amounts to an escape from one's ethical duty towards society, she stated more recently: 'I just don't want yet to give up on the possibility that things can improve.'

A member of the executive committee of Charter 88, which seeks constitutional reform, and of the management committee of the National Council for One Parent Families, Marina Warner takes her belief in citizenship seriously. Indeed she wonders whether her 'centrist' position and 'longing for connection' maintains her as a feminist in the eyes of modern feminists. She says: 'I think that certain things might improve but it's not from some delusion that women are virtuous, but that if their interests were served that might be better for men and children and for everyone.'

Curiously she displays a marked lack of confidence and is massively self-denigrating. Her work on myth and imagery surrounding women has undoubtedly earned her a place as a key feminist writer, but there have been critical reviews. Noel Malcolm, after publication of *From the Beast to the Blonde*, wrote in the *Sunday Telegraph*: 'Once upon a time, there was a very clever girl called Marina, who read lots and lots of books. Every book seemed to connect up with every other book, and they all told her something about images of womanhood in cultural history'. Her attempt to produce a 'world-relevant set of rules about how stories work' has been described as 'alarmingly generalist' by one academic, who tersely referred to the BBC's choice of her as only the second woman to deliver the Reith lectures since 1961 as 'venturesome'. Warner herself accepts that the BBC was thought to be 'quite barking' in its choice and took up the cross in full knowledge that a great deal of tokenism had gone into the decision.

But she is assessed as a person of enormous intellectual stature by professors in her field and one described her deliverance of the Reith lectures as 'masterful'. She has been assessed as an intellectual in the 'Continental sense', steeped in French structuralism, wide-ranging in scope. Marilyn Butler, rector of Exeter College, Oxford and professor of literature, acknowledges her 'deep interest in ideas' and her ability to unearth 'genuine topics'. Catherine Belsey, who chairs the Centre for Critical and Cultural Theory in Cardiff, said academe was badly in need of people who could take an overview. She said: 'I cannot get enough of sweeping pieces of cultural history. I want the excitement of the sweep. I think every academic wishes their work could be as brave as that. I use her books all the time.'

Joan of Arc, she said, became the model for approaching cultural history in a new kind of way: 'She caught a moment in that book. She set me off on a wholly new train of thought. In Shakespeare's comedies you always had girls dressed as boys, boys dressed as girls. The treatment of gender in the comedies was cast in a new light. Cross-dressing changes the identity of what you can be, it can bring about a new interpretation of ways of being. It was Marina who helped to bring that realisation about.'

Gillian Beer, professor of English literature and president of Clare Hall College, Cambridge, describes Marina Warner as a 'rare bird indeed, the freelance writer of considerable powers, not caught up in the academic web', a woman who often gets to contentious issues before others do, but who is scrupulous in her provision of references and generous in her acknowledgement of other people's work. Indeed she does this with the risk, at times, of making her work seem ponderous. Marina Warner feels she has to cover her back, says Beer, because much of her work is 'so speculative' and because of her sense of exposure through 'not having a proper academic background'.

She has become a woman of letters, the sort constantly invited to be in residence; a visiting scholar at the Getty in California; the Tinbergen professor in Rotterdam; a visiting professor at Queen Mary and Westfield College and visiting professor of women's studies at the University of Ulster. Yet she proposes that she did not choose an academic route after leaving Oxford, because she did not think she would be accepted.

It seems to be an abiding regret that she only gained a second as a student of French and Italian: 'I was very young when I went there, only 17. I didn't work. It was my first taste of freedom and I was very muddled. I had a number of disastrous personal problems, negotiating love. I think I was a bit overlooked. I did meet someone who was a young don who used to hang out with us and he said to me: "Gosh, of all the people of our generation at Oxford you were the last one I thought would have become a serious writer. You were just a pretty thing in a mini skirt." I've been expiating that mini skirt for many years.'

Having a long-standing passion for China, inspired by Joseph Needham's *Science and Civilisation in China* and his hypothesis that scientific inquiry in China, which frequently synchronised with Western advances, was often led by spiritual desire rather than practical considerations, Warner asked for time out from her job at *Vogue* to write her first book, *The Dragon Empress*. This was about the Empress Dowager Tz'u Hsi, who held supreme power in China for the second half of the nineteenth century. Its publication was a turning-point. She became gripped by the material and has been a workaholic ever since. That first scholarly incursion changed her for good.

She still seems to regret, however, that she is not taken seriously by the Oxford community. At a dinner at All Souls College, Oxford, to which she was invited, her professorship at Rotterdam was dismissed with 'utter contempt' 'by one of those gigantic ex-diplomats who live there'. Yet Lisa Jardine, the dean of arts and professor of English at London University's Queen Mary and Westfield College, describes her as a figure of 'real stature' who could have had a professorship elsewhere if she had wanted one. Jardine says: 'When she went to the Getty people flocked. Wherever she lectures rooms are packed to the gills. Young women queue up afterwards to ask her questions. Her books sell and sell and go on selling. The way her work moves between general cultural studies and cultural studies particular to women is an inspiration.' If Warner had taken up an academic post, says Jardine, she would have been surrounded by 'breathless students constantly feeding her new questions', avoiding the tendency to over-concentrate on her own questions and response to her critics, which, Jardine feels, is the one criticism she has to make of Warner's work.

Standing alone, in her freelance capacity, Marina Warner has been able to follow her nose. For all that that has left her exposed and vulnerable on occasions, it has also freed her from what she sees as the worst excesses of academic life. One can occasionally glimpse that ultimately she would not have had it any other way. The problem with academic life, she said, was not that people were too specialised, but that they got boxed into 'responding to discourses with each other so that you actually get people being sucked down tunnels – whole conferences with lots of students discussing Judith Butler's *Gender Trouble*'.

'It's not that the book is not worth discussing,' she continued with feeling, warming to criticism of her own, 'it's just that courses involving the fine-tuning of postmodernist texts is the worst kind of scholasticism of the twelfth century. I think students should read from primary sources, they should put pleasure first, working on that moment when interest crystallises and they are gripped. Then they can read the secondary texts. But if they begin with Judith Butler's *Gender Trouble* they'll end up on a course in accountancy.'

It is said Anthony Burgess once remarked how the English hate people who are prolific and flowery, which is why the poet Larkin is so revered. Marina Warner's turnover of writing is vast because she has had to make a living from it for herself and Conrad, the son from her first marriage to the writer William Shawcross. Her writing is rich and ornate. Looking at it that way she has sinned on two counts. *The Lost*

Father, an operatic novel based on the history of her mother's family, is extraordinarily sensuous. *Indigo*, which came later, an inversion of Shakespeare's *The Tempest*, works out the relationship of coloniser and colonised. Because her father's family was involved in the foundation of Empire, resembling Prospero's theft of the isle, she imagines in fiction the lives of Sycorax, Ariel and Caliban. A book of intricate construction, the language does indeed turn indigo in parts. But then Warner attributes this to her love of Continental literature and her avid reading of 'things that were very Italianate' when young. Dante, for example, was a first love. Rich 'plum-puddingy' writers were her early models: 'Dante is a writer who very much relies on the long extended simile which he took from the classics, from Homer, from Virgil. When I first started writing I was always told to cut my similes as people found them outlandish and flowery. It wasn't at all English minimalism or the wry, social observation that was current in the sixties.'

In the nineties her prose retains its plum pudding characteristic, but has settled down to being balanced, rhythmic and ornately elegant, displaying a basking pleasure in the musical nature of language. Yet characteristically Warner remains uneasy about that too. In future she would like her writing to have a more 'fragmented' quality to it, leaving more space for the reader.

She would also like to spend more time writing novels. She has in mind to write the story of a woman caught up in a civil war, building bridges between different ethnic communities. This is based on earlier research she did on women in the Crusades, when Conrad was small and she did not have time to follow the idea through.

She is making up a scrap-book of images and stories ready for the time when she can sit down to write. There are going to be spiders in the story, the imagery of webs will be important; the woman will be a make-up artist, a skin-changer, surviving through her role as a 'visagiste'; there is going to be a rape – 'a mythological rape like one of Zeus's rapes' – and there will be children born of rape.

Although Warner wants to create a greater sense of fracture, her love of weaving rich, fantastical stories and imagery will no doubt gain the upper hand. That, in the end, is probably her *raison d'être* as a writer. She says: 'If I have any role to play it is to bring back some kind of enjoyable presence; a lot of forgotten images and stories which not only produce entertainment and aesthetic delight, a rich cultural patterning, but can actually have some kind of – I don't want to sound too pious – helpful function in social terms.'

Publications include:

The Dragon Empress: Life and Times of Tz'u Hsi 1835–1900, Empress Dowager of China, 1972, 1993, Vintage.

Alone of All her Sex: The Myth and Cult of the Virgin Mary, 1985, Picador.

Monuments and Maidens: The Allegory of the Female Form, 1987, Picador.

Joan of Arc: The Image of Female Heroism, 1991, Vintage.

Mermaid in the Basement, 1993, Chatto.

Managing Monsters: Six Myths of Our Time, 1994, Vintage.

From the Beast to the Blonde: On Fairy Tales and their Tellers, 1994, Chatto and Windus.

Fiction
The Lost Father, 1988, Chatto.
In a Dark Wood, 1992, Vintage.
Indigo or Mapping the Waters, 1992, Chatto.

(© Elaine Williams)

Photograph by Neil Turner

Mary Warnock, DBE, Baroness Warnock of Weeke, born 1924, is one of Britain's best-known women philosophers. Former Mistress of Girton College, Cambridge and one of the 'great and good', she has frequently been called on to chair government enquiries and committees, including the committee of enquiry into human fertilisation and embryology.

Mary Warnock may have passed her seventieth birthday, but she is still learning. 'By nature I'm a perpetual undergraduate,' she says as she sits in the tiny living-room of her London flat. 'I've always been quite good at getting interested in whatever my next essay subject was, as it were. That was what I learned from doing Greats.'

The Oxford-educated philosopher and former Mistress of Girton College, Cambridge – her six-year tenure of that position ended in 1991 – is talking about her life as a public figure. For over twenty years, many an advisory committee or committee of inquiry, on a variety of subjects from environmental pollution to euthanasia, has included her – indeed, her *Who's Who* entry notes four occasions when she has been chairman of such a body.

'I have always been capable of asking questions until I thought I knew the subject,' says Baroness Warnock, whose name is probably indissolubly linked in the public mind with her chairmanship, in the early eighties, of the committee of inquiry into human fertilisation and embryology. Set up in 1982 and reporting in 1984, the committee recommended that experiments on human embryos should not be allowed after fourteen days; that surrogate motherhood agencies should be outlawed; and that test-tube baby clinics and embryology laboratories should be regulated by a licensing authority. That committee, she recalls, included a 'brilliant teacher' in member Ann McLaren (director of the MRC's Mammalian Development Unit) – 'it was like having a second undergraduate career' – but Warnock now feels that she is no longer up to date with the subject. In the ten years since her committee reported, she says: 'The whole subject has changed to genetic manipulation and the human genome. The science is becoming more and more difficult, at least for me. I'm quite happy with embryos, but not too good about cells.'

'So I find I'm called upon to give moral pronouncements on subjects that I'm not really master of, and I don't like that at all.' Moreover, she adds, the questions about embryology, as posed by the media, have become 'silly and trivial – whether it's morally right for women of seventy to have babies. I just cannot be interested in that kind of thing. It's never going to affect very many people.'

Despite this, she felt it necessary to speak on the matter in the House of Lords when an amendment to the Criminal Justice Bill introduced a new clause to ban foetal tissue experiments. (She opposed the amendment; it was defeated.)

She was also required to meditate on matters of life and death as a member of the Lords select committee on medical ethics (essentially a committee on euthanasia) which reported in 1994. Many saw her hand in the no-nonsense prose of that committee's report.

Her membership of the House of Lords goes back to 1985, when she was created Baroness Warnock of Weeke in the City of Winchester – her birthplace. She is an independent peer, but says 'I seem to have been a sort of honorary member of the opposition benches for all these education bills. That could change though. Being an independent is a very agreeable position to be in. I needn't come to the Lords unless I'm interested.' She lives in Wiltshire; the West London *pied-à-terre* is used only when duty and London calls.

It's philosophy, however, rather than her public career, that this interview is intended to be about. (Of course, there is a link; as Warnock notes in her collection of essays, *The Uses of Philosophy*, in both committee work and philosophy 'dialogue or discussion is not accidentally but essentially the proper mode of advance'.) We meet soon after the publication of her latest book, *Imagination and Time*. Not to be confused with her 1976 philosophical study, *Imagination*, the new book is based on her 1992 Gifford lectures at Glasgow University, and the Read-Tuckwell lecture at Bristol the same year. It is, she says, 'the last philosophical book I'm going to write'. Although it ranges widely, dealing with, for instance, story-telling and personal immortality as well as touching on epistemology, aesthetics and artificial intelligence, *Imagination and Time* has at its centre the argument that 'imagination is crucial in the acceptance of shared and continuing values', to use a phrase in the final chapter.

'Yes, the message is in the last chapter,' says its author. 'There are masses of accumulated apparently different topics which come together in this message about values, which is what I do believe in. That's my style of lecturing: I go rampaging around and then just at the end there is this moral.' It may be the final philosophical message of her own, but Warnock has not yet bidden farewell to the subject. Recently, she was editing an anthology of women philosophers. Reading through her forerunners in the Bodleian, she says, 'I've made the rather depressing but unsurprising discovery that most of the women who wrote before this century were terribly amateurish and slapdash.' Nevertheless, she is pleased to have found the 'absolutely wonderful' Anne Conway, the seventeenth-century metaphysical writer who may have had some influence on Leibnitz. 'Her book (*The Principles of the Most Ancient and Modern Philosophy*) is barking mad sometimes . . . but it was regarded very seriously at the time.'

Of course among the twentieth-century philosophers anthologised is her former Oxford colleague Iris Murdoch, a copy of whose

Metaphysics as a Guide to Morals lies on the coffee table in front of us as we talk. She was among a handful of women philosophers in the 1950s and 1960s, says Warnock, who 'began to develop a rather different style of doing moral philosophy . . . I think they were more interested in the concrete and what it was like to feel a moral dilemma – all the things Sartre was good at doing through his stories'. (Both Warnock and Murdoch have written books about Sartre and existentialism.)

Forty years ago, writing about morality had, in Warnock's words, 'come to a dead end'. Books with titles like *The Language of Morals* seemed to look not at ethical problems themselves but the way people talked about them. Warnock recalls her Oxford colleague Philippa Foot 'was quite influential in making people think that there had to be some content in moral philosophy again'. At the same time, ethics 'was thought to be very easy and therefore suitable for a woman'.

No doubt such thinking led Oxford University Press to ask Mary Warnock to write her first book, *Ethics Since 1900*, which came out in 1960. Apparently the commission had been offered first to – and turned down by – both Foot and Elizabeth Anscombe: 'I was just the next person on the list'. At the time, she was a fellow at St Hugh's College, teaching all branches of philosophy: Oxford, she says, did not encourage specialisation.

'You were very conscious of the history of the subject [at Oxford]. That was a very fruitful way of approaching philosophy for the general run-of-the-mill undergraduate. You could introduce them to what philosophy was like, but you could also get them to imagine how problems appeared to Descartes or Hume. This is a long way from today's specialisations in, for instance, medical ethics – disastrous, because they lose all contact with the sources of their ideas.'

The particular strain of post-war Oxford philosophy typified by J. L. Austin – a scepticism about metaphysical claims, combined with close attention to the use of language by both philosophers and ordinary people – is an obvious component of her own writing. 'I always admired Austin, and Geoffrey [whom she married in 1949 and who died in 1995] liked him very much – they got on terribly well as colleagues.' She recalls that her eldest daughter and Austin's youngest daughter 'used to play in the garden together while he did the nearest he ever got to gossip'. After Austin's death in 1960, Geoffrey Warnock edited some of his lecture notes to make *Sense and Sensibilia*, which Mary calls 'an absolute masterpiece – and a very funny book too'. It was Austin, she thinks, who recommended her to OUP, 'because he'd examined me in Greats, and he knew I could string words together'.

Ethics Since 1900 was followed by *Sartre, Existentialist Ethics* and *Existentialism*, but it was her 1976 book *Imagination* that gave her the most satisfaction – in fact, it is the only one of her fifteen books that did not arise from a commission. 'I felt as if all my life I'd been waiting to write that,' she says now, 'I was always terribly keen on Wordsworth and the Romantics, and as I went on doing philosophy I realised there were enormous links between Coleridge and Kant particularly.' Indeed, in the preface to her new book, she remarks that 'my interest in philosophy has always been an interest in the history of ideas'; *Imagination and Time*'s index has more references to Wordsworth than to Wittgenstein.

Imagination, the earlier book, was written immediately after Warnock had given up her post as headmistress of Oxford High School for Girls. Though it was indeed a contribution to the history of ideas, it also had an educational message: that we should cultivate imagination, the 'capacity in all human beings . . . to go beyond what is immediately in front of their noses'. Imagination, she argued, 'needs educating' – and this would be 'an education not only of the intelligence, but, going along with it, of the feelings'.

Born in April 1924, the daughter of a Winchester housemaster who died before her birth, Warnock went to Lady Margaret Hall, Oxford, as an undergraduate before becoming a fellow of St Hugh's at the age of twenty-five – incredibly the college's first married fellow. But she says she has never been a 'tremendously committed academic' and was 'always keener on teaching than research', so her 1966 move from an Oxford college to a high school was not a problem. Besides, she had worked as a school teacher during a break from wartime Oxford, and 'had always loved the whole atmosphere of school – it's so optimistic'.

Indeed, it was her involvement in the local education system, as chairman of the Oxfordshire schools' music subcommittee, that inspired Mary Warnock to take charge of the school where two of her daughters already were pupils. Her proudest achievement in her six years there was its musical improvement: 'I was very unpopular with the staff because they said – rightly – that I didn't care about anything but music. But they were very bright children, the staff were frightfully good, and all the departments ran themselves. But the school had dismal music, so we brought that up to the level of the other departments.'

Although the subject of music is strangely absent from her books on the imagination, it is indeed one of her passions: she grew up playing the flute (but 'sold it in a moment of poverty') and was also persuaded to learn the viola at the insistence of her older sister, who wanted to form a string quartet. 'I still think all my aches and pains are due to those few years I struggled with the viola. It's an awkward instrument,' she comments, stretching her left arm out to demonstrate.

She learned the French horn, too, while headmistress – in order to encourage the girls to take it up. Later, when she withdrew from the school orchestra to make way for players who had overtaken her in ability, she sold her horn to Sian Edwards, now a distinguished opera conductor.

Of the Warnock's five children, two are professional musicians – bassoonist son Felix helps run the Orchestra of the Age of Enlightenment and teaches at the Royal Academy of Music; daughter Fanny plays the cello. (Youngest daughter Box, though, teaches art and took the photograph of her mother that adorns the cover of *Imagination and Time*.) All five were born during the period that she was teaching at St Hugh's, and so had to spend some time in the care of nannies – 'I think children of academics have a ghastly time,' she has said. Nevertheless, it is her proud boast that she always cooked supper for the family while she was Oxford High School's headmistress.

It is for her family's sake that Warnock thinks that her next project, after the anthology of women philosophers, might be to edit her diaries. Begun in 1941 – the only year missing is, alas, the momentous one of 1945 – the diaries would be an 'embarrassment' for the Warnock children, she says, if nothing is done: 'They won't know what the hell to do with all these things, so it would be better to edit them. It's also something I promised my friend Frances Partridge I would do.

'But it's a bad diary; it has too many different forms. Partly it's to remind me what date I put in the broad beans last year so I can look it up. That's very difficult to mix with one's beautiful thoughts.'

It was her husband's appointment as principal of Hertford College that contributed to his wife's leaving Oxford High School; 'There was an awful lot of entertaining [at Hertford]. We moved from North Oxford and lived absolutely bang in the middle of Oxford. We had the most beautiful bedroom in Europe – a huge room looking out over Radcliffe Square.'

It was while Sir Geoffrey was fulfilling his duties as Oxford vice-chancellor that his wife was a member of the Lindop Committee of Inquiry into the validation of public-sector higher education, which reported in 1984. Its recommendations were not, on the whole, taken up: 'I'm afraid the handing out of the title of university to all comers has been a pretty awful move,' she observes.

Perhaps as a result, she is pessimistic about higher education in Britain today: 'There is a widespread indifference to what universities provide,' in her words. 'One can't say it's all the fault of Margaret Thatcher, but it's a Thatcher culture. It's becoming so unattractive now for a student to go to university that quite soon it will slip into a culture that thinks only fools go to university. If you want to get on, you get into the job market right away and make as much money as you can. The role model is Richard Branson, I should think. I admire him very much, actually, but it's a sad way to go.'

So what can be done? 'I don't see how higher education can improve at the moment. There's so little money that it's going to take some sort of extraordinary revolution to get back to anything like we were in the 1960s, and I don't see where that revolution can come from. I do feel very gloomy about it.'

'Having virtually always been connected with universities, one did feel that one was part of something that was terribly important, and that would never go away. I just don't feel that any more, which is sad.'

'In my worst nightmares I think we've got to go through a kind of dark ages, when all the libraries shut and nobody reads and there are no more publishing houses except for pornography. We've got somehow to get through all that before there's a renaissance.'

Publications include:

Imagination, 1976, Faber.
A Question of Life; Warnock Report on Human Fertilisation and Embryology, 1985, Blackwell.
A Common Policy for Education, 1988, Oxford University Press.
The Uses of Philosophy, 1992, Blackwell.
Imagination and Time, 1994, Blackwell.
Existentialism (new edition), 1996, Oxford University Press.
(Ed.) *Women Philosophers,* 1996, Everyman.

Shirley Williams, the Baroness Williams of Crosby, born 1930, is public service professor of electoral politics at Harvard University's John F. Kennedy School of Government. A Labour MP for fifteen years, she held two Cabinet posts and is one of the 'Gang of Four' who broke away from Labour to form the Social Democratic Party in the early eighties.

Photograph © Paul Salmon

House of Lords. Peers' entrance. An odd place to meet a professor of electoral politics, you might think. Yet Shirley Williams, a life peer since 1993, seems positively to revel in the rarified atmosphere. It is not the mouthful of a title – Baroness Williams of Crosby – that she likes. After all, she turned down a dameship and, as she reveals from behind a rather regal-looking desk in a refurbished Lords office: 'I haven't changed my cheque book, or anything like that'. Nor is it the hobnobbing with hereditary toffs, since her preference is for a second chamber elected regionally and on the basis of proportional representation. It is the fact that, in the cossetted upper chamber, the accent is on argument rather than artifice, issues rather than insults. As she remarked when first addressing the elderly members, if they 'walk a little more slowly' than in the House of Commons, they also 'think a little more deeply'.

That suits Williams very well. An overtly intellectual politician, she has, since 1988, been based at Harvard University, an overtly intellectual institution, where students play chess in the streets while sipping cappuccinos, where even local newsagents stock arcane academic journals alongside the daily newspapers. There, she holds one of a handful of professorships reserved for professionals – another is held by broadcasting bigwig Marvin Kalb, a former head of CBS television.

Located at the prestigious John F. Kennedy School of Government (Harvard's graduate school of public administration), Williams teaches three postgraduate courses: one, elective politics, focuses on the United States 'but draws comparisons with British parliamentary politics'; another, the development of the European Union, covers constitutional and legal mechanisms; and a third, democracy, deals with the challenges and lessons of alternative democratic systems. She is also director of Project Liberty, which has the goal of building democratic institutions in Central and Eastern Europe, and still finds time to nip round the world, giving classes in Paris and Brussels and establishing a Harvard-style Institute of Politics at the University of the Western Cape in South Africa.

She is plainly proud of her professorship, pointing out that her classes are delivered not to your run-of-the-mill Masters students but to high-powered high-fliers from the world of politics: 'people who are heads of government departments', 'top guys in the European Commission'. Yet there are those, especially in the party political world and even more especially in the Labour Party, who share the Shavian view of success – those who can 'do', those who can't 'teach' – and regard her professorship as evidence of professional failure, as evidence that she has 'taken herself out of politics', as one commentator puts it.

That a Harvard professorship can be deemed a failure is testimony to the extraordinary sense of expectancy that surrounded Williams' early party political endeavours. Born in 1930, she was, she says, 'in politics up to my neck from babyhood'. Her father, Sir George Catlin, was a Labour candidate in the 1931 election, who 'used to wheel me to Labour meetings in a pram'. Her mother, Vera Brittain, author of *Testament of Youth* , was an outspoken feminist and pacifist. Early on, she struck up a remarkable friendship with the Labour minister Herbert Morrison after, as she quaintly phrases it, 'bumping into him in an air raid shelter near Hyde Park' when she was thirteen. He became her 'first mentor', often inviting the awestruck teenager for lunch and for political chitchat at the Home Office. With such a political childhood, it was only natural that, on her sixteenth birthday, she joined the Labour Party – 'the first day I legally could'.

Two years later, she went up to Oxford, reading politics, philosophy and economics at Somerville and making a huge impression on the young battle-hardened male undergraduates who had just returned from the war. Today she has a reputation for not giving two hoots about her appearance – Lady Astor famously told her that 'you will never get on in politics, my dear, with *that* hair'. Harvard – where she says 'you have to look like a glamorous model of older women's clothes to be taken seriously' – would seem to have cured her of her more dowdy bluestocking habits. Around the Lords, she wears smart skirt suits, even a touch of make-up, and her grey-tinged hair shows no signs of the unkemptness which earned her the nickname 'Shetland pony'. But in her university days, there was never any question of her style, her fashionability. She was, as Sir Robin Day records, 'the most celebrated female undergraduate of her time' and, as another contemporary remembers, she had 'most of male Oxford in love with her'. A powerful speaker even then, and a chairman of the Oxford Labour Club, she was, says the Tory MP Julian Critchley, 'talked of as Britain's first woman prime minister'. Margaret Thatcher, another Somerville student and five years older, was never mentioned, let alone mentioned in the same hallowed breath.

Within ten years of first taking her parliamentary seat in 1964, Williams was topping the polls in the Shadow Cabinet elections, and although she never held one of the big offices of state (she was Secretary of State for prices and consumer protection from 1974 to 1976 and Secretary of State for education and science and Paymaster General over the next three years), she was being tipped as a future leader of the Labour Party. And then, of course, 1979 came along, apparently to change everything. She lost her seat, left the Labour Party within two years, co-launched the Social Democratic Party, and briefly held Crosby before being bundled unceremoniously out of the Commons after the Tory landslide victory at the post-Falklands general election in 1983.

This was a turning-point, for sure. And, on the face of it at least, it would seem to endorse the view that Williams did not live up to her early promise: she failed to reach high office, therefore she failed full-stop. But to take this view is mistakenly to overlook the fact that Williams' political instincts are, and have always been, more intellectual than pragmatic. For her, political parties matter, but political ideas matter most. As Ben Pimlott, biographer of Harold Wilson and professor of history at London's Birkbeck College, rightly observes: 'She was always more effective at the level of ideas than the level of administration'.

By becoming a professor, Williams was not choosing to follow a career path fundamentally different to the one she had always followed. For a start, she had long inhabited the two worlds of politics and academia. Her father was a professor and she has married two professors – the Oxford University philosopher Bernard Williams (whom she divorced in 1974 and with whom she had one child) and the Harvard University political scientist Richard Neustadt (whom she married in 1987).

More than this, she had herself developed a not inconsiderable academic reputation. After Oxford, she completed a postgraduate year at

Columbia University, majoring on trade unionism. She followed this with a spell as a journalist on the *Daily Mirror* and *Financial Times,* before becoming in 1960 the first female general secretary of the Fabian Society – the ideas factory of the labour movement. It was, she recalls, 'a time of tremendous intellectual excitement'.

Once in the Commons, she was regularly invited to give lectures in the US. Berkeley, Chicago, Columbia, Harvard, Princeton – you name the campus, she has probably given a lecture there. In the UK too, she became a familiar figure on the memorial lecture circuit. There was the Eleanor Rathbone lecture at Liverpool, the Thomas Baggs lecture at Birmingham, and the Charles Gittins lecture at Swansea. By the early 1980s, she could tell an audience that 'as lecturers go, I'm an old hand'.

Unusually for a minister, she had written her own political speeches – famously the 13-point speech in 1969 which called for financial reform in higher education – and university lectures, she maintains, are not a substantially different challenge. Back then, her pet subjects were economic policy, education, the future of the welfare state, human rights – and even on one occasion happiness. 'Spoken words are my stock in trade,' she once said, 'sometimes settling heavily over a subject, sometimes taking off like a wheeling flock of starlings.' If the subject of her lectures ranged widely, so did her source of quotation – everyone from Auden and Archibald McLeish to Solon and Wordsworth. Oxford, Harvard and the Policy Studies Institute were all sufficiently bowled over to offer her academic fellowships.

Even in her party political heyday, Williams was never far from the world of the academy. Nor was party politics the be-all-and-end-all of her existence, as it is for too many MPs. She was ready to give up her parliamentary seat, if that could have saved her marriage to Bernard Williams. And in 1976, two years after her divorce, she did opt out of the Labour leadership election partly because she believed it impossible to look after both the fortunes of the Labour Party and the future of her young daughter Rebecca.

This may suggest political feebleness, a lack of ambition even. But Williams does not understand politics as just a greasy pole which has to be slimed up. It is a set of ideas, a set of principles, which have to be developed, delineated and then defended. And if she has commanded a catalogue of Cabinet briefs in her time – from prices and consumer protection to education – she has been driven by two fundamental beliefs.

On the domestic front, she stands for classlessness, for social cohesion. 'Britain has to change socially and ethically,' she says. She is perturbed by the plight of the unemployed. Her parents participated in the famous Jarrow march against unemployment and carrying on the family tradition, she has campaigned for action, writing her book *A Job To Live* and recently speaking out during the Jobseekers Bill. Also, controversially, she favours a redistributive taxation system, and of course as a former education Secretary of State she sees education as a key to equality of opportunity, remaining proud of her role in extending the comprehensive school system.

Williams is often portrayed as the public-school girl who hypocritically expanded the state system, thereby denying thousands of children a similarly privileged education. But she points out that she only attended St Paul's Girls' School for two and a half years, and reveals that she 'learned my values and my ideals from my Church of England elementary school', one of eight she attended in all. Comprehensive schools, she insists, 'are – and remain – the best possible idea for a cohesive society'. When her daughter's school, Godolphin and Latymer, opted for independent status in the mid-1970s, she moved her to Camden High School for Girls, a distinguished comprehensive.

On the international front, Williams stands for the creation of supernational institutions. 'I'm an international idealist,' she explains, 'and I believe that the European Union, as well as the Commonwealth, are struggling attempts to find cross-border answers to huge global problems.' She dislikes nationalism, once remarking that it is 'the territorial imperative which man shares with lower animals', and she thinks the nation-state is fast losing its relevance. A long-time supporter of European union in particular – she wrote several Fabian pamphlets on the subject as far back as the mid-1950s – she now thinks the time has come for 'the creation of an orderly structure in Western Europe which will be an anchor for our continent, next door to those struggling, and in many ways, anarchic structures of the former Soviet Union'.

Her uncompromising commitment to these beliefs led to her party political downfall. By the late 1970s, the Labour Party had veered sharply to the left and, significantly, was ready to pull the UK out of Europe. This was the last straw. Europe had always been a non-negotiable issue. In 1971, she voted against a three-line whip in favour of Edward Heath's proposal to take the UK into the EEC, and temporarily sacrificed her Shadow Cabinet post as a result. Three years later, she threatened to resign when Labour toyed with abandoning the EEC.

After much soul-searching – Roy Jenkins and David Owen have revealed that she was the member of the Gang of Four who was most reluctant to leave – Williams abandoned her once-beloved party. For Labour Party *apparatchiks*, it was an unforgivable act of apostasy. Barbara Castle said that it was the loss of Williams, the darling of the party, 'which really hurt', and only fairly recently Tony Blair refused to share a platform with her at a Fabian Society meeting.

The whole episode is evidence that Williams places political principle above political position in the hierarchy of values. As she once told a lecture hall of listeners soon after the founding of the SDP: 'The pursuit of fame or esteem or great riches is self-defeating, for in the end such hollow crowns shatter in our hands'. This is not to say that she never harboured dreams of political power. Throughout the 1970s, she made compromise after compromise at the Cabinet table, being consistently voted down with Roy Jenkins on legislation proposals for human rights, freedom of information, and decentralisation.

But enough was enough. And she is now part of a party – the Liberal Democrats – which has no reasonable prospect of taking power. It is, however, big on what George Bush dubbed 'the vision thing', and in the last couple of years she has upped her intellectual input. After five years as a full-time professor, she rearranged the contract to spend six months in the Lords (occasionally popping across to Essex University where she has been given a visiting professorship) and six months in Harvard.

That sounds like a dream set-up for Shirley Williams because, in the final analysis, she is an academic politician rather than a political academic. If ideas are common currency between the professor and the parliamentarian, she says, working patterns and the psychology are wildly different. Politicians make up their minds quickly and then stick to their guns – and that for her is crucial. As she says: 'My basic bottom line is that if I'm fighting a real battle of principle, I'd much rather have another politician by me than another academic.'

Publications include:

Politics is for People, 1981, Harvard University Press.

A Job to Live, 1985, Penguin.

The New European Community: Decision-making and Institutional Change, 1991, Westview Press.

The Agony of Transition: From Communism to Democracy, 1992, The Edward Boyle Memorial Lecture.

Britain in Europe: Thoughts on the Constitution, 1992, The Charter 88 Sovereignty Lecture.

Europe: The Current Crisis, 1993, The Lothian Lecture Series.

Beyond Ambition: Career Paths of American Politics, 1993, with Edward Lascher, IGS, University of California Press.

'Britain and the European Union: a way forward', 1995, *Political Quarterly*, Winter.

(Simon Targett, © Times Higher Education Supplement)

Contributors

John Davies has worked as a journalist in London, Liverpool and Boston.

Sian Griffiths is features editor of the *Times Higher Education Supplement*.

Karen Gold is a freelance writer.

Lucy Hodges is a former education correspondent of *The Times*. She is currently a freelance writer.

Stella Hughes is France correspondent of the *Times Higher Education Supplement*.

Martin Ince is deputy editor of the *Times Higher Education Supplement* and author of seven books, including *The Dictionary of Astronomy*, to be published in 1996, Peter Collin Publishers.

Aisling Irwin is science correspondent of the *Times Higher Education Supplement*.

Celia Kitzinger is director of women's studies, University of Loughborough. Her books include *Social Construction of Lesbianism*, 1987, Sage.

Karen MacGregor is South African correspondent of the *Times Higher Education Supplement*.

Huw Richards is a journalist on the *Times Higher Education Supplement*. His history of the *Daily Herald* will be published by Pluto in 1997.

Andrew Robinson is literary editor of the *Times Higher Education Supplement*. His books include *The Story of Writing: Alphabets, Hieroglyphs and Pictograms*, 1995, Thames and Hudson; *Satyajit Ray: The Inner Eye*, 1989, Deutsch and *Rabindranath Tagore: The Myriad-Minded Man*, with Krishna Dutta, 1995, Bloomsbury.

Claire Sanders is news editor of the *Times Higher Education Supplement*.

Simon Targett is a journalist on the *Times Higher Education Supplement*.

Jon Turney is Wellcome fellow in science communcation at University College London. He is working on '*Frankenstein's Footsteps*', to be published by Yale University Press.

Gail Vines is a former features editor of the *New Scientist*. Her most recent book is *Raging Hormones*, 1994, Virago.

David Walker is a writer and former presenter of BBC Radio 4's 'Analysis' programme.

Jennifer Wallace is an official fellow and director of English studies at Peterhouse, Cambridge. Her book *Shelley and Greece: Rethinking Romantic Hellenism* will be published by McMillan in 1996.

Elaine Williams is an education writer.

Dorothy Zinberg teaches at the John F. Kennedy School of Government, Harvard.